Oracle9i™ For Dummies®

W9-CHV-044

Cool Tasks You Can Do with Oracle9i and Enterprise Manager Version 9.0

Task	Start in this tool	Uses
Run SQL from the Web	iSQL*Plus	View any data you want remotely
Get advice on tuning	Performance Overview Charts	Drill down any chart to get advice on how to tune the database
Create XML documents	XML Developer's Kit	Generate an XML Web page from a query
Search for an object by name	Schema Manager	Find any table, index, trigger, or whatever using a search window
Monitor your database from home	Web-Enabled Console	Run Console from any Internet browser that runs Java plug-ins
Create an HTML report create of table properties	Schema Manager	Click a button and instantly an HTML report from the table's attributes, including the SQL command to create the table

Place Your Login Information Here

Whenever you start Enterprise Manager Console or other tools, you must log in. Typically, you have three different Oracle user names: one for Enterprise Management Server, one for the database, and one for SQL*Plus.

Fill in this chart to help you remember which user name goes with each tool. Keep your cheat sheet in a secure place. **If you have no secure location, omit the passwords on the chart**.

My Login Chart

Tool	Username	Password
Console (Enterprise Management Server)		
SQL*Plus		
Console (stand-alone)		

For Dummies: Bestselling Book Series for Beginners

Oracle9i™ For Dummies®

Cheat Sheet

SQL Commands

SQL (Structured Query Language) gives you direct access to data in your Oracle9i tables. Use the following examples (taken from the book) to remind you of the correct syntax for SQL commands.

Create a table

```
CREATE TABLE CAR_SOLD
(CAR_ID_NO              NUMBER(16),
 MODEL_OF_CAR           VARCHAR2(30),
 DATE_SOLD              DATE,
 SUGGESTED_RETAIL_PRICE NUMBER(8,2),
 PRIMARY KEY (CAR_ID_NO));
```

Join two tables

```
SELECT SS.SAMPLE_ID, SS.SELLING_PRICE,
SS.SAMPLE_DESCRIPTION, TS.EDIBLE
FROM SEAWEED_SAMPLE SS, TYPE_OF_SEAWEED TS
WHERE TS.TYPE_ID = SS.TYPE_ID
ORDER BY SS.SAMPLE_ID;
```

Create an object type

```
CREATE OR REPLACE TYPE BREAD_TYPE AS OBJECT
( BREAD_NO NUMBER(5, 0),
  BREAD_NAME VARCHAR2(20),
  SALE_PRICE NUMBER(5, 2),
  IN_STOCK NUMBER(10, 0),
  RECIPE_TBL RECIPE_NEST );
```

Create a view

```
CREATE VIEW BREAD_VIEW AS
SELECT BREAD_NO BREADNO, BREAD_NAME
  BREADNAME,
IN_STOCK INSTOCK, SALE_PRICE SALEPRICE
FROM BAKERY_OBJ;
```

Create an object table

```
CREATE TABLE INGREDIENT_OBJ OF
  INGREDIENT_TYPE;
```

Insert one row

```
INSERT INTO SPY_MASTER
(CODE_NAME, COUNTRY, ACTUAL_NAME) VALUES
('Howie','US','James');
```

Insert many rows

```
INSERT INTO CLIENT
SELECT CUST_ID+125, NAME,
STREET_ADDRESS || ' ' ||CITY_STATE_ZIP,
NULL, NULL
FROM MILLIES_MAILING_LIST;
```

Update rows

```
UPDATE TICKET
SET EXTRA_TICKET = 'YES'
WHERE PURCHASE_DATE < TO_DATE('10-OCT-00');
```

Delete rows

```
DELETE FROM SEAWEED_SAMPLE
WHERE TYPE_ID IN (SELECT TYPE_ID FROM
  TYPE_OF_SEAWEED
      WHERE EDIBLE = 'INEDIBLE');
```

For Dummies: Bestselling Book Series for Beginners

TM

References for the Rest of Us!®

BESTSELLING BOOK SERIES

Do you find that traditional reference books are overloaded with technical details and advice you'll never use? Do you postpone important life decisions because you just don't want to deal with them? Then our *For Dummies*® business and general reference book series is for you.

For Dummies business and general reference books are written for those frustrated and hard-working souls who know they aren't dumb, but find that the myriad of personal and business issues and the accompanying horror stories make them feel helpless. *For Dummies* books use a lighthearted approach, a down-to-earth style, and even cartoons and humorous icons to dispel fears and build confidence. Lighthearted but not lightweight, these books are perfect survival guides to solve your everyday personal and business problems.

> *"More than a publishing phenomenon, 'Dummies' is a sign of the times."*
>
> — The New York Times

> *"A world of detailed and authoritative information is packed into them..."*
>
> — U.S. News and World Report

> *"...you won't go wrong buying them."*
>
> — Walter Mossberg, Wall Street Journal, on For Dummies books

Already, millions of satisfied readers agree. They have made For Dummies the #1 introductory level computer book series and a best-selling business book series. They have written asking for more. So, if you're looking for the best and easiest way to learn about business and other general reference topics, look to For Dummies to give you a helping hand.

Wiley Publishing, Inc.

5/09

Oracle9i™ FOR DUMMIES®

by Carol McCullough-Dieter

Foreword by Ned Dana
Principal Consultant and Toolmaster
Rare & Dear, Inc.

WILEY

Wiley Publishing, Inc.

Oracle9i™ For Dummies®

Published by
Wiley Publishing, Inc.
111 River Street
Hoboken, NJ 07030
www.wiley.com

Library of Congress Cataloging-in-Publication Data:

Library of Congress Control Number: 2001092899

ISBN: 0-7645-0880-6

Manufactured in the United States of America

10 9 8 7 6 5 4 3 2

3B/TQ/RR/QT/IN

About the Author

Carol McCullough-Dieter lives in Portland, Oregon, with her family. She is a consultant for the Pacific Disaster Center, a federally funded project for aiding in disaster mitigation and recovery serving Hawaii and many Pacific Island countries. She has written several online tutorials covering the Oracle DBA Certification exams for DigitalThink.com. She enjoys painting watercolor portraits and volunteering at her son's school.

This is the first edition of *Oracle9i For Dummies,* and Carol has authored all previous Oracle *For Dummies* books as well, beginning with *Oracle7 For Dummies* five years ago. She also co-authored several other books on Oracle software for IDG Books Worldwide, including the *Oracle8i DBA Bible, Oracle8Developer's Guide,* and *Creating Cool Web Databases.*

If you have questions about this book, you can visit Carol's Question and Answer Page at

www.geocities.com/carolmdieter/o9ifordum

And don't forget the Web site that contains all the examples and sample database tables on the *For Dummies* Web site:

www.dummies.com/extras/oracle_9i_fd

Carol's personal Web site featuring unusual Christmas holiday traditions from the past has received several awards. Surf on over to Maui and see it for yourself at

www.geocities.com/carolmdieter/xmas.htm

Her e-mail address is carolmdieter@yahoo.com.

Dedication

I dedicate this book to my Mom and Dad. Thank you both for a lifetime of good examples and funny adventures!

Author's Acknowledgments

Thanks to the great team of editors, copywriters, artists, and office staff headed by Jill Byus Schorr, as well as Susan Pink, Eric Rudie, the Media Development team, and all the others.

Finally, thanks to my husband, Pat, and my sons, Blue, Jesse, and Dustin. It's the greatest gift of all to have all three of my sons near me every day! I love you.

Publisher's Acknowledgments

We're proud of this book; please send us your comments through our Online Registration Form located at www.dummies.com./register

Some of the people who helped bring this book to market include the following:

Acquisitions, Editorial, and Media Development

Project Editor: Susan Pink

Sr. Acquisitions Editor: Grace Buechlein

Technical Editor: Eric Rudie

Editorial Manager: Constance Carlisle

Media Development Specialist: Heather Dismore

Editorial Assistant: Amanda Foxworth

Production

Project Coordinator: Dale White

Layout and Graphics: Joyce Haughey, Jackie Nicholas, Jill Piscitelli, Betty Schulte, Jeremey Unger, Mary J. Virgin

Proofreaders: David Faust, John Greenough, Angel Perez, Carl Pierce, TECHBOOKS Production Services

Indexer: TECHBOOKS Production Services

Special Help
Linda Morris

Publishing and Editorial for Consumer Dummies

Diane Graves Steele, Vice President and Publisher, Consumer Dummies

Joyce Pepple, Acquisitions Director, Consumer Dummies

Kristin A. Cocks, Product Development Director, Consumer Dummies

Michael Spring, Vice President and Publisher, Travel

Brice Gosnell, Associate Publisher, Travel

Suzanne Jannetta, Editorial Director, Travel

Publishing for Technology Dummies

Richard Swadley, Vice President and Executive Group Publisher

Andy Cummings, Vice President and Publisher

Composition Services

Gerry Fahey, Vice President of Production Services

Debbie Stailey, Director of Composition Services

Contents at a Glance

Cartoons at a Glance

By Rich Tennant

page 143

page 111

page 7

page 281

page 345

Cartoon Information:
Fax: 978-546-7747
E-Mail: richtennant@the5thwave.com
World Wide Web: www.the5thwave.com

Table of Contents

Foreword

*P*erhaps the subtitle for this book should be *An Aperitif*, because in a sense it is just that. Many volumes would be required to do justice to the entire Oracle9i meal because it consists of many courses, each with a large array of spices and condiments to enhance the experience. But although developing an appetite for such a meal takes time, this book's taste of what's ahead is quick and fun and won't leave you feeling ill the following day.

My introduction to Oracle came during a 1980 interview at Relational Software, Inc. (as the company was then known) when Bob Miner was showing me a few things on his terminal. Distinctly brilliant and a great guy who was much loved by the developers, Bob was current Oracle CEO Larry Ellison's partner on the technical side. I remember being particularly taken by the elegance and simplicity of SQL when Bob explained that the output of any query (on a table or set of tables) was itself another table. The next year, I was helping Bob, Bruce Scott (who played a key role in early development @md Bruce's cat's name is the password in Oracle's ubiquitous SCOTT/TIGER user), and others develop Oracle Version 3, a complete rewrite in C. This investment in portability was one of the early design decisions that enabled Oracle8i to become the best database on the market today.

If this book is your introduction to Oracle9i, you're in for a treat. Carol McCullough-Dieter covers complex and difficult material in a straightforward and conversational manner. But rather than boring you with details, she touches on key points and new features (such as XML Developer's Kit and Console). Doing so not only gets you started but also inspires you. Carol's lighthearted style is backed by many years of experience.

If you're new to relational databases, you'll appreciate this book's many examples of simple database designs. In the two chapters on relational theory alone, you find many examples, ranging from doctor's office information to bread making. As you consider each example, you begin to get a feel for how relational databases are used to model real-world situations.

Carol McCullough-Dieter's background as a database administrator is evident when she discusses important issues such as backup and recovery, security, space allocation, and the way Oracle9i actually works inside. Sections on using indexes and tuning SQL statements are a definite plus.

So if you're hungry to find out about the database that gives Bill Gates indigestion, this snack — *Oracle9i For Dummies* — is a great place to start!

My company, Rare & Dear, Inc., is a Hawaii-based consulting group focused on the design and administration of Oracle databases in high-performance Web sites. As our name indicates, we're committed to excellence in our staff, the work that we do, and of course, the place where we live! If you're interested in our company, you can reach us at 888-RareDear (888-727-3332) or check out our own (small) Web site at www.rare-dear.com.

Ned Dana
Principal Consultant and Toolmaster
Rare & Dear, Inc.

Introduction

Or-a-cle (noun) 1: a person (such as a priestess of ancient Greece) through whom a deity is believed to speak. 2: an authoritative or wise expression or answer. 3: an anagram of the name Carole.

That definition pretty much says it all, doesn't it? You have Oracle9i. You have the database to beat all databases. You have the cream of the crop, the tip of the top, the best of the best, the oracle from which all wisdom and answers flow. And if you only had your own Greek priestess to consult, you'd have no problem figuring out how to use the pesky thing!

Besides being one of the best relational database packages around, Oracle9i is one of the most complex. Oracle9i does some very fancy things, but the easy things are sometimes tricky.

Fear not, for you have come to the right place. This book is the Oracle's oracle, written by the high priestess of database knowledge. Well, all right, I'm just a normal human being, but I have lots of experience as a database programmer and database administrator with Oracle7 through Oracle9i. I had to find out the hard way — on the job, bribing nerds with doughnuts and even (shudder!) reading manuals. You can benefit from my experiences when you read this book, which easily guides you along the path to Oracle enlightenment with more fun than you're supposed to have at work.

This book focuses on Oracle9i. The vast majority of the subject matter applies to PCs, Macs, and mainframes and to all platforms from Windows to MacOS to UNIX. When appropriate, I show you how to use Enterprise Manager, Oracle9i's desktop toolset. Enterprise Manager comes as standard equipment with your basic Oracle9i database engine. All the figures used to illustrate the step-by-step instructions for Enterprise Manager are shown on a Windows 2000 computer. If you're using a different platform for Enterprise Manager, you may see some slight differences in the figures, but the steps should work on all platforms.

About This Book

Oracle9i puts its entire software documentation — the manuals — on a CD-ROM. Putting the documentation on CD saves a lot of trees but doesn't help you much because the CD version is cross-referenced about as well as a

Tom Robbins novel. If you know what the answer is before you start looking, the answer is really easy to find. If you don't know the answer, you may spend days trying to discover it.

This book gives you answers fast. Use it to get results quickly and easily. Hide it under your Oracle9i manuals and then dazzle your friends with your incredible know-how!

Conventions Used in This Book

For the most part, you don't need to do any special mouse functions because this book is mouse independent (like my home — I have two cats) and covers Oracle9i on a lot of different platforms. A line command is pretty much black and white. However, with the Internet and Java popping up everywhere, your mouse is probably getting a workout, even if you use UNIX or Linux.

Oracle9i's primary tools, Enterprise Manager and Console, have caught the Java wave and use the same mouse-driven screens no matter what operating system you're using. When I illustrate how to use these tools, here's the way I define mouse activities:

- ✔ **Select.** Highlight a word or phrase by clicking it. Sometimes you need to click, hold, and drag the mouse to the end of the word or phrase to highlight the entire section.
- ✔ **Click.** Select an object with the mouse by pointing at it and clicking one time with the left mouse button.
- ✔ **Double-click.** Point at an object and click twice with the left mouse button.
- ✔ **Right-click.** Point and click with the right mouse button.

When you see the kind of font on the next line, it means one of two things:

```
I am something you type into the computer.
```

or (where indicated)

```
I am what your computer says back to you.
```

Here's what words channeled from the little voice in my head look like:

> *You are so funny I could die.*

Just kidding on that last one.

In the sections that talk about Enterprise Manager tools, sometimes I tell you to use a menu command, such as File⇨Open. You can execute this command by moving your mouse pointer up to the File menu, clicking it, and then choosing the Open command from the submenu that pops up.

I also give you plenty of examples of SQL commands that you can copy. These are displayed in the book like this:

```
-- 02_objectquery_
SELECT * FROM INGREDIENT_OBJ
WHERE PRICE_PER_OUNCE > .1;
```

The first line of the command is a comment telling you the corresponding file that contains the command. All the examples can be downloaded from the For Dummies Web site at:

```
www.dummies.com/extras/oracle_9i_fd
```

To find the file containing the example you are reading, first go to the Samples directory. Next, open the directory for the chapter you are currently reading, and then open the file with the name matching the top line of the example you are reading.

The example SQL command is from Chapter 4. So, to open the file containing the command, I look in the Samples directory, then look in the Chapter04 directory, and then open the file named 02_objectquery.

On a final note, Oracle9i is not case sensitive (except for words enclosed in quotation marks), so you may see table, row, or column names or commands in uppercase or lowercase throughout this book.

What You're Not to Read

You don't want to get a reputation as a nerd, so be very careful to cover up the parts labeled with the Technical Stuff icon.

Be aware that reading all the chapters in this book in order will cause your head to explode. Jump around, skip over the boring parts — if you can find any — and get to the information you need.

Foolish Assumptions

To keep this book focused on database matters, I make some assumptions about your innate (or acquired) talents. You . . .

✔ **Own or have access to Oracle9i (on any platform).** Oracle9i is available for Windows 2000, Windows NT, Linux, UNIX, and Solaris and includes Enterprise Manager, a tool frequently featured in this book.

✔ **Use tables that others create and sometimes create tables yourself.**

✔ **Use and create queries and reports and sometimes enter data.**

✔ **Are comfortable using a mouse and Windows (not a requirement).**

How This Book Is Organized

So that you can quickly and easily find topics that you want to know more about, I've divided this book into five parts. Here's a quick look at what's inside.

Part I: Road Map

In Part I, you find important concepts and definitions that are used throughout the book. Chapter 1 is an introduction to Oracle9i; it includes a quick discussion of tasks that a database can (and can't) be used to accomplish. This part provides an in-depth look at the Console, a tool for browsing your database, and SQL*Plus, a utility that uses the SQL programming language to let you get at your data. Use it now and use it well.

Part II: Getting Started

An important aspect of using Oracle9i is knowing how an object-relational database puts together all the pieces of data that it stores. In Part II, I explain the basics about objects and show you how Oracle9i uses them.

You can use the database schema provided along with the Oracle sample files at the For Dummies Web site to experiment with SQL commands to view, add, change, and remove data in tables and objects. The samples on the Web site correspond with examples described in Part II.

Part II also takes a look backstage at the props Oracle9i uses to keep track of you and all the things that you and others create. You find a bit of technical stuff here, but it's carefully contained with the proper hexes and spells, so don't worry.

Part III: Putting Oracle9i to Work

Part III launches right into the heart of using Oracle9i. Here's where you find out how to create a table or two. Then you go right into creating objects. After you create some tables and objects, you may be upset if they get lost or get changed by some ham-handed programmer (possibly even someone who looks suspiciously like yourself). That's where the sections on security, backups, and sharing data come in handy.

Find out how to create a Web report with XML and Oracle9i. See how to combine SQL and Java and store a Java applet right inside the database. Experiment with the up-and-coming star of many a Web-based database system: XML Developer's Kit.

Finally, with tables in place, you're ready to find out whether you can actually use the data in some way. (Contrary to the opinion of many techno-systems analysts, data is intended for some purpose other than calculating disk storage space.)

You'll be so far ahead of the pack when you complete this section, you should just go ask for a higher salary right now!

Part IV: Tuning Up and Turbocharging

After you give SQL a whirl, you're ready to find out why executing a three-line SQL command takes three days. Part IV looks at what's slowing you down, how to speed everything up, and what to do when you hit a speed bump, a wall, or some other obstacle that can slow you down.

Find out how to make changes to the structure of already existing tables and objects using Enterprise Manager and SQL commands.

Part V: The Part of Tens

The wonderful Part of Tens. Does this part remind you of grade school, when you had to count ten sticks, wrap a rubber band around them, and then repeat the process ten times to make a hundred? Only me, huh? The Part of Tens focuses on quick, useful tips that can save you hours of research. Dazzle your toddler, your neighbor's dog, and maybe even your boss with your cunning.

Icons Used in This Book

All the *For Dummies* books use icons to help you find the important details without having to read the fine print. Here are the icons that you find sprinkled like confetti around the pages of this book.

Watch for this icon to highlight new Oracle9i features. This version of Oracle includes some fun new Web-related features that you might like.

This icon tells you that the paragraph contains an important reference to information found on the Internet. Go find that Web site using your Web browser.

Reserved for important and critical details, this icon is your cue to read carefully. Missing the stuff next to this icon can mean missing an important step and creating a query that never dies or some such freak of nature.

As you may have guessed, this icon marks some technical details that you can avoid or indulge in, depending on your mood. I take great pains to keep these sections to the size of your palm so that you can conveniently cover them up if you want.

This icon signifies hard-won information, from timesaving tricks to shortcuts.

Watch out here. You may have to walk through a minefield to get to your goal. This icon shows you the safest route to take.

Part I
Road Map

The 5th Wave — By Rich Tennant

"Please, Dad – do we have to hear the story of Snow White's SQL query and its 7 arrays again?"

In this part . . .

Before I launch you full tilt into the brave new world of Oracle9i, Part I paves the way with bits of knowledge.

The motto of Part I is "Forewarned is forearmed!" I figure it's better to have some idea of what's in the cupboard before you start making a birthday cake. Otherwise, you're pouring alum into the mixture instead of baking soda. With that in mind, Part I gives you a nice tour of all the tools that come as standard equipment with Oracle9i.

If you have a database to play with, this part also shows you how to create queries so you can see what you've gotten yourself into.

Chapter 1

A Quick Tour of Oracle9i

*W*ell, you lucky duck! Your world is about to expand into the great, undiscovered country called Oracle9i. Actually, the territory is not really unknown because some of us have boldly ventured there and returned with a map. I suppose that you would have preferred Chinese takeout or doughnuts. Sorry, Charlie.

This chapter is your guide. You look at what Oracle9i is all about and what components it includes; then you rev it up and give it a test drive.

Discovering Oracle9i: The Program That Runs It All

Once upon a time, back in the 1970s, a man named Larry Ellison built a great big software program called Oracle. The Oracle program lived in a giant mainframe, and when it fired up its boilers and started huffing and puffing, it expanded to the size of a house. Only the biggest mainframes had room for Oracle.

Then one day, a neighbor of Larry's saw what the big Oracle program could do and told Larry, "Hey! I want one, too, but my mainframe can't handle that really big program. If you make me a smaller one, I'll pay you big bucks."

Larry took the challenge and, in less than a year, created another Oracle program to fit into the smaller mainframe. He delivered it to his neighbor, who exclaimed, "It's a miracle!"

This exchange inspired Larry to think that other small-computer owners would want the Oracle program. So Larry went to all corners of the earth, found the best engineers, and gathered them together in the Promised Land of California to help him create Oracle for all sizes and shapes of computers.

Today, the Oracle engine is all that Larry dreamed it could be — and more. With Oracle9i, you're sitting on a database powerhouse. And they all lived happily ever after.

Oracle9i's core package

Figure 1-1 shows the Oracle9i database engine and the core utilities that are standard equipment with Oracle9i, regardless of your operating system or hardware. These core utilities and the database itself behave the same on all platforms. The differences are on the inside, where Oracle9i takes advantage of each computer's unique features for storage, reading, writing, and so on.

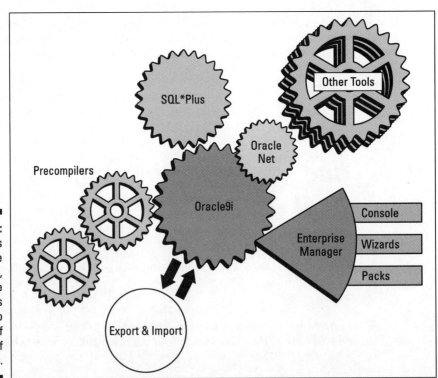

Figure 1-1: Oracle's powerhouse database, with its core utilities, is portable to dozens of kinds of computers.

Your Oracle9i software packages come with a bundle of CDs that contain the database engine and core utilities plus lots and lots of extra tools that you can try and then buy later if you like them. (Sometimes, it's not clear which parts you bought and which parts you're using on a trial basis, so look closely.) Although I can't cover all the cool playthings that Oracle tempts you with, I do cover the basics you need to get your database up and running and the power tools you use no matter what extras you buy (or don't buy) later.

Following are the core utilities:

✔ **Enterprise Manager.** Oracle9i continues to expand this user-friendly feature, which was introduced as an add-on for Oracle7. With Oracle9i, the tool is even more integrated with the database software. Enterprise Manager gets installed automatically with the database. This tool saves a great deal of code writing by aiding you with menus and windows for many database administrator (DBA) tasks, such as adding tables or indexes. The utility's easy-to-use tools make anyone a savvy DBA in no time! You'll love it!

The latest edition of Enterprise Manager (Version 9.0) is packed with great tools, lots of documentation, and many advanced features that I can't even get to in this book. So much data, so little time! You can install Enterprise Manager also by itself on another computer that links to a database using the Internet or an internal company network.

Much of this book focuses on how to use this versatile and timesaving utility. Read on in this chapter for a better look at Enterprise Manager.

The Enterprise Manager contains many tools and utilities. The three important ones featured in this book are

• **Console.** This component of Enterprise Manager now contains a fully integrated Console. Prior to Oracle9i, Console was a stand-alone tool only partially integrated into Enterprise Manager. Now Console combines in one place all the Enterprise Manager tools you use to manage your database. Look over storage space or table column names or user profiles. Check out which users are logged in right now. You can even work on table data in a convenient spreadsheet format. I feature Console in several chapters. Here's the best part: You don't need to know SQL (pronounced *sequel*) to use this tool! Console can even be customized to do fancy work. For example, Console can watch a database for certain conditions, such as running out of space or security violations, and then page your cell phone! Super DBA to the rescue!

• **Wizards.** Get out your magic wand. The wizards are here. Oracle9i packs a whole group of wizards (would that be a cauldron of wizards?) into the house. You can get a wizard to help you back up and recover your database, or tune and analyze data. Those are just a few of the wizards available.

- **Packs.** Oracle has many add-on tools that you can snap into your existing Enterprise Manager structure. *Packs,* which are sets of related tools, are available for trial use and for sale from Oracle. The Tuning Pack, for example, contains tools such as the Tablespace Map tool, SQL Analyze, and Oracle Expert. I look into some of these add-on tools so you have an idea of what is available.

✔ **SQL*Plus.** This tool allows you to create and run queries, add rows, modify data, and write reports. To use SQL*Plus, you must figure out SQL, the Structured Query Language. You can use this language in nearly any relational database. The Oracle9i version is called SQL*Plus because Oracle embellished the usual SQL suite of commands. These embellishments allow you to customize reports, edit and save files, define variables, and do other cool stuff. You can even perform duties that are typically reserved for database administrators, such as creating new users and starting and stopping the database engine.

Whenever I need to show you SQL commands, I use SQL*Plus to demonstrate. You see SQL examples that you can run in SQL*Plus in many of the chapters.

✔ **Oracle Net.** This tool is your key to communicating with a remote database. Oracle Net comes with a wizard and an assistant to help you configure your networked computer to reach any remote Oracle database on your network. Oracle Net is a key component that glues other pieces of the system together.

✔ **Export and Import.** You can export (EXP) data to or import (IMP) data from any Oracle9i database. For example, you can use EXP on a PC to copy to a file data and tables that you created. You can move this file to a UNIX computer, an IBM mainframe, or any other platform that has an Oracle9i database, and then use IMP to place the information in that database. In addition to the export function, Oracle9i provides wizards and tools for backup and recovery that run inside Enterprise Manager or as stand-alone components.

✔ **Precompilers.** A bunch of precompilers are available; actually, there's one for each programming language, including Ada, C, C++, Pascal, and FORTRAN. The mix varies on different platforms (hardware and operating systems). I don't cover precompilers at all in this book; you need to know a programming language to use them.

Oracle9i's newest star: XML Developer's Kit

Larry Ellison was serious about making Oracle9i the Internet database! The Oracle9i database handles XML and Enterprise Java Beans as if they were its own inventions.

Use Oracle's XML Developer's kit to create Web pages without any fancy programming. What fun! You can try it on for size and create some templates for the sample tables found with the Oracle9i bonus text on the For Dummies Web site at `www.dummies.com/ext ras/Oracle9i.html`.

The new look of Enterprise Manager

Whether you're working with Oracle9i on an IBM mainframe, Windows 2000, Windows NT, or UNIX, you get the awesome Enterprise Manager toolbox. Enterprise Manager has a bunch of nice utilities that bring Oracle into the Windows world better than ever.

Enterprise Manager Version 9.0 looks similar to the previous version, except Enterprise Manager's Console now looks more like the DBA Studio from the previous version. The new Console integrates all the features of the old Console and the old DBA Studio into a single tool. Another new feature is the capability to log into Console in stand-alone mode, which is sometimes faster in response time than the alternative mode, which is called Enterprise Management Server mode (what a mouthful). You can use Enterprise Manager in three ways:

- ✔ **Direct access.** Access Console or some other Enterprise Manager tool directly. This is the easiest way to use Enterprise Manager and requires minimal setup. I use this way of accessing Console most of the time in the book.

- ✔ **Management Server access.** Access Console and then access any Enterprise Manager tool through Console. This is the best way to go when you have to handle multiple databases. Remember, you must configure Enterprise Management Server before you can access Console in this way. Plus, you have to configure your Console correctly before you can get Web access (described in the following bullet) to work at all.

- ✔ **Web access.** Most Enterprise Manager tools are available through a Web connection, including the essential Console with its suite of DBA tools. The steps for setting up Web access are a bit tricky, but I show you how to get it ready to use later in this chapter. And who knows — you may have to run these tools while you are on vacation in Idaho next summer. All you need is a coffeehouse with an Internet connection!

Console packs four all-star components

Now for a closer look at Console, which is the part of Enterprise Manager that I use the most in this book. Much of this book describes step-by-step instructions on how to use the components of Console to administer your

database easily — without requiring you to figure out SQL. Figure 1-2 shows
the first screen you see when you start Console. As you can see, it's designed
to look like a tree-style directory of objects.

TIP

Take some time to run the Quick Tour (click the button labeled Quick Tour in
the lower-right part of the screen). The Quick Tour gives you some great
insights into how to use the tool.

Console includes many tools. Following are the four primary components for
database administration:

- **Instance.** Sometimes, two or more Oracle databases are running on the
  same computer or in the same network configuration. Each database is
  called an *instance*. The Instance component lets you see an overview of
  the activity in one instance at a time. You see who is logged in, what the
  user is doing, and whether the user is in trouble. Even if you have only
  one instance running, this tool is a troubleshooting aid. It is also a convenient place to start and stop the database.

- **Schema.** This component allows you to see your database much like
  your Explorer (Windows NT, 2000 and so on) layout, using icons for
  tables, users, and other parts of the database. You can arrange all the
  objects in your database by type or by owner. You can add or change
  tables, indexes, views, keys, and columns here. I give you lots of examples of using this component in the book.

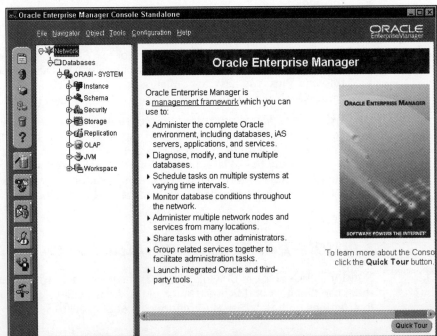

Figure 1-2:
Console
combines in
one location
nearly all
the tools
you need for
database
adminis-
tration.

✔ **Security.** This component makes creating users, setting and changing passwords, and assigning roles so easy that it's hard to make a mistake.

✔ **Storage.** Add more space to your database as easily as you create a new directory on your hard drive. This handy component allows you to review and modify the data files and tablespaces you use in your database.

Now that you've seen an overview, get busy with a quick tour of your database.

Looking Around with Enterprise Manager Console

First, make sure your Oracle9i database is running by following the steps in the preceding section. Then start Console by following these steps:

1. Start Console.

On Windows platforms, choose Start➪Programs➪Oracle HOME2➪Enterprise Manager Console. Note that the Oracle HOME2 label may have a different name, such as ORAHOME81, on your computer. The person who installed the software on your machine designates the name.

On UNIX, Linux, or any other platform, type **oemapp console** at the operating-system command line.

You see the logo screen for Oracle Enterprise Manager, and then the Oracle Enterprise Manager Console login window appears, as shown in Figure 1-3.

Figure 1-3: The initial login window for Enterprise Manager appears before you reach Console.

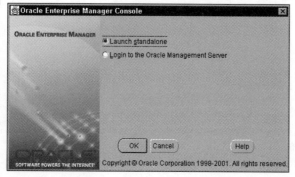

2. Make sure the Launch Standalone option is selected, and then click OK.

Console's initial screen appears.

3. Double-click the Databases folder.

All available databases are listed.

4. Double-click the name of the database that you want to work on.

If this is the first time you have used Console or if you have not saved your login settings, you see a login screen. Otherwise, you see a list of Managers (including Instance, Schema, Security, and Storage).

5. If you see a login screen, follow these steps to log in:

a. For the Username, type SYSTEM.

b. For the Password, type MANAGER or whatever the current password is for SYSTEM on your database.

c. For the Connect As option, select Normal.

d. Click to add a check mark to the Save As Local Preferred Credentials option.

Your screen should now look like Figure 1-4.

e. Click OK.

Console asks whether it's okay to save your credentials in a local encrypted file.

f. Click OK to continue.

The list of Managers (including Instance, Schema, Security, and Storage) appears.

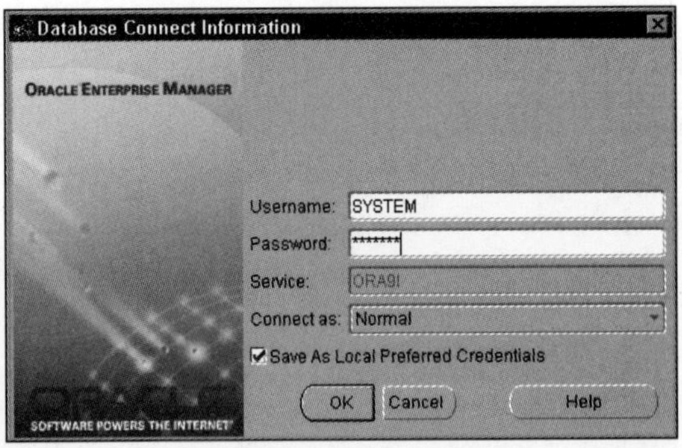

Figure 1-4:
Console
saves the
login data
in an
encrypted
file so you
don't have
to repeat
that data
next time.

Database Connect Information

ORACLE ENTERPRISE MANAGER

Username: SYSTEM
Password: *******
Service: ORA9I
Connect as: Normal
☑ Save As Local Preferred Credentials

OK Cancel Help

SOFTWARE POWERS THE INTERNET

6. **In the left half of the window, double-click the Schema icon.**

   This action opens Schema Manager within Console. A list of schema objects appears below the Schema icon.

7. **In the left half of the window, double-click the Table folder.**

   A list of tables appears in the right half. A list of schemas (table owners) appears under the Table folder in the left half of the window, as shown in Figure 1-5.

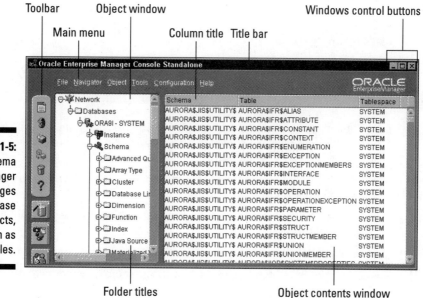

Figure 1-5:
Schema
Manager
manages
database
objects,
such as
tables.

Notice how neatly Schema Manager arranges the files, icons, and buttons you use to work with Oracle9i. (This setup is certainly much neater than my husband's arrangement of tools, documents, and other assorted items on his workbench.)

Figuring out the parts of Schema Manager that I highlight in Figure 1-5 helps you get around like a pro. Think of the figure as a VCR manual. No, actually, it's a lot simpler than that. Just don't try to set the clock.

The Schema Manager window has two important groups of elements: One group consists of the Object window and the Object contents window; the other group is what I call the "Other Elements" group and consists of everything else.

The Object and Object contents windows

The Object (left side) and Object contents (right side) windows give you a visual representation of all the objects that you can access in Oracle9i. *Objects* are any of several kinds of things in a database, such as indexes, tables, packages, views, and synonyms. This book shows you many examples of how to use Schema Manager to create and correct database tables, indexes, views, and synonyms.

Some of the other objects — such as packages, procedures, and clusters — are beyond the scope of this book, and you don't need them for starters anyway. These objects come into play when you perform advanced DBA tasks that only a supergeek enjoys.

The cool thing about Schema Manager is that it uses many of the basics about getting around that you probably already know from Windows 98, Windows 2000, or NT Explorer. Here are some examples:

- The left window shows a hierarchy of objects available for you to look at. The right window shows the contents of whatever you select (via a mouse click) on the left side.
- Click the plus (+) or minus (–) signs next to the icons in the left window to expand or contract the contents.
- Right-click an object to get a little menu that tells what you can do with the object.
- Double-click objects in the left window to expand or contract them.
- Click the Table icon to see a list of all the tables owned by all the users in the database.
- Click the column headers in the right window to rearrange the list, sorting by the heading that you click.
- Adjust the column width by clicking and dragging the dividing line between columns.
- Click the menu items across the top to see context-sensitive menu selections.
- Click and drag the edges of the window or dividing frame to change the dimensions of the window or frame.
- If you get lost, click the Help button, which offers context-sensitive instructions.

All the Managers available in Console work in similar ways. As you discover how to use Schema Manager, you develop skills that you can use later with the other Enterprise Manager tools.

By the way, if you have Windows 2000 and are not familiar with it, check out *Windows 2000 Professional For Dummies* by Andy Rathbone and Sharon Crawford (published by Hungry Minds, Inc.) for a good start.

The other Schema Manager elements

The Object window and the Object Contents window are far from the only elements in Schema Manager. Look for these additional goodies:

- **Windows control buttons.** These buttons are standard Windows controls for moving the window to the bottom taskbar, enlarging the window so that it fills the entire screen, and closing the window. (Close the window; I feel a draft.)

- **Title bar.** If you aren't sure where you are, the title bar tells you. If you still aren't sure, go ask your mother. Also, if you click the title bar and drag, you move the entire window. (I wish I could do that with the window over my sink; it's too close to the refrigerator.)

- **Main menu bar.** In this menu bar, you find the usual collection of menus, such as File, View, and Help. A click on any of them shows the options that are available.

- **Toolbar.** This bar shows little buttons of tools that you have available. You use most of these tools only occasionally. Nearly all the tools are available by right-clicking or by clicking a menu bar. The buttons are (from top to bottom):

  - **Create Report.** By clicking the Create Report button, you can generate and save a report based on your database information. The Create Report window that appears lets you choose from a long list of predefined reports, such as the Initialization parameters report or the Storage space of the database report. The report is automatically formatted as a Web page! This is great for documentation, if you ever have time to write it.

  - **Refresh.** Surprise! This button updates your windows with the latest data. Aaaaaaaah! How refreshing!

  - **Create.** Creates an object of the type that is highlighted.

  - **Create Like.** Copies something, such as a table or an index.

  - **Remove.** Drops the selected object from the database.

  - **Help.** Provides context-sensitive help. This button seems to work only in the menu bar and toolbar. Otherwise, you get into the Help screens at the table of contents.

Try clicking some of the elements and see what appears.

When you start digging into Enterprise Manager's Console, you reveal another layer of detail. To reveal this layer, follow these steps:

1. **If needed, start Console and open Schema Manager.**

   For details, see the preceding section ("Looking Around with Enterprise Manager Console").

2. **In the left window, double-click the Table folder.**

   A list of table owners appears in both the left and right windows.

3. **In the left window, double-click the first owner name.**

   This reveals a list of tables below the name.

4. **In the left window, click the first table in the list.**

   The right window changes to display a tabbed window describing the highlighted table.

   Figure 1-6 shows the components of this window. The basic structure that you see in the figure is common to all Console components (the Security, Schema, Instance, and Storage Managers). This basic structure also applies to most of the other Enterprise Manager tools, such as Recovery Manager.

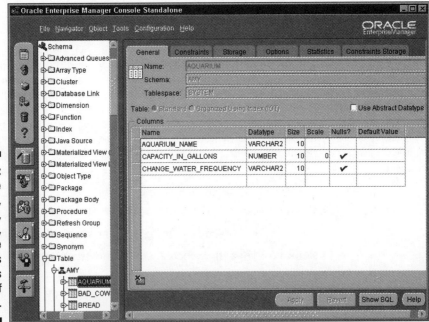

Figure 1-6: The Schema, Instance, Security, and Storage Managers all have this sort of layout.

You get these buttons at the bottom of the window:

- **Apply.** Use this button to finalize any changes that you made in the window.

- **Revert.** Put the details in the window back to the state they were in before you started messing around. This button does not reverse changes that you have already applied — only those that you have not yet applied!

- **Show SQL/Hide SQL.** As you make changes, you create SQL code, and this code is run when you click the Apply button. Click the Show SQL button to open a small window displaying the SQL code that you generated. After you click the button, it transforms into the Hide SQL button. Click that button, and the code window shuts.

- **Help.** Click this button to zoom in on context-sensitive help.

5. **Right-click the same table and choose Table Data Editor.**

   Figure 1-7 shows you this awesome new feature: a spreadsheet where you can view and edit the data in any table in the database! I take another look at this feature in Chapter 5.

Figure 1-7:
Use Table Editor inside Schema Manager to view or change data in a table without writing any SQL commands!

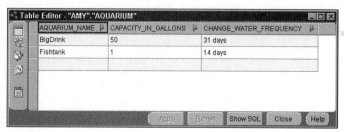

6. **Click the X button in the top-right corner of the Table Editor window.**

   This closes the window and returns you to Console.

7. **Click the X button in the top-right corner of the Console window to close it.**

Here are other chapters where you find various information about Schema Manager:

- Chapter 5 gives you a good review of Schema Manager.
- Chapter 9 shows you how to create tables using Schema Manager.
- Chapter 10 lets you create an object with Schema Manager.
- Chapter 19 shows you how to correct or change table layouts with Schema Manager.

The next section shows you one important feature of Oracle9i: SQL*Plus. Here is where you can use SQL, the powerful relational database language, to perform various miracles.

Getting Acquainted with SQL: The Messenger Priestess of Oracle9i

So how do you see and manipulate data stored in Oracle9i? You have three choices:

- **Schema Manager's editor feature.** As you see in the preceding section, you get a simple spreadsheet format in which to view and edit the data of any single table.
- **SQL*Plus.** This has been part of Oracle's software system from the start. SQL*Plus can be run in command-line mode or window mode, and it requires a knowledge of the relational database language called SQL.
- **SQL*Plus Worksheet.** This tool is part of the Enterprise Manager suite of tools and adds a useful function for scrolling back through previous SQL commands in SQL*Plus.

You can execute SQL commands in SQL*Plus Worksheet or SQL*Plus. In the majority of the book, I show you the steps for running most SQL commands only in SQL*Plus because it is more convenient. You can execute just about every example shown in SQL*Plus or the SQL*Plus Worksheet without any change.

Chapter 3 zooms in on SQL*Plus to show you how to write basic queries and how to add, remove, or change data using SQL. Chapter 4 rushes right in on how to query the new kids on the block: Oracle objects.

Starting and stopping SQL*Plus on a desktop

SQL*Plus is one of the tools included with your Oracle9i database. To begin using it, follow these steps:

1. **Start SQL*Plus.**

   On Windows platforms, choose Start➪Programs➪Oracle HOME➪ Application Development➪SQL*Plus.

   On UNIX, Linux, or any other platform, type **sqlplus** at the operating-system prompt to start the command-line version of SQL*Plus.

2. **Log in as the DBA user.**

   If you see a login window, follow these steps:

   a. **In the Name box, type** SYSTEM.

   b. **For the Password, type MANAGER or whatever the current password is for SYSTEM on your database.**

   c. **In the Host String box, type the Oracle Net name of the Oracle9i instance on your local computer or on your network.** For a local database, you can usually leave this blank. For a database on a network, ask your administrator to provide you with a valid host string.

   d. **Click OK.**

   The SQL*Plus window appears.

   If instead of a login window you see a prompt for a user name, follow these steps:

   a. **In the Username box, type** SYSTEM@*XXXX*, **replacing *XXXX* with the Oracle Net name of the Oracle9i instance on your local computer or on your network.**

   For example, if you want to log into the ORCL database as SYSTEM, you would type SYSTEM@ORCL.

   b. **Press Enter.**

   c. **When you are prompted for a password, type the current password for SYSTEM. The default password is MANAGER.**

   d. **Press Enter.**

   The SQL prompt line appears. Your session may or may not have the Windows-like screen, but all the commands work the same.

Figure 1-8 shows the SQL*Plus window that you can use to type your commands. Simply type the SQL command you need, press Enter, and voila! The results appear magically in the window.

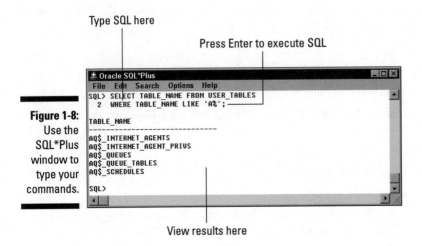

Type SQL here

Press Enter to execute SQL

Figure 1-8:
Use the
SQL*Plus
window to
type your
commands.

View results here

This tool is convenient because if you make a mistake (not *you,* the *other* readers!), you can edit the command and run it again. To edit a command, type **edit** and then press Enter. SQL*Plus creates a file with your command in it, and you can use your favorite text editor to fix the command. Close the file and you automatically return to SQL*Plus with the corrected command ready to go.

The menu selections along the top should look familiar if you use Windows. These controls open and close the window, resize and move the window, and get help.

The File menu has a few extras that you see when you click it:

> ✔ **Spool.** Use this to save to a file the typing and displayed results you see in your window.
>
> ✔ **Run.** Use this to reexecute the SQL command shown in the window.

The Edit menu works with the context of your cursor to cut, paste, and so on. In addition, the Edit menu lets you define the editor you want to use while working in SQL*Plus. As a test, type the following SQL command and press Enter. (You don't have to type the first line because it's a comment.)

```
-- 01_sample
SELECT TABLE_NAME FROM USER_TABLES
WHERE TABLE_NAME LIKE 'A%';
```

Both SQL*Plus and the SQL*Plus Worksheet require one of these two symbols to end a command and allow it to execute:

- The semicolon (;) at the end of the command.
- The forward slash (/) alone on the line immediately following the end of the command.

For example, you can write the preceding SQL query as the following and then press Enter:

```
-- 02_sample
SELECT TABLE_NAME FROM USER_TABLES
WHERE TABLE_NAME LIKE 'A%'
/
```

When in SQL*Plus Worksheet, click the Run icon (the lightning bolt) to execute your command. You see results miraculously appear in the bottom half of the screen. (Captain! We're being hailed! Onscreen, Mr. Data!) You should see something like Figure 1-9. Use the scroll bar on the bottom right side and on the bottom of the lower window to scroll up, down, left, and right to view all the results, if necessary.

Figure 1-9:
The SQL*Plus Worksheet displays results in the lower half of the screen.

Close the SQL*Plus window by clicking the X button in the top-right corner of the window. That was easy!

Using SQL*Plus in command-line mode

Unlike several Windows-based programs that are out today, SQL*Plus still works in ancient ways. No point-and-click mousing around with SQL*Plus — only command-line input is involved. You run SQL*Plus from a command line on any platform by typing this command:

```
sqlplus username/password@netname
```

Replace *username* with your Oracle9i user name. Replace *password* with your actual password. If you are not a person according to Oracle9i, log in as the default DBA user in Oracle9i; type **SYSTEM** as the *username* and MANAGER (or whatever the current password is for SYSTEM) as the *password*. If you are running a local database, you can leave off the *@netname*. Otherwise, type the @ symbol and replace *netname* with the Oracle Net name of the database to which you connect. You get a few status messages; then your prompt changes to this one:

```
SQL>
```

This prompt means that you are in SQL*Plus and are ready to go! Now you can create queries and tables to your heart's content. You can do one right now! Type this line and then press Enter to run it:

```
SELECT TABLE_NAME FROM USER_TABLES
WHERE TABLE_NAME LIKE 'A%';
```

Oracle9i lists the results on your screen, which look just like the results shown in Figure 1-9, except without the window around it. When you're finished, you leave SQL*Plus by typing the following command and pressing Enter:

```
EXIT;
```

You return to your operating system, and the prompt returns to its normal state.

Many of the chapters contain examples of SQL code that you can type in SQL*Plus and run. It doesn't matter which mode you use in SQL*Plus (window or command line) because the SQL and SQL*Plus commands work the same in either mode.

When running SQL commands in SQL*Plus, you must end the command with a semicolon (;) or a forward slash (/). If you use a slash, it must be on a line by itself. The semicolon can be in the last line of the command.

Getting to know Oracle9i . . . and Scott and Tiger

Every Oracle database comes with demonstration tables that you may want to become familiar with. And if you do, you quickly notice references to Scott or Scott and Tiger. Perhaps you have already noticed these references in the Oracle9i documentation.

So who are Scott and Tiger? I hear that Scott is a real human (or was at one time). Now he's a legend whose name is engraved in every Oracle database around the world. You can use his name as an acceptable user name. Scott's cat, Tiger, is a legend in his own right, immortalized as Scott's password.

In the Oracle9i demonstration tables, Scott is one of only two highly paid analysts in a small company that is set on selling something. The head honcho's name is King. This company has four departments in four cities across America. All the salespeople get commissions, although one poor guy gets a zero commission. Nobody has ever earned a bonus. You can find out more about the people who work for Scott by typing these SQL commands in SQL*Plus:

```
select * from emp;
select * from dept;
select * from bonus;
select * from salgrade;
```

You can see that the big boss lives in New York; the analysts, who all get paid more than their manager, live in Dallas; and the salespeople live in Chicago. Apparently, a puppet office exists in Boston — probably as a shady tax write-off. No doubt Tiger's behind it all!

Getting Help: Let Your Mouse Do the Walking

The Oracle9i tools have a ton of documentation dragging along with them. The documentation actually holds a great deal of valuable information and is indexed and cross-referenced ad nauseum. Your mouse may get dizzy running the maze of trails through backtracks, side streets, riddles, and CMI (Completely Meaningless Information).

Here are several ways to find the Oracle9i documentation:

- ✔ Click the Help button that is located in almost every Enterprise Manager window.
- ✔ Select one of the documentation icons from the Start menu.
- ✔ Click the Documentation link on the Enterprise Manager Web site (if you've implemented it).

As of Oracle9i, you must install the documentation from a special documentation CD-ROM. If you do not do this additional step, you have to insert the Documentation CD-ROM to look up any of the Help documents.

Oracle has put all of its documentation in Web format (HTML) and includes a Java-based window with an Interactive search tool that can search across many documents.

Figure 1-10 shows the main search window that begins your exploration of the documentation.

For those of you who want to do a search, click the letter of the word you want to find. For example, you may want to read up on initialization parameters, so you click the letter *I*. This pops up the I listing for the Master Index. The Master Index combines index entries from all of Oracle's documentation into a single searchable, alphabetized listing. After you find the words *initialization parameters* for our example, you will find a detailed list of links for every initialization parameter, plus links for migration issues, concepts, and how-to instructions for changing parameter settings. To view the corresponding entry, just click it.

If you need additional help resources, go to the Oracle Web site called Technet. It's great! The membership is free, and there are discussion groups on all the latest topics: e-commerce, Enterprise Manager, Oracle Forms, and so on. Visit the Web site at `technet.oracle.com/`.

Figure 1-10:
Go hunting
for subjects
using this
versatile
document
search tool.

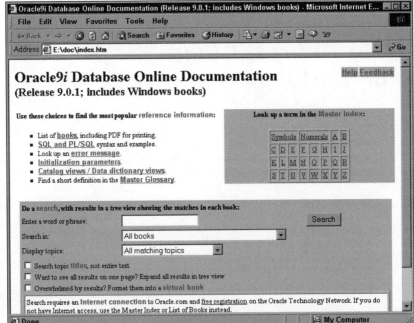

Chapter 2

Data Whaaat? A Database Primer

*S*o you just installed Oracle9i, you have the shiny new box sitting on your office shelf for your colleagues to envy, and you're ready to do some heavy-duty computing with databases. That's great. But first — ssssshh! Be vewy, vewy quiet! — wouldn't it be nice if you knew something about databases?

This chapter focuses on databases, tables, rows, and columns and how they all join to form one big, happy family. The chapter also has a section on the new kid on the relational block: the object.

For the most part, databases are designed to make your life easier. I offer lots of cute examples and scenarios in this chapter, just to show you how practical databases really are.

If, after reading this chapter, your head is spinning like that girl's in *The Exorcist,* please do not fret. After sifting through this book, you'll be creating relational and object-relational databases in your sleep.

Dataspeak Definitions for the Techno-Impaired

Shakespeare wrote, "A rose by any other name would smell as sweet" — but when you order one over the Internet, you should probably call it a rose. Similarly, you should probably understand some common database terms, including

 ✔ Databases

 ✔ Users and roles

 ✔ Tables

 ✔ Columns and rows

 ✔ Relationships

 ✔ Object types

 ✔ Object tables

 ✔ Object views

 ✔ Methods

 ✔ Arrays

 ✔ Nested tables

Sections throughout this chapter provide an expanded look at each of these terms and how they relate to Oracle9i users.

The term *database* has many meanings, depending on the context. In the world of *Oracle9i For Dummies,* this term refers to all tables, all data inside the tables, and all the users, views, synonyms, and many more items that the Oracle9i software keeps track of for you. Your database has a name (you type the database name when you install a new database). If your operation uses two databases, each has a unique name and each has its own set of tables, data, users, and so on. Each database is called an Oracle9i *instance*.

A *relational database* is a collection of tables connected in a series of relationships so that they reflect a small part of the real world. An *object-oriented database* uses objects, rather than tables, to store information. Objects also contain *methods,* which are predefined ways to manipulate the data. Oracle9i is a combination of a traditional relational database and an object-oriented database. I call this an *object-relational database*. So should you.

Here are a few of the many reasons why databases are great for storing information:

 ✔ Databases keep similar pieces of information, such as names and addresses, in one place so that you can use them in many places.

 ✔ Databases categorize, sort, filter, and pool items in multiple ways without duplicating the data.

You can harness databases to manage and reorganize your information. Suppose that you have two address books: one for clients and one for friends. Helen started as just a client but has become your friend. Would you copy her address to the Friends address book? Would you leave Helen's address in the Clients book and remember to look for her there? Would you give up and make a new book with both clients and friends in it? Would Helen really put up with all these address-book shenanigans? I think not!

If you have both address books in tables in Oracle9i, the program can combine the tables for you, as illustrated in Figure 2-1. Click a button and Oracle9i opens with your friends' addresses, including Helen's, in alphabetical order. Close the file and click another button and Oracle9i opens with your clients' addresses, including Helen's, in alphabetical order. Best of all, Oracle9i does not duplicate entries. Each entry contains an identifying field that tells the database whether the entry is a friend, a client, or both. You entered Helen's address only once, but you may feel as though you recorded it twice. How practical of you! Soon, you may need to start paying yourself twice.

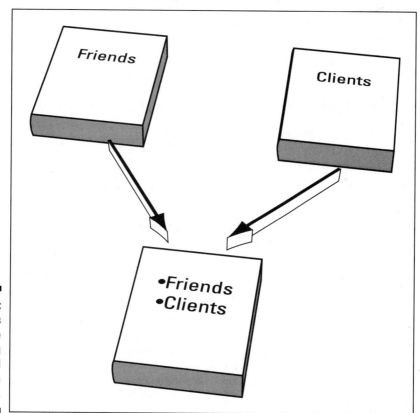

Figure 2-1:
Databases
make
managing
related
information
easier.

Relational Database Concepts

The traditional relational database has been around for many years. It still is very popular for business applications of all kinds, including banking, airline, and manufacturing applications. Ask anyone!

Today, the relational database is still hot stuff as it finds its niche on the Internet. E-commerce, Internet banking, virtual shopping malls, and even dating services use relational database engines behind their Web sites. For example, the popular online bookstore Amazon.com uses an Oracle database to handle online searching and purchasing. Amazon.com uses its database also to display information related to a book — for example, when you view the page for *Oracle9i For Dummies,* you see a list of other books that have been purchased by people who bought *Oracle9i For Dummies.*

This section describes the main ideas you should be familiar with when using a relational database.

Users and roles

A *user* is a unique login name in Oracle9i. Before any data goes into your database, you must have users to own the data. All users in the Oracle9i database have these characteristics:

- A unique name that is 1 to 30 characters long.

- A password (which does not have to be unique) that is 1 to 30 characters long. The database, your operating system, or even your Web site can validate the password. Traditionally, the database does this.

- At least one role assignment. *Roles* determine the capabilities and privileges that a user has inside the database. Although you can assign privileges to each user directly, the easiest way to manage privileges is to assign them to roles. (I discuss users and roles in Chapter 8.) The database administrator (DBA) can add and remove roles.

An Oracle9i user usually corresponds to one person in the real world. That person has his or her own user name and password. Sometimes, for convenience, several people share an Oracle9i user name, and all of them know the user name and password. This arrangement can have legitimate uses, such as in these situations:

- A team of programmers is working on one project. One Oracle9i user owns all the tables and other elements.

✔ You must give a large and continually changing group of people limited access to the database. Administering all the changes is too difficult. For convenience, you distribute a single user name and password to all these people. Generally, you do this only for a user name that has restricted access to prevent inadvertent damage to data.

✔ A large public or government bureau needs to find more effective ways to waste money training everyone and his brother to log in to Oracle9i so that next year's budget will be larger.

Tablespaces and datafiles

I could write an entire chapter on how Oracle9i stores your data as compressed, indexed, validated chunks in your database. However, even a DBA has little use for the details because Oracle9i handles so much of the storage process automatically. This section shows you all the basics you need to know without bogging down in a mire of details.

The basic storage components for an Oracle9i database are

✔ **Tablespace.** This is the largest piece of storage. Your initial database came configured with at least four tablespaces. One tablespace may contain a single table or hundreds of tables. A special kind of table (a really huge rascal called a *partitioned table*) crosses over several tablespaces.

✔ **Datafile.** This is a file you can see on your hard drive. Each tablespace uses the storage space contained in at least one datafile. As tables within a tablespace grow, more datafiles can be added to that tablespace. Or the original datafile can expand. Or both! See Chapter 9 for all the exciting details.

Figure 2-2 illustrates the contents of a basic Oracle9i database. Oracle9i stores data differently than, say, your word processing program, which stores one document in one file. Oracle9i stores data from many tables inside one file. As rows are inserted in a table, Oracle9i uses a chunk of a datafile. The chunks of space for a particular table don't need to be next to each other. The first chunk is data you added to the first table, the second chunk could be data in a second table, and the third chunk could be additional data for the first table. Chapter 9 goes into more detail about assigning space to tables and tables to tablespaces.

The memory that Oracle9i uses is called the System Global Area, or *SGA*. This memory contains specific sections for various tasks. For now, think of it as the RAM behind the database. Chapter 18 describes how you can tune this area using Memory Manager.

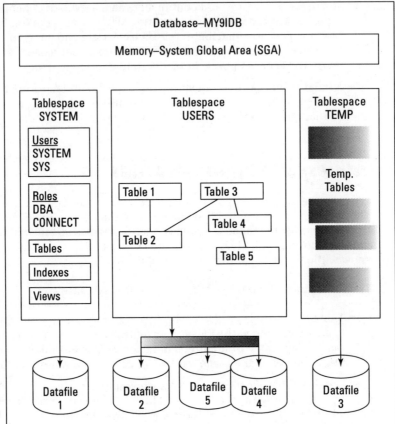

Figure 2-2:
This is your
brain on
Oracle9i.

In Figure 2-2, you see one database, which is named MY9IDB. This database contains three tablespaces, which are created automatically when you create a new Oracle9i database:

✔ SYSTEM. This tablespace contains a lot of the overhead, or system, tables needed to maintain and run your database. Lists of users (such as SYSTEM and SYS) and lists of roles (such as DBA and CONNECT) are stored here as well as lists of tables, indexes, views, and more. Chapter 7 tells you the whole story.

✔ USERS. The USERS tablespace comes as the default storage location for your tables when you create a new Oracle9i database. This tablespace is intended to store the tables that you create. For example, if you create sample tables for AMY and BAKERY (which I provide), these tables most likely end up in the USERS tablespace. I can't guarantee that they will because you can always create new tablespaces and store your tables in these other tablespaces instead of the USERS tablespace. It is entirely up to you.

✔ **TEMP.** This tablespace is the default storage location for temporary tables, such as the ones that are created (if needed) during the execution of a complex query. Again, after the database is created, you have the option of creating other tablespaces for this purpose.

Tables

A *table* holds information inside a database. Oracle9i stores the information in an orderly fashion, using rows and columns. A table is easy to sort, filter, add, average, find, combine, and otherwise manipulate. Every bit of information that goes into a relational database must also go into a table. Even Oracle9i itself keeps track of its own information in tables (refer to Chapter 7).

Tables are real-life objects and database objects. Table 2-1 shows the similarities and differences between the table in your dining room and the one in your computer.

Table 2-1	The Table versus the Table
Furniture Table	*Database Table*
Built of wood	Created out of thin air
Holds coffee cups	Holds the description and price of a coffee cup
Holds many kinds of objects	Holds information about only one kind of object
Runs out of space	Runs out of space
Has four legs	Has at least one column
Usually one per room	Usually many per database
Gets scratched	Gets fragmented

Chapter 9 goes into nauseating detail on how to build a better database table. Oracle9i stores information about your tables and your data in its own system tables, which are tables of tables.

Every table has a name. Try to make table names singular nouns or noun phrases. Descriptive table names are helpful. A table named CAR probably has something to do with automobiles, toy cars, train cars, or even cable cars. A table named X1000 probably requires a comment explaining its contents. Without a comment attached, you may need to ask someone for help, which could definitely interfere with your ultra-cool image at the office.

Tables always have columns and rows, which I cover in the very next section. Tables also have a *size*. Here are the main reasons for defining the size of a table:

- ✔ **To reserve room in the database for the table (initial space).** The database can store the table's data in one place, which makes the data more efficient to service. By reserving space, you help Oracle keep your table physically stored in a single chunk rather than in many smaller chunks. This arrangement is similar to going to a restaurant with a big group. If you call ahead and reserve space, the waiter seats your group together and can take your orders and deliver your food more efficiently. If you scatter yourselves all over the restaurant, the waiter works harder, and you have less fun. (On the other hand, watching the wait staff try to total multiple checks in a table configuration like this one is especially fun.) Keep your tables (and wait staff) happy and reserve the right amount of space for them.

- ✔ **To prevent a table from taking over the entire database (maximum space).** You may encounter a situation in which you are unable to predict how much information the table will store. All you know is that you want the table to stop growing when it eats up all the available database space. (This condition is known in some circles as the Rush Limbaugh syndrome.) Fortunately, a cure exists: the maximum space parameter. This method is not one of those dashboard buttons on the *Enterprise*. ("More power, Scotty!" "I'm givin' 'er all she's got, Cap'n! Any more, and she's going to blow!")

- ✔ **To control growth in a way that keeps the table from becoming scattered in the database (incremental space).** Some tables contain a great deal of data in one row. Tables containing video or graphics have rows that are much larger than the average bear. Larger tables benefit from having large chunks of space. Getting back to the restaurant example, suppose that your group grows in 50-person increments because members are arriving on buses. The wait staff would be wise to seat the group in one of the restaurant's larger areas instead of seating the group at random tables throughout the restaurant. If you use this method, be sure to add an automatic 15 percent gratuity.

Tables also usually have a primary key (a column or group of columns that uniquely identifies each row in the table), one or more indexes (see Chapter 18), and relationships (see Chapter 6).

Columns and rows

Columns are the vertical parts of tables. *Rows,* on the other hand, are the horizontal parts of tables.

Do other differences between the two exist? Absolutely. Columns and rows have different purposes in a table. A row holds different kinds of information about one item. The row for my Maui cruiser in Figure 2-3, for example, tells you that the car is a Buick Century, has four doors, and was made in 1982.

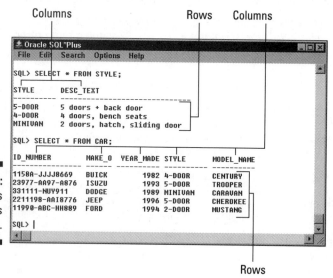

Columns   Rows   Columns

```
± Oracle SQL*Plus                                    _ □ ☒
 File   Edit   Search   Options   Help

SQL> SELECT * FROM STYLE;

STYLE       DESC_TEXT
----------  -----------------------------
5-DOOR      5 doors + back door
4-DOOR      4 doors, bench seats
MINIVAN     2 doors, hatch, sliding door

SQL> SELECT * FROM CAR;

ID_NUMBER       MAKE_O  YEAR_MADE STYLE    MODEL_NAME
--------------  ------  --------- -------- ----------
1158A-JJJJ8669  BUICK        1982 4-DOOR   CENTURY
23977-AA97-A876 ISUZU        1993 5-DOOR   TROOPER
331111-NUY911   DODGE        1989 MINIVAN  CARAVAN
2211198-AAI8776 JEEP         1996 5-DOOR   CHEROKEE
11990-ABC-HH889 FORD         1994 2-DOOR   MUSTANG
SQL> |
```

Rows

Figure 2-3: Two tables with parts labeled.

A column holds the same kind of information about many items. The YEAR_MADE column in Figure 2-3, for example, tells you when all the vehicles in the table were made.

Columns determine all the information that you allow in a table. These items can be cars, animals, people, sales figures, or whatever you choose. But if you don't have a column for the item, you can't enter it in your table. You use the CAR table, for example, to gather only certain information about cars: the ID number, make, year, style, and model name. Cars also have owners, color, options, tires, mileage, selling prices, and so on, but you can't place all these other categories of information in the CAR table until you add an appropriate column for each one. As Figure 2-3 stands, you know only five distinct kinds of information about the cars in the table.

When you create a table, the columns exist but the rows don't. *Columns* are like ground rules, which must be in place before the game starts. As you can in some games, you can later refine, add, modify, or even remove the rules (that is, the set of columns). See Chapter 19 for commentary on how to change your table's columns.

Each column holds one piece of information. You define a column by giving it a name and some guidelines about what it contains. Here are the components of a column:

✔ **Datatype.** This component helps classify data. High-class data own Cadillacs. Actually, the most popular classes break down like this:

- VARCHAR2. This class has a funny name that stands for *variable character string, Version 2.* VARCHAR2 is used most often for any kind of text data, such as names, addresses, favorite colors, or eye colors.

- NUMBER. Obviously, this class holds numbers.

- DATE. Oracle9i keeps dates in a special format that enables it to perform date math faster. Dates can fluster some databases but not Oracle9i. The Oracle9i date contains not only a four-digit year but also the time of day if you need it.

✔ **Length.** You need this component for VARCHAR2 and NUMBER datatypes. If you don't specify a length, Oracle9i plugs in a big default length. Putting in a reasonable length prevents you from getting an enormous essay in the FAVORITE_COLOR column.

✔ **Null/not null.** *Null* means *unknown* or *missing.* You can create a row in a table without filling in all the columns in that row. Columns in which no data has been entered are defined as containing a *null value.* For example, suppose that you have a table called APPLICATION_FORM that contains columns representing lines on an application form that prospective employees fill in. Any line that is not filled in on the form can be left blank in the database as well by allowing nulls in the corresponding column. Suppose that you have a line on the application for spouse name, for which you create a column called SPOUSE_NAME and allow null values. Later, when you are creating new rows in the table for new applicants, you can leave that column blank for single applicants and fill in the spouse name for married applicants. Nulls are okay in any column except the primary-key column, which by definition cannot be null. You add the not null parameter to primary-key columns.

Chapter 9 goes into more detail on defining columns. Chapter 3 shows you how to make changes in data in your table by using SQL*Plus. Take a look at Chapter 19 for complete instructions on adding columns to or removing columns from your tables.

Relationships

A database *relationship* is how two tables fit together. When two tables kiss, they're in a relationship. Even if they don't kiss, any connection between tables is a relationship, in database lingo.

Continuing with the car example, cars can be divided into categories such as 2-door, 4-door, SUV, and so on. By creating a new table called STYLE, you can relate any car in the CAR table to one particular style in the STYLE table. Figure 2-4 highlights the relationship of the CAR and STYLE tables from the preceding section. The CAR and STYLE tables have the STYLE column in common. The relationship between the tables looks like this:

- ✔ A car in the CAR table can have one style, which exists in the STYLE table.
- ✔ A style in the STYLE table can be selected for none, one, or many of the cars in the CAR table.

Two cars have the same style

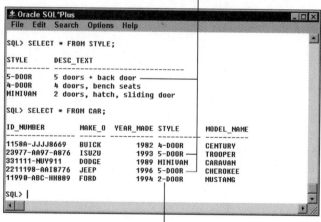

Figure 2-4:
The STYLE column creates a relationship between these two tables.

Every car has a STYLE found in the STYLE table

The key to the power of a database is the integrity of its relationships. When you say that a person has integrity, you imply that you trust him or her — that person does not say one thing and do another. *Integrity* in table relationships means that after you define the relationship, every row in both tables fits into the relationship. In the CAR and STYLE example, integrity means that no cars in the CAR table have a style that you do not find in the STYLE table.

The lines between tables in a diagram define relationships.

Object-Relational Database Concepts

Technically, you can call Oracle9i an *object-relational database.* This term means that Oracle9i contains all the features of a relational database combined with some of the features of an object-oriented database. Because the program is a hybrid, it allows you to make some choices about how to set up your database design.

This section covers the basic definitions of Oracle9i's world of objects and describes the main ideas you want to be familiar with when using object-relational structures such as methods and object tables.

Many of the object-oriented features of Oracle9i can be used with plain SQL, which you see in this book. SQL (Structured Query Language) is an English-like set of commands for defining database objects and querying and modifying data in those objects. The features that can't be used with plain SQL require you to use a programming language. The current release of Oracle9i supports Java, C++, and PL/SQL as languages in which you can program applications that use Oracle9i objects.

I cover programming in Java very lightly in Chapter 13 and 14 to demonstrate the Java Virtual Machine. Demonstrating C++ or PL/SQL is beyond the scope of this book. If you're interested, you can find out about C++ in *C++ For Dummies Quick Reference,* 2nd Edition (published by Hungry Minds, Inc.). *Oracle8i DBA Bible,* which I wrote with Gerrit-Jan Linker and Jonathan Gennick (also published by Hungry Minds, Inc.), shows you everything you need to know about programming in PL/SQL. Check it out. As for Java, check out *Java For Dummies,* 3rd Edition, by Aaron E. Walsh.

An object defined

An *object* is like a table with extra features. In both tables and objects, you use columns to define what information you'll store in each new row of the table. Object columns, which are called *attributes,* have extra features. You can define an attribute as

- ✔ **A regular column.** For example, your EMPLOYEE object may contain an attribute called BIRTH_DATE with the DATE datatype.

- ✔ **A list.** In object terms, a list is called an *array.* Your EMPLOYEE object may need to store a list of children's names for each employee. You could use an array called KID_NAMES defined as one to ten VAR-CHAR2(25) fields. This lets you store up to ten children's names, each with a length of up to 25 characters.

✔ **An embedded table.** Called a *nested table*, this kind of attribute allows you store a table of data (which you must predefine) within an object. In your EMPLOYEE object, for example, you could define a nested table that has four columns for storing past job history: START_DATE, END_DATE, EMPLOYER, and JOB_TITLE. The nested table stores as many job records as needed for each employee, right inside the EMPLOYEE object. If you have five employees, your object will contain five nested tables: one for each employee row.

✔ **Another object.** The object (which you must predefine) is treated like another column. However, unlike a column, it has its own list of attributes that can be made up of regular columns, arrays, nested tables, or more objects! The EMPLOYEE object could use a predefined object to store a mailing address. For example, suppose that a MAILING_ADDRESS object has attributes for STREET, CITY, STATE, and ZIP. You simply define an attribute in EMPLOYEE with a datatype of MAILING_ADDRESS. The advantage is that you can reuse the MAILING_ADDRESS object in many other objects for consistency.

Finally, an object has one more special feature that sets it apart from a table: an embedded program, called a method. A *method* tells Oracle how to change the values in your object. For example, you may want a method that calculates the employee's age and places it in a column in the EMPLOYEE object when you record the employee's birth date. Attributes, arrays, nested tables, and methods get scrutinized in the next sections in this chapter, so hold on to your tinfoil hat.

The scoop on object types

An *object type* enables you to extend the definition of datatypes (classes of data) into customized *user-defined datatypes*. Oracle calls these special datatypes *object types*.

For example, suppose that a fishery owner wants to use certain data about fish in many ways, so she creates an object type called FISH_TYPE. This object type contains three elements:

✔ **Fish name** (VARCHAR2 datatype)

✔ **Date of birth** (DATE datatype)

✔ **Date of death** (DATE datatype)

VARCHAR2 and DATE are normal datatypes.

You can also embed object types in other object types. For example, the FISH_DESC_TYPE object type contains three elements:

- ✔ **Fish name, birth, and death** (FISH_TYPE datatype)
- ✔ **Reference to the fish's aquarium** (REF datatype)
- ✔ **A text description of the fish** (VARCHAR2 datatype)

In this example, the first element's datatype is the user-defined datatype FISH_TYPE. The second is a column with a REF datatype, which is a normal datatype for connecting objects. The third column has a normal datatype of VARCHAR2.

Object types are used in these kinds of places in Oracle9i:

- ✔ **As a column datatype.** Object types can be used in place of the usual datatypes when you define a column in a table. The column is called an *object column*. A table can contain more than one object column and can contain a mixture of object columns and regular columns.

- ✔ **As a definition for an object table row.** One object type is used in place of a list of columns when you define an *object table*. You can define an object table as a table of one object type. Each row of the object table contains all the attributes in the object type.

- ✔ **As an element in another object type.** As you saw in the FISH_DESC_TYPE example, object types can be separated into modules and then composed into complex object types.

Chapter 10 shows you how to create and remove object types.

The connection of relational tables with objects

I mentioned that Oracle9i is a hybrid of both relational and object-oriented databases. To allow you to combine the two for the best of both worlds, Oracle9i provides three bridges between relational tables and objects:

- ✔ **Object view.** An *object view* maps relational tables into an object table. Like relational views, the object view doesn't actually have data of its own; it's merely a way of looking at the underlying tables. The object view allows you to use existing relational tables in an object-oriented way. If you use the object view, you can use the usual SQL commands or object methods to update the underlying data in relational tables.

✔ **Object table made of one object type.** An *object table* is a table whose rows are defined by an object type rather than by explicit columns. The elements in the object type define what data is stored in the object table.

In addition, an object table can have object methods, which manipulate data and are stored with the table's definition. In other words, object tables have both data and application functionality wrapped up into one object. Kind of like a corn dog.

Object tables also can have primary keys (unique identifiers) and indexes (fast retrieval paths).

✔ **Object table that combines object columns and relational columns.** An *object column* is a column with an object-type attribute as its datatype.

Chapter 10 demonstrates the creation of an object view and both kinds of object tables. Getting a room with a view is my object when visiting relatives in the Far East.

Object reference

An object reference, or REF, is a special datatype created for object tables. It acts like a foreign key because it defines a relationship between two object types.

Say you have an object table called AQUARIUM_OBJ with a primary key. Another object table, the FISH_OBJ, has a column that shows which aquarium each fish is in. This column is assigned the REF datatype, and AQUARIUM_OBJ is named as the referenced object.

Unlike a relational table's foreign key column, the contents of the REF column can't be shown by using a normal SQL query. Even so, you can use the REF column to find details from the referenced object. For examples of how to use REF columns in queries, refer to Chapter 4.

Methods to their madness

An *object method* is a program stored in the database to perform special tasks on data in an object table. Object methods are great fun.

Methods are self-contained bits of programming code that travel with an object, delivering parts or modifying data according to the method code. Methods are the heart of object-oriented technology.

Suppose that you're working with an object-relational database schema (a set of related tables and objects) that contains information about making a model airplane. A model airplane has several subassemblies, such as the engine and the instrument panel, which are made up of individual parts. A change in any individual part may affect the assembly of the entire plane. If the fuel gauge in the cockpit is changed to a different diameter, for example, the hole drilled in the instrument panel must also be changed. You can use *object types* to define the individual parts, the subassemblies, and the entire airplane. *Object methods* define how these object types interact with one another. One program uses the object types and methods to handle changes in the data. Another program can use the objects and their associated methods to extract a complete instruction booklet for the plane.

Nested tables

My parents now have two homes: one in Arizona and one in Wisconsin. And I have two addresses for my friends on Maui: their post office box and their street address. I have to use two entries in my address book for each of them. When I go to computerize all my addresses into my database, I have to figure out how to store two different addresses for each person. And what happens if someone gets a third home, like my rich cousin Elmer? I want to have one record for each person with an expandable area for any number of addresses.

A *nested table* does this kind of cool trick. You can store multiple rows of one kind of data in a table that's nested in the column of another table.

Nested tables are a form of *collection,* which means a table within tables. Another form of collection is the array, which I describe in the following section.

Chapter 10 shows how to create a nested table. Chapter 4 shows how to query a nested table. Go for it!

Arrays

Have you ever been stuck scribbling your friend's new cell phone number below her home, business, and fax numbers in your sorry little black book? What if you could magically expand that little one-line phone number spot so it could hold any number of phone numbers and then just tuck back into that one line when you didn't need it?

An *array* holds a finite number of rows of data and allows you to add repeated data into a row in a table. An array is an alternative to defining two relational tables that store related information.

The difference between a nested table and an array is that the nested table has an unlimited number of rows whereas the array has a predefined maximum number of rows. Typically, you use an array for a simple collection, such as a list of phone numbers for a customer, and a nested table for more complex collections, such as the detailed items in a catalog order form.

Chapter 10 shows how to create an array for your viewing pleasure. Chapter 4 shows how to query an array, which happens to be a process that is identical to querying a nested table.

Databases, users, roles, tables, rows, columns, relationships, objects, nested tables, and arrays are not the only terms that are common to database development. Many more terms appear in this book and in the Oracle9i manuals. Look in the glossary in the back of this book for more definitions.

Database Things That You Can Do with Oracle9i

This section shows three scenarios that help you get a feel for what databases do in real life. I hope you enjoy these examples. Let your imagination run wild, and think about what you want your database to do for you.

Keeping track of a fishbowl (the easy example)

Why are aquarium fish so nervous when their world is quiet, rocking them in an endless cradle of gentle bubbles and waves? Well, I guess I would be nervous, too, if 12-foot eyeballs kept popping up in my picture window.

I have a small aquarium with one little gold guppy named Wesley, who was born on January 1, 2000. The aquarium used to contained four guppies, but Wesley ate the other three. Your mission, if you choose to accept it, is to design a set of tables that accurately depicts the world of my aquarium.

When you create a set of related tables and all the database things that go with these tables, you create a *schema*.

Continuing with the aquarium example, here are the facts that you have to work with:

✔ I have one aquarium that holds one gallon of water, if my 11-year-old doesn't get to it with his Ninja-stealth-throwing stars.

✔ I feed Wesley once a day, whether he asks for it or not.

✔ I change the water once every 14 days, even if I can still see Wesley.

✔ Three fish died. Their headstones in the garden read:

  • Fish Two (black-and-tan female guppy), born 12/11/99, died 3/15/00

  • Fish Three (red-and-white male guppy), born 2/18/00, died 4/8/00

  • Fish Four (transparent guppy), born 3/1/00, died on an unknown date under very suspicious circumstances while I was out of town

You can easily track all this information in a simple two-table schema, as shown in Figure 2-5. I discuss the kind of diagram shown in this figure in more detail in Chapter 6.

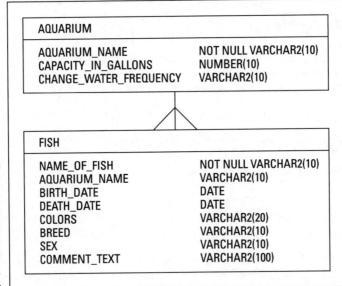

Figure 2-5:
My water world has two related tables: AQUARIUM and FISH.

Running a pet shop (the medium example)

I buy fish food at the pet shop around the corner from my house. The owner stocks the pet shop with bird cages, dog collars, flea powder, and a few hundred other items — including birds, rabbits, and even a monkey. Here are sundry activities that the shopkeeper handles with her database:

- Logging every item, purchase price, selling price, and number in stock
- Tallying tax on every sale
- Adjusting in-stock numbers on all inventory as sales occur
- Creating monthly accounting statements
- Creating annual tax reports
- Tracking names and addresses of customers
- Printing customized letters for advertising to customers
- Printing mailing labels

Keeping tabs on the pet shop — or any business that does similar tasks — is a great use for Oracle9i! The power of the relational model allows you to store your data one time and use it in a variety of ways.

For your information, if you were to try implementing the pet-shop system by using only the Oracle9i database and the tools that are part of the basic package, you would have to do some advanced programming or get some additional tools. The portions that you cannot do easily with your Oracle9i database are

- **Automatically adjusting inventory.** This requires programming a database trigger, which is beyond the scope of this book.
- **Tallying tax on every sale.** You need a database trigger or an additional tool (such as Oracle Forms) to calculate tax at the time of the sale.

Tracking endangered species globally (the hard example)

Tracking endangered species globally is a worthy cause, for sure. If I were creating a database design for the effort, here are the features that I would include:

- Information-gathering from around the world by using the Internet
- Massive text archiving of news articles about both positive and negative activities
- Full-text search capabilities
- Pictures of cute little animals to adopt by sending monthly payments
- Letters from cute little animals to their sponsors
- A Save the Guppies program, with a multibillion-dollar government grant
- Engraved ID tags for all the animals, identifying them as members of endangered species

✔ A clearinghouse of resources available to people and organizations, cross-referenced by needs, skills, locations, and funding

✔ Maps showing populations of animals, color coded by level of danger of extinction

✔ Internet search capabilities linked to maps of areas — clicking the map zooms you to a more detailed map

✔ Maps that allow you to click an area and go to a screen that shows all the data about the animals, resources, organizations, and any other items related to the area that you select in the map

✔ Automatic coffee dispensers in every cubicle at state offices

Read Chapters 6 and 7 before diving in and designing your own relational database. Those chapters offer invaluable insights on how to put your world into the relational-database format. Remember — the best design for your situation may not be the obvious choice.

As you find out more about databases, you discover that you can fit many pieces of information into the database world. Just remember to allow the databases, like art, to imitate life. When you start expecting life to imitate your database, come up for air. You could turn into one of those nerds who write database books.

Chapter 3

SQL Nuts and Bolts

· ·

· ·

*I*n this chapter, I cover information that spans about 300 pages of Oracle9i documentation. You may want to get your coffeepot going, put on your sunspot-deflecting glasses, and break out the little tinfoil hat. (Hey! Put down the pocket protector! Easy, now! Just hand it over and there won't be any trouble.)

You may have heard rumors about Oracle9i being so new that you can just write Java scripts to create and run the entire database. Sorry; not quite! You still need a healthy helping of SQL. This entire chapter is about SQL and relational tables. I include lots of examples for you to review and try out. I first cover some background information about SQL. Then I show you how to get some great results by using this powerful tool. You're going to wear out the book flipping to this chapter so often.

Chapter 4 has more SQL to dazzle and delight you. There, I show you how to use SQL to look at and revise data stored in object tables, nested tables, and arrays. Something to look forward to!

*Starting SQL*Plus*

You may want to follow along by typing the examples I show you in this chapter. To do so, you need to do two things:

1. **Add the sample schema that goes with this book.**

   For the schema, go to the Oracle9i portion of the For Dummies Web site at `www.dummies.com/extras/oracle9i.html`.

   * **Start SQL*Plus, logging in as AMY (the owner of the sample schema).**

After you complete those steps, you have a user called AMY who has a password of AMY123 and owns a set of tables, indexes, views, and other goodies for you to use.

Follow these steps, and you're in business:

1. **Start SQL*Plus.**

2. **Log in as the Oracle user.**

   If you see a login window, follow these steps:

   a. **In the Name box, type AMY.**

   b. **For the Password, type AMY123.**

   c. **In the Host String box, type the Oracle Net name of the Oracle9i instance on your local computer or on your network.** For a local database, you can usually leave this blank. For a database on a network, ask your administrator to provide you with a valid host string.

   d. **Click OK.**

   The SQL*Plus window appears, as shown in Figure 3-1.

Figure 3-1:
SQL*Plus
looks like
this when
you first
start it in its
Windows
mode.

```
± Oracle SQL*Plus                                          _ □ ✕
 File  Edit  Search  Options  Help

SQL*Plus: Release 9.0.1.0.1 - Production on Wed Oct 31 12:03:35 2001

(c) Copyright 2001 Oracle Corporation.  All rights reserved.


Connected to:
Oracle9i Enterprise Edition Release 9.0.1.1.1 - Production
With the Partitioning option
JServer Release 9.0.1.1.1 - Production

SQL> |
```

If instead of a login window you see a prompt for a user name, follow these steps:

    a. In the Username box, type AMY@*XXXX*, **replacing** *XXXX* **with the Oracle Net name of the Oracle9i instance on your local computer or on your network.**

        For example, if you want to log into the ORCL database as AMY, you would type SYSTEM@ORCL.

    b. Press Enter.

    c. When you are prompted for a password, type AMY123.

    d. Press Enter.

        The SQL prompt line appears, as shown in Figure 3-2. Your session may or may not have the Windows-like screen, but all the commands work the same.

Figure 3-2:
SQL*Plus looks like this when you run it in its command-line mode. Your colors may vary.

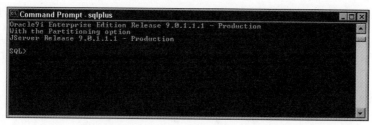

Follow along and type the examples shown in this chapter to become familiar with SQL and SQL*Plus. This chapter goes from very basic to very powerful SQL examples in a few short, sweet pages. Hold onto your hat, tinfoil or otherwise.

Here are some hints to help you get started when typing examples in SQL*Plus:

  ✔ To type an example, begin typing at the SQL> prompt line.

  ✔ To go to the next line and continue typing, press Enter.

  ✔ When you have finished typing a command, you can end it by typing a semicolon (:).

  ✔ To both end a command and execute it, type a semicolon and press Enter. Alternatively, you can press Enter, type a forward slash (/) on the next line, and press Enter.

- ✓ The results appear below your command. If the results are long, the page scrolls and you no longer see your command above the results.
- ✓ To run another command, just start typing it.

Asking a Question in SQL

In SQL, you ask a question when you write a *query.* The example queries in this book all begin with SELECT, which is your clue that they're queries. Your best weapon when you look at your data is a good knowledge of the *schema* (your set of tables) and how the tables relate to one another. You may want to read the stuff about keys in Chapter 6 before you go further in this chapter.

Simply put, anything that goes into tables in the database can come out when you use a query. With queries, you can do interesting things such as calculate average sales, find the highest-paid employee, and sort by employees' middle initials.

Here's the magic formula for constructing queries: Know what you want and where it is. Knowing the proper syntax (format) of SQL queries also helps. One of the goals of this chapter is to give you a good working knowledge of how to construct some basic SQL queries for getting data out of a table.

The basic SQL query

A SQL query has five main parts (or clauses):

- ✓ SELECT. Put the list of columns that you want to see here. List all the columns, even if they are from several tables, and separate them with commas.
- ✓ FROM. Put the table name here. If you have more than one table, list them all and separate them with commas.
- ✓ WHERE **(optional).** Put comparisons, limits, and connections between tables here and list them with AND or OR between each set. The WHERE clause is optional. When the WHERE clause is left out, all rows are chosen.
- ✓ GROUP BY **(optional).** Tell how you want data summarized here. You need this clause only for a query that summarizes data. See the "Grouping and Summarizing Data" section later in this chapter.
- ✓ ORDER BY **(optional).** List columns to use for sorting here. When there is no ORDER BY clause, rows are returned in no specific order.

A few other types of clauses can go into a query, but the preceding clauses are the primary ones.

Here's how the five parts fit together in a single SQL query:

```
SELECT COLUMN, COLUMN, ...
FROM TABLE
WHERE CLAUSE
GROUP BY CLAUSE
ORDER BY CLAUSE;
```

Some sample queries

Pretend that you are ruler of the universe, and you're visiting Earth. Pour a glass of wine, have a little cheese, and light up that great contraband Cuban cigar. For all the property you've cataloged so far, you want a list that shows the ID number of the human who currently owns the property, the ID number of the property itself, and a short description of the property. The query looks like this:

```
-- 01_basic_query
SELECT HUMAN_ID, PROPERTY_ID, LAND_DESC
FROM PROPERTY_LIST;
```

Three columns are chosen from one table. The results may look like this:

```
HUMAN_ID    PROPERTY_ID LAND_DESC
----------  ----------- ---------
MA-0015487 A-100        LOT ON NORTH SIDE OF LAKE
NY-0000145 B-999        APARTMENT
MA-0015487 A-102        HOUSE IN TOWN
3 rows selected.
```

You want the list in order by human, so you add an ORDER BY clause like this:

```
SELECT HUMAN_ID, PROPERTY_ID, LAND_DESC
FROM PROPERTY_LIST
ORDER BY HUMAN_ID;
```

You execute the query, with this result:

```
HUMAN_ID    PROPERTY_ID LAND_DESC
----------  ----------- ---------
MA-0015487 A-100        LOT ON NORTH SIDE OF LAKE
MA-0015487 A-102        HOUSE IN TOWN
NY-0000145 B-999        APARTMENT
```

Suppose you want only the property owned by one human, the one whose ID number is NY-0000145. Add the WHERE clause to narrow down your selection. The WHERE clause comes between the FROM clause and the ORDER BY clause. When you use a word or phrase in the WHERE clause, you enclose it in single quotes. Any entry other than a number must be in single quotes. Otherwise, Oracle9i assumes that the entry is a column name.

```
-- 02_basic_orderby
SELECT HUMAN_ID, PROPERTY_ID, LAND_DESC
FROM PROPERTY_LIST
WHERE HUMAN_ID = 'NY-0000145'
ORDER BY HUMAN_ID;
```

Oracle9i looks for rows that have NY-0000145 in the HUMAN_ID column and then sorts the rows in proper order. Sorting does not do much when you have only one row, but there it is anyway.

```
HUMAN_ID    PROPERTY_I  LAND_DESC
----------  ----------  ---------
NY-0000145  B-999       APARTMENT
```

Some tips to help you write good queries

The following tips may help you write good queries. Some of these tips are guidelines or hints for good form; others are simply possibilities — options you have available that you may not be aware of.

- ✔ List columns in the sequence in which they appear in your report. The SELECT clause is your only chance to specify which column comes first, second, and so on.

- ✔ Use the asterisk to select all the columns in a table to save yourself some typing time when you need all the columns (in the sequence they appear in your table) in your query.

```
SELECT * FROM HUMAN;
```

- ✔ List columns in the order in which you sort them. This is not a requirement, but it is logical — like listing people's names in the phone book with their last name first to facilitate quick visual searching.

```
SELECT COUNTRY. CITY. STREET ...
ORDER BY COUNTRY, CITY, STREET;
```

- ✔ Add words or phrases in your SELECT statement if you need them to make your report clearer, as in this example:

```
SELECT 'My name is'. FIRST NAME
FROM HUMAN;
```

- ✔ Sort by multiple columns if you need to do so. List the columns in the ORDER BY clause, as in this example:

```
... ORDER BY COUNTRY, CITY, STREET;
```

✔ Oracle9i is sensitive to uppercase and lowercase in the words or phrases that you place inside single quotes. For example:

```
... WHERE FIRST_NAME = 'Jane';
```

is not the same as

```
... WHERE FIRST_NAME = 'JANE';
```

✔ Oracle9i does not differentiate between uppercase and lowercase for column names, table names, and SELECT statement clauses. For example:

```
SELECT TOWN FROM HUMAN;
```

is identical to

```
select town from human;
```

In fact, you can mix and match, which I do all the time. Oracle9i sees the following line as the same as the preceding two examples:

```
Select Town from HuMaN;
```

✔ Oracle9i does not care how you arrange your query as far as blank spaces and line breaks are concerned. For example:

```
SELECT TOWN, COUNTRY FROM HUMAN ORDER BY TOWN;
```

is identical to

```
SELECT TOWN, COUNTRY
FROM HUMAN
ORDER BY TOWN;
```

Purely for aesthetics, my preference is to start each clause (SELECT, FROM, WHERE, and ORDER BY) on a new line.

✔ When you are working in SQL*Plus, the closing semicolon (;) marks the end of the SQL command. If you are writing a series of queries, separate each one with a semicolon.

*Using an Editor While Running SQL*Plus*

I call up my editor to beg for a deadline extension. You can call up an editor to save files, edit files, and start up files. When you are in SQL*Plus, you can type the following editing commands right in the command line:

✔ EDIT. Opens a temporary file and starts the local text editor for the current SQL query. When you close the file, its contents are written to your current SQL*Plus session.

✔ EDIT filename. Opens a file with the name specified. This command lets you make permanent SQL scripts. You replace filename with the actual file name and, if you want, include the path and suffix. For example, to edit a file called humans.sql, type this:

```
EDIT humans
```

The suffix is assumed to be .sql. If it's different, you need to type it with the file name.

✔ SAVE filename. Saves the current SQL query in a file. As with the EDIT command, replace filename with the actual file name and, if you want, include the path and suffix. For example, to save your current query in a file called testquery.sql, type this:

```
SAVE testquery
```

✔ GET filename. Retrieves a SQL query from the file that you name. The file must contain only one SQL statement, for example, a SELECT statement or an UPDATE statement. If the file contains more than one SQL statement, use the START command.

✔ START filename. Retrieves a file and runs it in the current SQL*Plus session.

✔ LIST. Lists your current SQL command.

SQL*Plus has some little rules that you need to know about regarding saving and running files. If you need to put more than one SQL command into a file, you can use only the EDIT and START commands with the file. Using the other commands causes errors or loses portions of the file. The GET, SAVE, and RUN commands deal strictly with a single SQL command at a time.

Pulling Out Data without Breaking Anything

"Don't touch that! I said *don't!* There — you broke it! Are you happy now?" Do these phrases sound familiar? If so, you may have a nagging hesitation about constructing a new query.

Don't worry. Data is never changed when you run a query — never. You may slow the entire company to a halt and black out the lights on a city block, but the data is okay.

I wander around in the park and lie awake nights worrying that you may break your fingers if you spend a great deal of time typing long, involved queries. When this insomnia occurs, I just slip on my handy little tinfoil hat to filter out excess sunspot radiation. In an effort to save your fingers, I want to share with you the secret of the alias. An *alias* is an alternative name for a table or a column in a query. Using aliases in the FROM clause of a query saves typing.

A table alias is defined by placing it immediately after the table name and is separated from the table name by a space. In the following query, H is the alias for the HUMAN table:

```
-- 03_alias
SELECT H.HUMAN_ID, H.FIRST_NAME, P.LAND_DESC
FROM HUMAN H, PROPERTY_LIST P
WHERE H.HUMAN_ID = P.HUMAN_ID;
```

The HUMAN table's alias is the letter H. The PROPERTY_LIST table's alias is the letter P. The letters are used as a prefix in the SELECT and the WHERE clauses to save typing out the table names.

You can also define a column alias. This alias appears as the column heading when you execute the SQL. For example, the following query has a column alias for each of its columns:

```
-- 04_column_alias
SELECT HUMAN_ID "Human ID", PROPERTY_ID "Prop#",
LAND_DESC Description
FROM PROPERTY_LIST
WHERE PROPERTY_ID > 'B';
```

Notice that I used double quotes around two of the aliases. Quotes are only needed if you use special characters such as the # sign or spaces, commas, and percent signs or if you want to preserve lowercase letters in the heading. Take careful note that I did not use the column alias in the WHERE clause. The WHERE clause must reference the actual column name. The results look like this:

```
Human ID    Prop#       DESCRIPTION
----------  ----------  -----------
NY-0000145  B-999       APARTMENT
```

Now that you have determined the whereabouts of Human B-999, you turn over the coordinates to your general and continue into the next galaxy.

Oracle's documentation of SQL commands

Oracle has created an interesting map-style diagram for documenting all the SQL commands and their variations. It takes a bit of examination to determine what it all means. Here is a quick outline of how to use the diagrams. The figure shows the diagram used to document the basic SELECT command I just described. As you can see, I have not elaborated on all the many optional features of the SELECT command. You build more details into it later in the chapter. The figure is just one part of the diagram, which is about three pages long. If you need to know all the gory details for any SQL command, you have to be able to read this kind of diagram. I've added notes to describe the key features of this kind of diagram. Don't say I didn't warn you! Oracle's documentation is a language all its own.

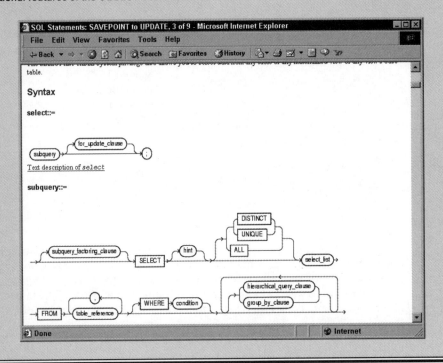

Combining Tables: The Meat and Potatoes of SQL

When a query combines data from two tables, the query is called a *join* (or *joining tables*). The key to joining tables is just that — the key! Know your tables, their keys, and how they connect. I've created examples for you in this section, beginning with simple ones and moving on to more complex ones.

Basic join query structure

The basic structure of a join is the same as that of any other query. The primary differences are that you list columns from several tables in the SELECT clause and that you list several tables and tell SQL how they fit together in the WHERE clause. Here's the basic layout:

```
SELECT ALIAS1.COLUMN, ALIAS2.COLUMN, ...
FROM TABLE ALIAS1, TABLE ALIAS2, ...
WHERE ALIAS1.COLUMN = ALIAS2.COLUMN
AND CLAUSE        --(optional)
GROUP BY CLAUSE   --(optional)
ORDER BY CLAUSE;  --(optional)
```

The last three lines are optional additions to a join that are sometimes used, but not required.

A table alias (indicated in the preceding query as ALIAS1 and ALIAS2) assigns each table in the FROM clause a shorthand nickname. Use the alias (followed by a period) as an identifier to show which table is the source of each column in the other parts of the query (the SELECT, WHERE, GROUP BY, and ORDER BY clauses). Although a table alias is not technically required unless two columns in different tables have identical names, I find it to be important for creating clear and easy-to-follow join queries.

The next section shows several examples of join queries in action. As a general rule, the more tables you add to a query, the more complex the WHERE clause becomes.

Build your query gradually by starting with one table in the query and getting it to run. Next, add one more table and get the query working with two tables. Build onto the query, always stopping to test your results to make sure that your query still works. This way, if you do run into problems, figuring out what part of the query caused the problem — most likely, where you made your most recent change — is much easier. This simple technique saves hours of guesswork, after you've constructed an entire query, in trying to figure out which part doesn't work.

Examples of join queries

Now for the fun part! Imagine that you are a mermaid. You have categorized and catalogued your fantastic collection of rare seaweed in your Oracle9i tables. You have two tables: one called TYPE_OF_SEAWEED for the kind of seaweed and one called SEAWEED_SAMPLE for each unique specimen in your collection. Figure 3-3 shows the two tables, their relationship, and some of the data.

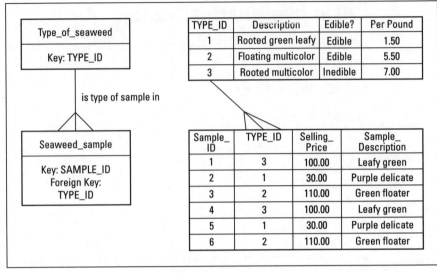

Figure 3-3:
The ultimate
mermaid
treasure —
and it's all
yours!

You want a simple report that lists the seaweed samples and shows whether they are edible. Here's the SQL code:

```
-- 05_basic_join
SELECT SS.SAMPLE_ID, SS.SELLING_PRICE,
SS.SAMPLE_DESCRIPTION, TS.EDIBLE
FROM SEAWEED_SAMPLE SS, TYPE_OF_SEAWEED TS
WHERE TS.TYPE_ID = SS.TYPE_ID
ORDER BY SS.SAMPLE_ID;
```

Here are the results:

```
SAMPLE_ID  SELLING_PRICE SAMPLE_DESCRIPTION    EDIBLE
---------- ------------- --------------------- ----------
         1           100 Leafy green           INEDIBLE
         2            30 Purple delicate       EDIBLE
         3           110 Green floater         EDIBLE
         4           100 Leafy green           INEDIBLE
         5            30 Purple delicate       EDIBLE
         6           110 Green floater         EDIBLE
```

Your seaweed is in big demand because of the tidal wave that wiped out all the seaweed farms in the area. You begin selling your seaweed collection. You want to keep track of the people who buy from you in case you want to send them a flyer next year, so you add a table called CLIENT to your database. Now you have three tables, as shown in Figure 3-4. You add a new column to the SEAWEED_SAMPLE table, which is a foreign key to the CLIENT table. (If you don't know what a foreign key is, look it up in Chapter 6.)

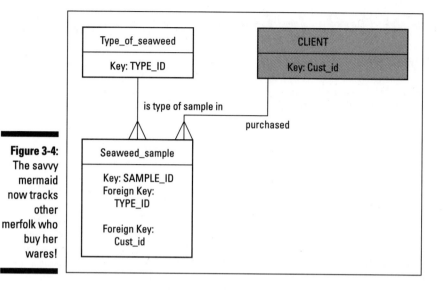

Figure 3-4:
The savvy
mermaid
now tracks
other
merfolk who
buy her
wares!

This query combines all three tables:

```
-- 06_join_3_tables
SELECT SAMPLE_ID, TS.EDIBLE, C.NAME
FROM SEAWEED_SAMPLE SS,
TYPE_OF_SEAWEED TS,
CLIENT C
WHERE TS.TYPE_ID = SS.TYPE_ID
AND SS.CUST_ID = C.CUST_ID;
```

The results look something like this:

```
SAMPLE_ID   EDIBLE       NAME
----------  ----------   --------
         1  INEDIBLE     Jane
         4  INEDIBLE     Jane
         3  EDIBLE       Joe
         6  EDIBLE       Joe
         2  EDIBLE       Harry
         5  EDIBLE       Amy
```

The results show a list of the samples, which types of seaweed are edible or inedible, and which of your little mermaid friends bought the sample. You are such an enterprising mermaid!

In the previous exercises, you use SQL commands to get a basic report from the database. The next section looks at some interesting extras that you get with SQL.

Using the Built-in Functions of Oracle9i

Oracle9i comes with many built-in functions. You can use some of these to manipulate the output of your query. In fact, you can use these functions in the WHERE clause to create truly unique queries. In the next two sections, I discuss two that are most commonly used: TO_CHAR and CONCATENATE.

Reformatting a date with TO_CHAR

One commonly used function is TO_CHAR, which allows you to reformat a date when it is displayed.

Swimming right along with my mermaid example, you determine that you want to send a few clients a birthday card. Query the CLIENT table to see each client's birth date. As a fun trick, you can use the TO_CHAR function also to find out the day of the week that each client was born. Here is the query:

```
-- 07_to_char
SELECT CUST_ID, NAME,
 TO_CHAR(BIRTH_DATE,'MM/DD/YY') "BIRTHDATE",
 TO_CHAR(BIRTH_DATE,'Day') "BIRTHDAY"
FROM CLIENT
ORDER BY BIRTH_DATE;
```

And the results look like this:

```
   CUST_ID NAME                                    BIRTHDAT BIRTHDAY
---------- ------------------------------- -------- ---------
         1 Jane                                     06/11/59 Thursday
         4 Amy                                      09/25/63 Wednesday
         2 Joe                                      05/30/66 Monday
         3 Harry                                    10/14/71 Thursday
         5 Jimmy                                    01/07/74 Monday
```

The TO_CHAR function has a few dozen parameters you can use to format the date any way you please.

The DATE datatype contains both time and date. If you do not specify a time, Oracle9i assigns the default time of midnight. Use the TO_CHAR function to view the time. For example, the following displays the birth date and time:

```
TO_CHAR(birthdate,'MM/DD/YY HH:MI')
```

Concatenating columns with concatenate (||)

You can squeeze two columns together into a single display column just as easily as you put salami in a Kaiser roll. Here's how.

Place the CONCATENATE symbol (||) between two columns. If one of the columns is a DATE datatype column, add the TO_CHAR function around it to make it into a plain character column.

Here's another mermaid dream: You list your seaweed samples by name and put the edibility of each one in parentheses after its name. Here is the query:

```
-- 08_concatenate
SELECT SAMPLE_ID,
SAMPLE_DESCRIPTION || ' (' || EDIBLE || ')' FULL_DESCRIPTION
FROM SEAWEED_SAMPLE SS,
TYPE_OF_SEAWEED TS
WHERE TS.TYPE_ID = SS.TYPE_ID
ORDER BY SAMPLE_ID;
```

Two columns, SAMPLE_DESCRIPTION and EDIBLE, were combined. The parentheses are not in the data and were added as literal values enclosed in single quotes. The entire string was concatenated with three sets of concatenation marks (each concatenation mark consists of a pair of vertical bars). The whole mess was named DESCRIPTION by using a column alias. Here are the results:

```
SAMPLE_ID FULL_DESCRIPTION
--------- ------------------------
        1 Leafy green (INEDIBLE)
        2 Purple delicate (EDIBLE)
        3 Green floater (EDIBLE)
        4 Leafy green (INEDIBLE)
        5 Purple delicate (EDIBLE)
        6 Green floater (EDIBLE)
```

In the following section, you can see another fine technique that can help you gain friends down at that new bar, The Database Connection Dot Com.

Grouping and Summarizing Data

Here's a simple question: How do you find the total number of phone book numbers in your telephone book table without waiting all day for your query results to scroll by? Or how do you figure out the list of dates on which more than 100 traffic tickets were issued?

The answer is: Summarize! In Oracle-speak, you use a group function. A *group function* performs a routine of some kind to a whole group of rows and then displays the results. Group functions do not modify the underlying database.

A number of group functions exist. The most commonly used group functions are

✔ SUM. Add a column for the selected rows.

✔ MIN. Find the lowest value in a column for the selected rows.

✔ MAX. Find the highest value in a column for the selected rows.

✔ COUNT. Count the number of rows selected.

The basic syntax of the group function is

```
SELECT groupfunction(columnname)
FROM ....
GROUP BY .... -- optional clause
HAVING ....   -- optional clause
ORDER BY ....;  -- optional clause
```

Replace *groupfunction* with the function name, and replace *columnname* with the column that requires the function. (In the case of COUNT, you can use * instead of a column name.)

The mermaid really needs to know exactly how many clients she has, so she issues the COUNT function on the CLIENT table like this:

```
-- 09_count
SELECT COUNT(*)
FROM CLIENT;
```

The results are

```
COUNT(*)
--------
       5
```

Now, suppose that the mermaid (that's you, so start swishing your seashells, honey) wants to know how many seaweed samples each client has purchased. This calculation requires the use of a group function (COUNT) and the GROUP BY clause in the query. Here is what the query looks like:

```
-- 10_group_by
select name, count(sample_id)
from client c,
  SEAWEED_SAMPLE SS
WHERE SS.CUST_ID = C.CUST_ID
GROUP BY NAME
ORDER BY NAME;
```

The results are

```
NAME                 COUNT(SAMPLE_ID)
-----------------    ----------------
Amy                                 1
Harry                               1
Jane                                2
Joe                                 2
```

Use any group function in the HAVING clause of a query to find subsets of data. For example, suppose that a friend asks you, "Which type of seaweed in your collection has the most value?" You decide to query the database to discover which types of seaweed contain samples totaling more than $100 in value. The following query, which uses a SUM function in the HAVING clause, answers the question:

```
-- 11_sum
SELECT TS.TYPE_ID, TS.DESCRIPTION_TEXT,
SUM(SS.SELLING_PRICE)
FROM SEAWEED_SAMPLE SS, TYPE_OF_SEAWEED TS
WHERE TS.TYPE_ID = SS.TYPE_ID
GROUP BY TS.TYPE_ID, TS.DESCRIPTION_TEXT
HAVING SUM(SS.SELLING_PRICE) > 100
ORDER BY TS.TYPE_ID;
```

The results are

```
  TYPE_ID DESCRIPTION_TEXT        SUM(SS.SELLING_PRICE)
--------- ---------------------   ---------------------
        2 Floating, multi-color                     220
        3 Rooted, multi-color                       200
```

In the next section, you can look at the other really powerful feature of SQL: modifying your data.

Making Power Changes in Data

The real power of SQL is evident in the way that it operates on many rows of data at one time. A single line of code can change every row in a table. You can use the techniques for gathering rows for a report to modify many rows at the same time. I break down the process for you in this section. The three basic commands are UPDATE, INSERT, and DELETE. Each command has some interesting subtleties.

Modifying data with the UPDATE command

This overworked command allows you to modify data that you previously put in a table. Maybe you muffed it and put everyone's first name in the last-name field. Maybe you added a column and need to plug in data. The UPDATE command can help you. The command has several forms. The next two sections cover the two basic forms of the UPDATE command.

Using literals

The most common form of the UPDATE command involves manipulating columns using data from the same row. The basic format of the statement looks like this:

```
UPDATE tablename SET columnname = expression,
columnname2 = expression2
WHERE where clause; -- optional clause
```

Replace *tablename* with your table's name, and replace *columnname* and *columnname2* with the names of the columns that you want to modify. You can use *expression* (and *expression2*) to modify many things: a literal (such as today's date), another column, or some combination of both. Replace *where clause* with any valid WHERE clause to tell Oracle9i which rows you want to include in the update. You can update all the rows in a table by not including the WHERE clause.

For example, you head the ticket sales committee for an upcoming benefit dinner. Your job involves tracking every ticket sale, printing nametags for all the guests, and building a mailing list of all the guests. Naturally, you set up a table (TICKET) in your Oracle database to help you. You start with columns for FIRST_NAME and LAST_NAME. Later, you decide to combine those columns into a new column called FULL_NAME. Now you want to combine every first and last name that you've put in the table and put the results in this new column. Here's the statement:

```
-- 12_update_all_rows
UPDATE TICKET
SET FULL_NAME =
FIRST_NAME || ' ' || LAST_NAME;
```

Oracle9i replies with this:

```
9 rows updated.
```

Simple yet effective. This statement updates every row in the table because no WHERE clause is on the end.

You now want to update all the rows of ticket holders who bought their tickets before October 10. You want to give these people an extra raffle ticket for the grand prize drawing because they were the early birds. You create a new column called EXTRA_TICKET that has YES in it for the early birds and NO in it for everyone else. Although I can think of several ways to update this column, I will show you the most straightforward method. This method does the work in two separate statements: one for all the early birds and one for everyone else. Here is the UPDATE command for the early birds:

```
-- 13_update_some_rows
UPDATE TICKET
SET EXTRA_TICKET = 'YES'
WHERE PURCHASE_DATE < TO_DATE('10-OCT-00');
```

Oracle9i replies with this:

```
5 rows updated.
```

The UPDATE command for Johnny-come-latelies looks like this:

```
-- 14_update_some_rows
UPDATE TICKET
SET EXTRA_TICKET = 'NO'
WHERE PURCHASE_DATE >= TO_DATE('10-OCT-00');
```

Oracle9i replies with this:

```
4 rows updated.
```

Now, to save your updates, commit the transaction by typing:

```
COMMIT;
```

Oracle9i replies:

```
Commit complete.
```

Oracle's date format

Oracle has a standard default format for displaying dates. This standard also affects how you write literal dates in all SQL statements. The format is

```
DD-MON-YY[YY]
```

DD is the day of the month, MON is the first three letters of the month, and YY[YY] is the year. For example, July 5, 1956 is 05-JUL-56.

The month can be in uppercase, lowercase, or any combination of uppercase and lowercase. For example, November 1, 2045 is 01-NOV-45, 01-nov-45, or 01-Nov-45.

April 13, 2005 is `13-Apr-2005`. When you leave the century off the year, Oracle assigns it to 20, the current century if the last two digits are less than 50. If the last two digits are 50 or greater, Oracle assigns the previous century (19) to the date.

When you write a literal date in SQL, place it inside the `TO_DATE` function, which converts characters to a date. For example, `TO_DATE('01-OCT-96')` converts October 10, 1996, to Oracle's date format.

If, for some reason, you have dates that are in a different format, you can tell Oracle what to expect. `TO_DATE('10/15/87','mm/dd/yy')` converts October 15, 1987, to the Oracle date format. You can use many variations of this format.

Using subqueries

The second variation on the `UPDATE` command has a great amount of flexibility because it uses a subquery — a query within the `UPDATE` command. The basic format goes like this:

```
UPDATE tablename SET (columnname, columnname2, ...) =
(SELECT columnname3, columnname4, ...
FROM tablename2
WHERE subquery where clause)
WHERE update where clause;
```

The placement of parentheses is very important.

Replace *tablename* with the table you are updating. Replace *columnname*, *columnname2*, and so on with a list of columns you are updating. The subquery is everything inside the parentheses after the equal sign. Inside the subquery, you can place any query you want, so long as the columns in the subquery (*columnname3*, *columnname4*, ...) match the columns in the `UPDATE` command. *The subquery must return exactly one row.*

Notice the two `WHERE` clauses. The first one (*subquery where clause*) corresponds to the subquery `SELECT` statement. The second one (*update where clause*) corresponds to the `UPDATE` command and tells Oracle9i which rows to update with the data retrieved in the subquery.

The subquery has incredible power! I love using subqueries! Subqueries save so much time and effort and show you how much you can do in SQL. Gush, gush. I put together a few examples to give you some ideas on how to use the subquery format. This format has so many variations that listing them all is impossible.

Suppose that you run an art gallery. You have a table called `MONTHLY_SALES`. You update it at the end of the month with the sum of all sold art from the `DAILY_SALES` table. Here's your `UPDATE` command for January 2001:

```
-- 15_update_subquery
UPDATE MONTHLY_SALES
SET (SALES_AMOUNT) =
(SELECT SUM(SALES_AMOUNT)
FROM DAILY_SALES
WHERE SALES_DATE BETWEEN TO_DATE('01-JAN-2001')
AND TO_DATE('31-JAN-2001'))
WHERE SALES_MONTH = '01-JAN-2001';
```

Oracle9i tells you it's finished with this:

```
1 row updated.
```

I enclose the subquery in parentheses. The first WHERE clause in this statement relates to the subquery only. The second WHERE clause relates to the UPDATE statement, causing only one row in the MONTHLY_SALES table to be updated (the one for January 2001).

Using correlated subqueries

The third variation on the UPDATE command is more difficult to understand, but it is also one of the most flexible of the UPDATE commands. This variation is similar to the preceding UPDATE command syntax, except that the subquery is slightly different. The basic format goes like this:

```
UPDATE tablename SET (columnname, columnname2, ...) =
(SELECT columnname3, columnname4, ...
FROM tablename2
WHERE tablename2.columnname5 = tablename.columnname6 AND
            subquery where clause)
WHERE update where clause;
```

Replace *tablename* with the table to be updated. Replace *columnname*, *columnname2*, and so on with a list of columns to be updated. The subquery is everything inside the parentheses after the equal sign. You can place any query you want inside the subquery. Columns in the subquery must correspond with the UPDATE command's list of columns. *The subquery must return exactly one row for each row updated.*

Notice the two WHERE clauses. The first one (beginning at the WHERE and ending with *subquery where clause*) corresponds to the correlated subquery SELECT statement. Replace *tablename2.columnname5 = tablename.columnname6* with a join clause that connects (correlates) the table that you're updating with the table in the subquery. The second WHERE clause (*update where clause*) corresponds to the UPDATE command and tells Oracle9i which rows to update with the data retrieved in the subquery.

Now suppose that you are a mermaid — don't argue with me! You categorized and catalogued your seaweed collection beautifully in your Oracle tables. You have two tables: one called TYPE_OF_SEAWEED for the kind of seaweed and one called SEAWEED_SAMPLE for each unique specimen in your collection.

One day, a tsunami of incredible force sweeps through your corner of the ocean, which makes certain types of seaweed suddenly very rare. You immediately decide to increase the price per pound of all the edible seaweed. That means you have to update two of your tables: Double the price per pound (PER_POUND column) for all edible seaweed types in the TYPE_OF_SEAWEED table, and use the new price per pound to calculate the new SELLING_PRICE of all the edible seaweed in your SEAWEED_SAMPLE table.

Figure 3-5 shows a simple query of the TYPE_OF_SEAWEED table before the price hike. Four rows include edible seaweed types that range in price from $1.50 to $5.50.

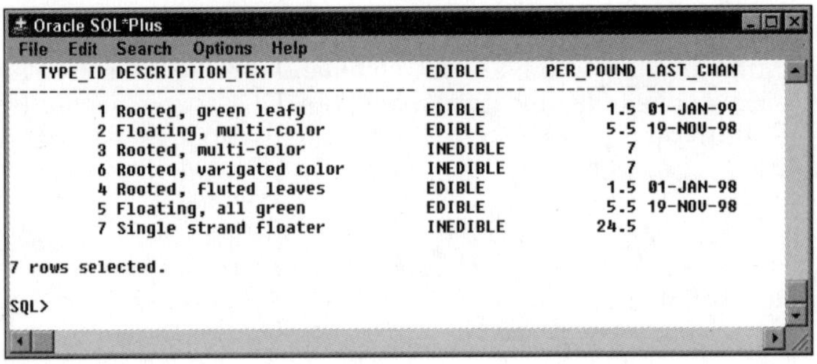

TYPE_ID	DESCRIPTION_TEXT	EDIBLE	PER_POUND	LAST_CHAN
1	Rooted, green leafy	EDIBLE	1.5	01-JAN-99
2	Floating, multi-color	EDIBLE	5.5	19-NOV-98
3	Rooted, multi-color	INEDIBLE	7	
6	Rooted, varigated color	INEDIBLE	7	
4	Rooted, fluted leaves	EDIBLE	1.5	01-JAN-98
5	Floating, all green	EDIBLE	5.5	19-NOV-98
7	Single strand floater	INEDIBLE	24.5	

```
7 rows selected.

SQL>
```

Figure 3-5: The sequestered seaweed selection of the solitary mermaid.

First, you want to double the price per pound of your edible seaweed. The price per pound is kept in the TYPE_OF_SEAWEED table. Here is the SQL code to double the price:

```
-- 16_update_some
UPDATE TYPE_OF_SEAWEED
SET PER_POUND = 2 * PER_POUND,
LAST_CHANGE = SYSDATE
WHERE EDIBLE = 'EDIBLE';
```

Oracle9i tells you this:

```
4 rows updated.
```

The preceding UPDATE command doesn't have a correlated subquery. However, after the update is performed, the SQL code that updates the SEAWEED_SAMPLE table refers to the new PER_POUND price in a *correlated subquery*.

Update the selling price of all your edible samples by recalculating the selling price using your updated TYPE_OF_SEAWEED table. The recalculation takes the PER_POUND column value for the correct type of seaweed and multiplies it by 20 (because all your samples are 20 pounds). The SQL code for changing the selling price of edible seaweed looks like this:

```
-- 17_update_correlated
UPDATE SEAWEED_SAMPLE SS SET (SELLING_PRICE) =
(SELECT TS.PER_POUND * 20    -- start of correlated subquery
FROM TYPE_OF_SEAWEED TS
WHERE TS.TYPE_ID = SS.TYPE_ID
 AND EDIBLE = 'EDIBLE')      -- end of correlated subquery
WHERE SS.TYPE_ID IN (SELECT TS1.TYPE_ID
        FROM TYPE_OF_SEAWEED TS1
        WHERE TS1.EDIBLE = 'EDIBLE');
```

Oracle9i complies and says

```
4 rows updated.
```

The correlated subquery begins on the third line of code and ends on the sixth line. The TS alias tells you that the first TYPE_ID in the subquery refers to the TYPE_OF_SEAWEED table. The SS alias tells you that the second TYPE_ID comes from the SEAWEED_SAMPLE table, which is not in the sub-query but is in the outer part of the UPDATE command.

The last three lines are another WHERE clause that narrows the rows to be updated by saying, "Update only those rows that have a TYPE_ID that is in a list of TYPE_IDs that are edible."

The correlated subquery is a powerful tool, and getting the hang of it may take some experimentation and study.

When you're trying an UPDATE command, remember that ROLLBACK can undo the updates.

Inserting new rows with grace and style

I'll be brief: The INSERT command has three forms that are similar to the UPDATE command.

Inserting a single row

Here's the way to insert a row where you know exactly what the row will look like:

```
INSERT INTO tablename (columnname1, columnname2, ...) values
(value1, value2, ...);
```

Replace *tablename* with the table into which you insert the row. Replace *columnname1*, *columnname2*, and so on with the names of the columns you insert data into. You can omit the entire list of columns as long as your list of values matches the table's columns exactly.

Replace *value1*, *value2*, and so on with the actual data. You must enclose everything except numbers in single quotes. Dates must be in the standard Oracle format (*dd-mon-yy*) and in single quotes.

Make sure your list of values is in the same order as your list of columns. When you omit the list of columns, your list of values must be in the same order as the columns, as they are defined in the table.

You, the enterprising mermaid, have discovered a type of seaweed that has never before been identified. Your immediate response is, of course, to add it to the TYPE_OF_SEAWEED table in your fabulous underwater Oracle database. You currently have seven types of seaweed in your table. Here's the code to add an eighth variety:

```
-- 18_insert_one_row
INSERT INTO TYPE_OF_SEAWEED
(TYPE_ID, DESCRIPTION_TEXT, EDIBLE, PER_POUND) VALUES
(8, 'Mutant strain of green goo','INEDIBLE',7.50);
```

Oracle replies

```
1 row created.
```

Don't forget to COMMIT your changes to the database. Type:

```
COMMIT;
```

Oracle replies

```
Commit complete.
```

Inserting with a subquery or correlated subquery

INSERT is similar to the subquery used in updates. Review the section on updates using subqueries for a detailed look at how to write a subquery. I will not repeat myself again and again this time.

The basic format for this kind of INSERT command is

```
INSERT INTO tablename (column1, column2, ... ) subquery;
```

The main difference between UPDATE and INSERT is that the INSERT command has no parentheses around the subquery. Again, you can leave the list of columns out if you are including every column in the table. You list the columns in the same order in which they appear in the table.

At the risk of getting hate mail from mermaids, I continue to play with this plausible example in which you are indeed a mermaid. Swish your tail and take a deep breath of water as you prepare to try this example.

Your neighbor, Millie Mermaid, gave you a disk with her mailing list on it. You want to insert all the merfolk into your CLIENT table. Here's the command:

```
-- 19_insert_many_rows
INSERT INTO CLIENT
SELECT CUST_ID+125, NAME,
STREET_ADDRESS || ' ' ||CITY_STATE_ZIP,
NULL, NULL
FROM MILLIES_MAILING_LIST;
```

Oracle9i replies

```
3 rows created.
```

Because you include every column in the right order (the last two columns are designated with null values), you do not have the column list in the command. Millie's table, called MILLIES_MAILING_LIST, has a CUST_ID, as yours does. You do have to accommodate some differences between her list and yours:

- Her address is broken into two columns, which you combine in your ADDRESS column by using the concatenate function, ||.

- You already have CUST_IDs from 1 to 125, so you add 125 to Millie's CUST_ID to make sure that you get a unique CUST_ID.

- Millie does not have a COUNTRY column, so you substitute NULL in this column for all the inserted rows.

- Millie does not have a BIRTH_DATE column, so you substitute NULL in this column also.

If you prefer, you can include a list of columns in the INSERT command so you do not have to add null value placeholders to your subquery. Here is what it would look like:

```
-- 20_insert_many_rows
INSERT INTO CLIENT (CUST_ID, NAME, ADDRESS)
SELECT CUST_ID+125, NAME,
STREET_ADDRESS || ' ' ||CITY_STATE_ZIP
FROM MILLIES_MAILING_LIST;
```

The results of the command are the same: Rows are inserted with values in three of the five columns for each row. The remaining two columns contain null values in all the inserted rows.

Deleting rows with distinction

The DELETE command is simple and to the point:

```
DELETE FROM tablename
WHERE clause;
```

Replace *tablename* with the actual table name. Replace *clause* with any valid WHERE clause, like one that you would put in a query. The WHERE clause can include subqueries or correlated subqueries if you want.

You have changed your mind — not that this ever happens to you, I'm sure! You decide to throw out every inedible seaweed sample that you own because you're moving to a smaller sea cave. Here's the code:

```
-- 21_delete
DELETE FROM SEAWEED_SAMPLE
WHERE TYPE_ID IN (SELECT TYPE_ID FROM TYPE_OF_SEAWEED
  WHERE EDIBLE = 'INEDIBLE');
```

Oracle9i says

```
2 rows deleted.
```

This code uses a subquery that creates a list of all inedible seaweed types. Then the main WHERE clause uses that list to choose which rows to delete.

Test your DELETE statement by creating a SELECT statement that uses the same WHERE clause. This way, you can look at which rows are being selected for deletion before you delete them.

Fixing Mistakes, or Where's the Brake?

When Oracle9i makes a change permanent, it calls this a *commit,* or *committing* the change, because you use the COMMIT command. Before the commit occurs, you can undo a command with the ROLLBACK command.

Oracle9i allows you to reverse a committed change with a new command: UNDO. So, if all else fails, you can recover from changes even after they are saved with the COMMIT command.

The COMMIT and ROLLBACK commands

When you use the COMMIT and ROLLBACK commands, here's what you tell Oracle9i to do:

- *COMMIT:* Save as permanent all changes made since the last commit was implemented in the database.
- *ROLLBACK:* Remove all changes since the last commit was implemented.

One interesting thing about the COMMIT command becomes evident when you look at data using SQL*Plus. Suppose I update ten rows in a table. When I select the ten rows, I see my data with the changes. However, as in life, until you commit to change, others can't see the change. In other words, Joe can query *the same ten rows* before I commit my changes, and he sees them as unchanged even though I see them as changed. After I commit, Joe's next query shows the ten rows with the changes, just as I see them.

Another interesting point that comes up only when you share your database with others is the *locked row.* After I make a change to a row, Oracle9i *locks* that row to prevent others from changing it. Others can still query the data, and they see the data as if it were not changed. If they attempt to change the data, they receive an error message. When I commit, the lock goes away. The lock prevents two people from overlaying each other's updates.

Commands that can't be undone, even with ROLLBACK

Some insidious commands have an automatic commit built in, which means that if you make changes that you have not yet committed to the database and you execute one of these commands, the changes get committed automatically. The most commonly used commands that automatically commit prior changes are

- ALTER. You can alter a table, index, tablespace, and more.
- CREATE. You can create tables, indexes, tablespaces, database links, synonyms, views, users, roles, and so on.
- DROP. You can drop just about anything you create.
- RENAME. You can change the name of a table, view, or index.

The next section looks at a new feature that lets you peer into a window where you can look and even restore old data.

Traveling Back in Time with Flashback Queries

A Flashback Query takes you on a trip. Far out, man! Can you dig it? Flashback Query is a new feature of Oracle9i that resets all the data you look at to a date and time in the past that you name. It is easy to use because after you set the Flashback date and time, you simply use SQL as usual, and Oracle9i delivers the data from the past to you.

Imagine that you instructed your assistant to use SQL*Plus to update a list of phone numbers in your CLIENT table. He goes to lunch, after committing the changes he made. Because you routinely work during lunch hours (you really need a break!), you have decided to finish updating the table yourself. How are you going to figure out where he left off? You can use Flashback Query to roll back the database to before he went to lunch. Then you use SQL queries to compare the old and new phone numbers to quickly locate the remaining numbers that need to be changed.

 This all sounds great, but the default settings allow only 900 seconds of time travel. That calculates out to 15 minutes. If you need more time, you must increase the time span by increasing the value of the UNDO_RETENTION initialization parameter.

Now, it's time to experiment with this flashback technology. Hold onto your tinfoil hat!

When you want to view data from the past, you must sandwich your queries between flashback commands. The first command (DBMS_FLASHBACK. ENABLE_AT_TIME) turns on the flashback and sets time back a few minutes or hours, according to your specifications. Then you write your query or other commands as usual. Finally, revert time to normal, by issuing the second flashback command: DBMS_FLASHBACK.DISABLE.

Follow along with this example to see how to run a Flashback Query.

You, the mermaid entrepreneur, have just completed updates of all the prices on your seaweed samples. A client calls and reminds you that you promised her a sample at the price in your database last Tuesday (eight hours ago). You have to go find that price.

Note: This example assumes that the UNDO_RETENTION parameter was set to 36000 (ten hours in seconds) last week sometime, which allowed Oracle9i to record historical data for more than the eight-hour period you need.

To change the UNDO_RETENTION, type these commands, replacing PWD with the actual password of the SYS user and DatabaseName with your database name:

```
CONNECT SYS/PWD@DatabaseName AS SYSDBA;
ALTER SYSTEM SET UNDO_RETENTION=3600 SCOPE=BOTH;
```

Then wait a day before trying the flashback query so the system has time to gather the data it needs.

First, you must allow AMY to use the flashback package provided by Oracle. To accomplish this, type these commands, replacing PWD with the actual password of the SYS user and DatabaseName with your database name:

```
CONNECT SYS/PWD@DatabaseName AS SYSDBA;
GRANT EXECUTE ON DBMS_FLASHBACK TO PUBLIC;
CONNECT AMY/AMY123@DatabaseName;
```

Next, set the clock back, so to speak, by issuing the ENABLE_AT_TIME command.

```
EXECUTE DBMS_FLASHBACK.ENABLE_AT_TIME(TO_TIMESTAMP
        (TO_CHAR(SYSDATE-10/24), 'DD-MM-YYYY HH24:MI:SS'));
```

Finally, reset your session so any further queries occur during normal time:

```
EXECUTE DBMS_FLASHBACK.DISABLE;
```

Oracle9i replies:

```
Succeeded.
```

You can run as many queries as you want after initiating the Flashback session.

It is possible to use Flashback Query to retrieve old data and restore it to the database even after updates or deletions are committed. However, you have to know PL/SQL along with Flashback Query. Refer to Oracle9i's "Application Developer's Guide — Fundamentals" documentation for a complete example. Now that you have your feet wet with SQL for relational tables, you may want to batten down the hatches and launch into SQL for objects in the next chapter.

Chapter 4

Object SQL: The New Stuff

● ●

● ●

*T*here is more to the imagination than is dreamed of in your universe. How's that for a misquoted quote? Reading the Oracle9i documentation about objects and how to use them is a lot like reading the study guide for a Shakespearean play — the poetry gets lost in the translation.

This chapter gives you not only the facts but also the *feel* of objects. (They'll seem like old friends.) After reading this chapter, you'll be just as comfortable querying object tables as you are querying good old relational tables.

To get the most out of this chapter, you need to understand the basic construction of a SQL query. If you want to brush up on this subject, page back to Chapter 3 and look it over.

All the examples in this chapter use a sample object schema called BAKERY. You can create this schema by going to the For Dummies Web site at www.dummies.com/extras/Oracle9i.html and using the schema found with the Oracle9i extras. There you also find the instructions for creating the BAKERY schema.

The BAKERY schema contains two object tables, in which each row is a single object type:

> ✔ INGREDIENT_OBJ. This table contains a list of ingredients that the bakery has on hand for mixing all the different kinds of bread.
>
> ✔ BREAD_OBJ. This table contains a nested table of ingredients and amounts that make up the RECIPE_TBL column.

The BAKERY schema also contains a CUSTOMER table, which has a combination of regular columns and object columns. An *object column* is a column with a user-defined datatype (aka an object type). This table has two object columns:

- ✔ **BREAD_LIST.** An array containing a list of the breads that a particular customer has purchased. (Chapter 2 has a good definition of an *array.*)
- ✔ **FULLADDRESS.** An object made up of columns for the customer's postal box, street address, city, state, and country.

The names of the objects, columns, types, and attributes indicate what kind of object they are. Table 4-1 shows all the pieces and parts that I use in this chapter.

Table 4-1	Sample Types, Objects, and Attributes for Chapter 4		
Name	*Kind of Item*	*Attribute*	*Attribute Datatype*
INGREDIENT_TYPE	Object type	INGREDIENT_NO	NUMBER(5)
		INGREDIENT_NAME	VARCHAR2(30)
		PRICE_PER_OUNCE	NUMBER(8,4)
		OUNCES_IN_STOCK	NUMBER(10,1)
BREAD_TYPE	Object type	BREAD_NO	NUMBER(5)
		BREAD_NAME	VARCHAR2(20)
		SALE_PRICE	NUMBER(5,2)
		IN_STOCK	NUMBER(10)
		RECIPE_TBL	RECIPE_NEST
RECIPE_TYPE	Object type	INGREDIENT_REF	REF of INGREDIENT_TYPE
		AMOUNT_IN_OUNCES	NUMBER(10,1)
RECIPE_NEST	Table type		Table of RECIPE_TYPE
BREAD_ARRAY	Array type		Array (10) of NUMBER(5)
BREAD_OBJ	Object table		Row of BREAD_TYPE

Name	Kind of Item	Attribute	Attribute Datatype
INGREDIENT_ OBJ	Object table		Row of INGREDIENT_ TYPE
ADDRESS_ TYPE	Object type	POBOX	VARCHAR2(20)
		STREET	VARCHAR2(50)
		CITY	VARCHAR2(35)
		STATE	VARCHAR2(20)
		COUNTRY	VARCHAR2(25)
CUSTOMER	Object table	CUSTOMER_ID	NUMBER(5)
		FIRST_NAME	VARCHAR2(15)
		LAST_NAME	VARCHAR2(25)
		FULLADDRESS	ADDRESS_TYPE
		PHONENUMBER	VARCHAR2(25)
		BREAD_LIST	BREAD_ARRAY

The SQL examples in this chapter use the items shown in Table 4-1. Notice that an object type always has the suffix _TYPE, an array type has the suffix _ARRAY, and so on. I named them this way so that you can easily distinguish when to use the type name and when to use the attribute name in the sample SQL. This distinction becomes clearer when you make your own objects and work with them.

Starting SQL*Plus

To follow along with the examples in this chapter, you must start SQL*Plus and log in with your Oracle9i user name and password. Follow these steps:

1. **Start SQL*Plus.**

   On Windows platforms, choose Start⇨Programs⇨Oracle HOME⇨Application Development⇨SQL*Plus.

   On UNIX, Linux, or any other platform, type **sqlplus** at the operating-system prompt to start the command-line version of SQL*Plus.

2. **Log in as the Oracle user.**

   If you see a login window, follow these steps:

    a. In the Name box, type the user name. If you installed the sample schema, type BAKERY**.**

    b. In the Password box, type the password. If you installed the sample schema, type BAKERY**.**

    c. In the Host String box, type the Oracle Net name of the Oracle9i instance on your local computer or on your network. For a local database, you can usually leave this blank. For a database on a network, ask your administrator to provide you with a valid host string.

    d. Click OK.

If instead of a login window you see a prompt for a user name, follow these steps:

    a. In the Username box, type BAKERY@*XXXX***, replacing XXXX with the Oracle Net name of the Oracle9i instance on your local computer or on your network.**

    For example, if you want to log into the `ORCL.TEST.NET` database as BAKERY, you would type **BAKERY@ORCL.TEST.NET.**

    b. Press Enter.

    c. When you are prompted for a password, type BAKERY**, the current password for BAKERY.**

    d. Press Enter.

    Your session may or may not have the Windows-like screen, but all the commands work the same.

Now you can follow along and type the examples in this chapter to familiarize yourself with SQL for object tables. You're gonna love it.

Querying Object Tables in SQL

Object tables might seem tricky to use. In Oracle9i, however, most relational techniques for querying have been adapted to handle many situations that arise with object tables. (Find out how to create your own object tables in Chapter 10.)

All object tables have a built-in set of methods that can be used only in PL/SQL blocks. You can't use these methods with plain old SQL; you need to know PL/SQL. These methods involve sorting, comparing, and adding null rows to nested tables and deleting rows from arrays. I don't cover PL/SQL in this book because it is an advanced topic. If you want to learn about PL/SQL, check out a book I wrote with Gerrit-Jan Linker and Jonathan Gennick: *Oracle 8i DBA Bible* (published by Hungry Minds, Inc.).

With SQL, you can do the basics: query, insert, update, and delete. And you find out how to do all these in the next few sections. So, put on your favorite CD, grab your best brain-stimulating beverage, don your solar-ray-deflecting cap, and dive in.

The basic object-oriented SQL query

If your object table contains nothing but the usual datatypes in its object type attributes, you can proceed with a query that is just like a query you would use for a relational table.

For example, INGREDIENT_OBJ contains rows made up of INGREDIENT_TYPE. Looking at Table 4-1, you can see that INGREDIENT_TYPE is an object type with attributes that are NUMBER or VARCHAR2. Because these attributes are standard to Oracle9i, you can create a simple query like this to display your ingredients:

```
-- 01_objectquery
SELECT * FROM INGREDIENT_OBJ;
```

SQL*Plus displays the results:

```
INGREDIENT_NO INGREDIENT_NAME PRICE_PER_OUNCE OUNCES_IN_STOCK
------------- --------------- --------------- ---------------
          101 Cinnamon                      2             150
          102 Flour                       .04            3500
          103 Bananas                     .06             680
          104 Nuts                        .22             425
          105 Yeast                        .2             995
          106 Salt                        .03             245
```

You can add a WHERE clause to this query, just as you would with a relational table query. The following query lists any ingredients that have a price per ounce over ten cents:

```
-- 02_objectquery_
SELECT * FROM INGREDIENT_OBJ
WHERE PRICE_PER_OUNCE > .1;
```

Oracle9i shows these results:

```
INGREDIENT_NO INGREDIENT_NAME PRICE_PER_OUNCE OUNCES_IN_STOCK
------------- --------------- --------------- ---------------
          101 Cinnamon                      2             150
          104 Nuts                        .22             425
          105 Yeast                        .2             995
```

Suppose that you try this query on a table that contains another object type, a nested table, or an array in one of its columns. The column that is an object type, nested table, or array shows up with identifying data inside the record. Here is an example:

```
-- 03_queryobject
SELECT LAST_NAME, FULLADDRESS FROM CUSTOMER;
```

The table — CUSTOMER — contains the FULLADDRESS column, which uses ADDRESS_TYPE as its datatype. The results of the query are shown in Figure 4-1.

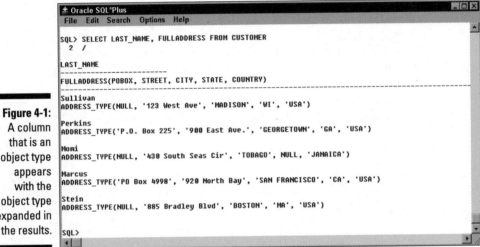

Figure 4-1:
A column that is an object type appears with the object type expanded in the results.

To remove the attributes from the column that contains the object type, use this format in the SELECT clause:

```
tablealias.columnname.attributename
```

where *tablealias* is the alias that you must specify in the FROM clause, *columnname* is the column from the table, and *attributename* is the attribute from the object type that defines the column. I define the concept of table aliases completely in Chapter 3.

For example, use this query to grab the last name, street address, and city of each of your customers:

```
-- 04_querywithtype
SELECT C.LAST_NAME,
C.FULLADDRESS.STREET,
C.FULLADDRESS.CITY
FROM CUSTOMER C;
```

The table alias is the letter C, the column name is FULLADDRESS, and the attribute names are STREET and CITY. Here are the results of the query:

```
LAST_NAME            FULLADDRESS.STREET     FULLADDRESS.CITY
----------------     ----------------------  ------------------
Sullivan             123 West Ave           MADISON
Perkins              900 East Ave           GEORGETOWN
Momi                 430 South Seas Cir     TOBAGO
Marcus               920 North Bay          SAN FRANCISCO
Stein                885 Bradley Blvd       BOSTON
```

The moment that you add anything related to objects to your SQL query, you must use a table alias. If you don't use an alias, you get this error:

```
ORA-00904: invalid column name
```

Queries using a nested table

A *nested table* is a table embedded inside another table's column. By definition, you can get more than one row of data from the nested table for each row in the primary table. How do you do this?

Oracle9i has a technique called *flattening* a nested table. In effect, you pretend that the nested table is a stand-alone table, but in the FROM clause, you don't name a table. Instead, you include an entire query (a subquery) that grabs the column containing the nested table. The basic format of the query is

```
SELECT alias1.ntattribute, ...
FROM TABLE (SELECT alias2.ntcolumn
  FROM tablename alias2
  WHERE clause) alias1;
```

Using the new technique of flattening a nested table, you replace

- ✔ *alias1* with the alias that you create for the subquery
- ✔ *ntattribute* with the nested table attribute that you want to view
- ✔ *tablename* with the main table that contains the nested table
- ✔ *alias2* with an alias for the main table
- ✔ *clause* with a query criteria that makes the subquery return a single row of data from the main table (each main table row contains one complete nested table)

One fully flattened nested table is queried.

For example, the BAKERY schema contains a bread table that stores the bread names. One of the columns in the bread table contains a nested table that consists of a set of rows: one row for each ingredient that you need to make the bread. This column is named RECIPE_TBL. Find RECIPE_NEST in Table 4-1 to review the attributes in the nested table. Use the following query to return the ingredients needed to make a loaf of Cinnamon Swirl bread (bread number 1):

```
-- 05_querynestedtable
SELECT P.INGREDIENT_REF.INGREDIENT_NAME,
    P.AMOUNT_IN_OUNCES
FROM TABLE (SELECT B.RECIPE_TBL
    FROM BREAD_OBJ B
    WHERE BREAD_NO = 1) P;
```

The query returns this list of ingredients:

```
INGREDIENT_NO_REF.INGREDIENT_N AMOUNT_IN_OUNCES
------------------------------ ----------------
Cinnamon                                      2
Flour                                        64
Yeast                                         2
Salt                                         .3
```

Here's a cool trick: The following query shows you how to pull out *all* the rows from the bread table and list their recipe ingredients. The key is to use the CURSOR keyword in the SELECT clause and place a subquery in the SELECT clause. Clever. Too clever to make sense, but you can definitely win some points for this kind of query. Here it is:

```
-- 06_querynestedtable
SELECT B.BREAD_NO, B.BREAD_NAME,
CURSOR (SELECT NT.INGREDIENT_REF.INGREDIENT_NAME,
    NT.AMOUNT_IN_OUNCES
    FROM TABLE (B.RECIPE_TBL) NT )
FROM BREAD_OBJ B;
```

Oracle displays this list of recipes:

```
BREAD_NO    BREAD_NAME              CURSOR(SELECTNT.INGR
---------   --------------------    --------------------
       1    Cinnamon Swirl          CURSOR STATEMENT : 3
CURSOR STATEMENT : 3
INGREDIENT_REF.INGREDIENT_N     AMOUNT_IN_OUNCES
---------------------------     ----------------
Cinnamon                                       2
Flour                                         64
Yeast                                          2
Salt                                          .3
       3    Plain White             CURSOR STATEMENT : 3
CURSOR STATEMENT : 3
INGREDIENT_REF.INGREDIENT_N     AMOUNT_IN_OUNCES
```

```
-----------------------          -------------------
Flour                                            72
Yeast                                             2
Salt                                             .5
        2       Nutty Banana        CURSOR STATEMENT : 3
CURSOR STATEMENT : 3
INGREDIENT_REF.INGREDIENT_N      AMOUNT_IN_OUNCES
-----------------------          -------------------
Flour                                            72
Bananas                                           4
Yeast                                             2
Salt                                             .5
```

Notice the attribute named NT.INGREDIENT_REF.INGREDIENT_NAME in the preceding query. This attribute is like an embedded join connecting to another table. Here's how it works:

✔ The NT table alias refers to the nested table column.

✔ The INGREDIENT_REF column contains the object ID (OID) of one row in INGREDIENT_OBJ. This column is similar to a foreign-key column, which contains the value of the primary key for one row of another table. The datatype of the OID attribute is always REF, which is a special datatype for object tables.

✔ INGREDIENT_OBJ contains an attribute named INGREDIENT_NAME. Only object tables can be referenced with an OID. The OID is similar to a ROWID in a relational table.

✔ By stringing everything together, you get the ingredient name — for example, Cinnamon — for each row of the nested table.

Now, how about some fun with arrays?

Queries using an array

As you know, an array is like a nested table, except for one important difference: An array has a predefined maximum number of rows whereas a nested table has no maximum number of rows.

An excellent use for an array is storing a simple repeating value in a column, such as a list of ten favorite colors. In the example schema, the array stores up to ten values that tell what kind of bread a customer has purchased.

You can see the values stored in the array by using two different kinds of query techniques. The first technique simply allows Oracle9i to display its interpretation of the array in a long string. Just name the array column in your SELECT clause. For example, the CUSTOMER contains an array. You can query the CUSTOMER_ID column and the array column as follows:

```
-- 07_queryarray
SELECT CUSTOMER_ID, BREAD_LIST
FROM CUSTOMER;
```

The results are messy but accurate, as shown in Figure 4-2.

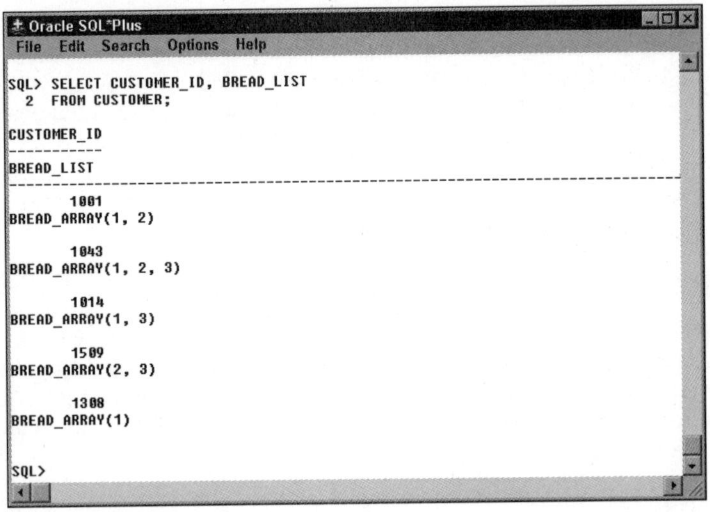

Figure 4-2:
An array
shows up
with its
parts
dissected in
this query.

The second technique yields results that are more like the query of a nested table, using the same flattening technique:

```
-- 08_queryarray
SELECT COLUMN_VALUE
FROM TABLE (SELECT CUST.BREAD_LIST
FROM CUSTOMER CUST
WHERE CUST.CUSTOMER_ID = 1001) PURCHASES;
```

These results show the data inside the array for customer number 1001:

```
COLUMN_VALUE
------------
           1
           2
```

Note: The COLUMN_VALUE column is the default name of the column in an array of numbers or other basic Oracle datatypes such as dates and characters.

Now you have a good start on arrays.

Making Changes to Object Table Data

When making changes to an object table, you use the UPDATE, INSERT, and DELETE commands, just as you do in relational SQL. The only difference is that with an object table, you must use an alias on the table. And if you're dealing with a nested table, you must flatten it first.

For more information on flattening a nested table, see the "Queries using a nested table" section earlier in this chapter. Flattening allows you to make changes to a nested table in the same way that you make changes to a relational table or object table (depending on the characteristics of the nested table).

Updating an object

Suppose that you want to change the street address of one of your bakery customers. The street address is stored in a column with an object type as its datatype. How do you tell Oracle9i to update just one attribute within that column? Here's how:

```
-- 09_updateobject
UPDATE CUSTOMER C
SET C.FULLADDRESS.STREET = '987 West Side Ave.'
WHERE CUSTOMER_ID = 1001;
```

Updating one row in a nested table

To update one row in a nested table, you need to flatten the nested table and then update it as if it were a regular table.

Suppose that you've made a change to your famous Nutty Banana bread (bread number 2) recipe by increasing the amount of bananas. Use this update command to change the amount of that one ingredient:

```
-- 10_updatenestedtable
UPDATE TABLE (SELECT B.RECIPE_TBL
    FROM BREAD_OBJ B
    WHERE BREAD_NO = 2) RECIPE_LIST
SET RECIPE_LIST.AMOUNT_IN_OUNCES = 100 WHERE
RECIPE_LIST.INGREDIENT_REF.INGREDIENT_NAME =
'Bananas';
```

SQL*Plus replies:

```
1 row updated.
```

Inserting rows into an object table

The For Dummies Web site at www.dummies.com/extras/Oracle9i.html includes lots of examples of inserting data in object tables. Take a look at the Bakery.sql file in the Make directory.

The trick to inserting rows into an object is to name the object type and follow it with a list of the values in parentheses. For example, suppose that you just got another regular customer at your bakery to fill in your questionnaire. To add this person to CUSTOMER, enter this SQL command:

```
-- 11_insertobject
INSERT INTO CUSTOMER VALUES
(1041, 'Joe','Smith',
ADDRESS_TYPE('PO Box 100', NULL,'MADISON','WI','USA'),
'222-333-4444',
BREAD_ARRAY());
```

The preceding SQL command shows you how to add data to an object type column. The object type column is called FULLADDRESS, but you don't see that name in the command. Instead, you see the object type name followed by a list of data in parentheses:

```
ADDRESS_TYPE('PO Box 100', NULL,'MADISON','WI','USA')
```

Each field inside the parentheses is a value for one attribute in the ADDRESS_TYPE object.

Here's how you insert a row into an object table that contains a nested table, when you want no data in the nested table:

```
-- 12_insertemptynestedtable
INSERT INTO BREAD_OBJ VALUES
(4,'Sourdough',.95, 12,RECIPE_NEST());
```

You list the nested table *type* (not the nested table *column*) and follow it with an empty pair of parentheses:

```
RECIPE_NEST()
```

A later section shows you how to insert rows into the nested table.

Inserting rows into an array

You can use SQL to insert data into an array at the same time that you insert the entire row. Here's an example:

```
-- 13_insertarray
INSERT INTO CUSTOMER VALUES
(1041, 'Joe','Smith',
ADDRESS_TYPE('PO Box 100',
'123 West Ave','MADISON','WI','USA'),
'222-333-4444',
BREAD_ARRAY(1,2));
```

The array column is named BREAD_LIST, but it is *not used* in the preceding INSERT command. Instead, you see the array *type* named, followed by a list of values inside parentheses:

```
BREAD_ARRAY(1,2)
```

In this case, the BREAD_ARRAY contains an array of numbers, so you simply list the numbers and separate them with commas.

If the array is an *object type* datatype rather than of a number or other standard datatype, you need to list the object type and then the values. For example, if the array is made up of a list of addresses of the type ADDRESS_TYPE, an array of two addresses looks like this:

```
ADDRESS_TYPE('PO Box 100',
'123 West Ave','MADISON','WI','USA'),
ADDRESS_TYPE('PO BOX 119',
'4000 East River Street','CHICAGO','IL','USA')
```

"How do I add data to a nested table?" you ask, anticipating my very next move as if you were reading my mind. (I'd better put on my tinfoil hat!)

Inserting rows into a nested table

To insert a row in a nested table, the flattening technique comes to the rescue once again. The INSERT command looks clumsy, but hey, it works!

Here are the two basic syntaxes for inserting rows into a nested table:

```
INSERT INTO TABLE (subquery of nested table column)
VALUES (...)
```

or

```
INSERT INTO TABLE (subquery of nested table column)
SELECT ...
```

Remember that the subquery must return one row. And just as you can with a relational table, you can sometimes use a list of values or a SELECT statement to fill the data in a row in your nested table.

For example, in the RECIPE_TBL nested table, add the first row for the new sourdough bread that you just added to the database. This row represents the first ingredient in the recipe for sourdough bread. Here is the SQL:

```
-- 14_insertnestedtable
INSERT INTO TABLE (
SELECT B.RECIPE_TBL
FROM BREAD_OBJ B
WHERE B.BREAD_NO = 3
)
SELECT REF(I), 2
FROM INGREDIENT_OBJ I
WHERE I.INGREDIENT_NO = 102;
```

Notice that the subquery retrieves the nested table column for one row in BREAD_OBJ. When BREAD_OBJ was created, the column containing the nested table was named RECIPE_TBL. The attributes of each row in the nested table are defined in the RECIPE_TYPE object type. Refer to Table 4-1 to review the attributes.

When using object types, you must prefix attributes with table aliases. Otherwise, you receive syntax errors when you try to execute your SQL code.

The first attribute in the nested table is a reference to the INGREDIENT_TYPE object type. You know this because the first attribute is of the REF datatype and has been defined to reference INGREDIENT_TYPE, which means that you must place an OID in this attribute. Use the REF function to grab the OID for you. The syntax is

```
SELECT REF(tablealias)
```

Replace tablealias with the alias of the table you're querying.

Deleting rows from an object table

Deleting rows from an object table is just like deleting rows from a relational table. Remember that if your object table has a nested table in one of its columns, Oracle9i also deletes the corresponding nested table inside that row.

Suppose that you're never going to use cinnamon (ingredient 101) in your bakery again because it was discovered that dolphins were harmed in the harvesting of cinnamon. So you want to delete the row from your list of ingredients, which you store in INGREDIENT_OBJ. Do it like so:

```
-- 15_deleteobject
DELETE FROM INGREDIENT_OBJ I
WHERE INGREDIENT_NO = 101;
```

SQL*Plus replies:

```
1 row deleted.
```

Watch out for dangling refs! Those guys could fall on you as you leave the stadium. Seriously, you must avoid dangling refs in your object tables. A *dangling ref* is a condition in which a row references a row that has been deleted. Oracle9i lets you do this without warning.

The previous example actually creates a dangling ref because you have existing bread recipes that use cinnamon. You can find the dangling refs in the RECIPE_TBL column of BREAD_OBJ. Figure 4-3 shows a query that hunts down dangling refs caused by deleting a referenced row in the bread recipes.

```
± Oracle SQL*Plus                                             _ □ X
 File   Edit   Search   Options   Help
SQL> SELECT B.BREAD_NO, B.BREAD_NAME,
  2    CURSOR
  3    (SELECT NVL(NT.INGREDIENT_REF.INGREDIENT_NAME,
  4       'Dangling ref found!')
  5    FROM TABLE (B.RECIPE_TBL) NT
  6    WHERE NT.INGREDIENT_REF IS DANGLING)
  7    FROM BREAD_OBJ B;

  BREAD_NO BREAD_NAME              CURSOR(SELECTNVL(NT.
  ---------- --------------------- --------------------
         1 Cinnamon Swirl          CURSOR STATEMENT : 3

CURSOR STATEMENT : 3

NVL(NT.INGREDIENT_REF.INGREDIE
------------------------------
Dangling ref found!

         3 Plain White            CURSOR STATEMENT : 3

CURSOR STATEMENT : 3

no rows selected
```

Figure 4-3: Cinnamon Swirl bread contains a dangling ref, but Plain White bread does not.

Deleting a row from a nested table

I bet that you've already guessed how to delete a row from a nested table. That's right, the great and powerful flattened nested table. When deleting a row from a nested table, your WHERE clause refers to attributes of the nested table.

Suppose that, because you've stopped using cinnamon in your Cinnamon Swirl bread, you want to delete that ingredient from your recipe. The recipe is stored in a nested table, so you flatten the nested table by grabbing the nested table inside a single row of the object table. Then you use this flattened table and delete one row from it. Here is the SQL:

```
-- 17_deletenestedtable
DELETE TABLE (SELECT B.RECIPE TBL
    FROM BREAD_OBJ B
    WHERE B.BREAD_NO = 1) RECIPE_LIST
WHERE
RECIPE_LIST.INGREDIENT_REF.INGREDIENT_NO = 101;
```

SQL*Plus replies:

```
1 row deleted.
```

You have passed through the gauntlet and deserve one cream-puff pie (or a great crab-and-chives salad if you live in California).

Chapter 5

Using Enterprise Manager's DBA Tools

● ●

In This Chapter

▶ Reviewing the major DBA components

▶ Discovering what's useful to an application designer

▶ Exploring all the miscellaneous parts and what they do

● ●

This chapter is like going to a school prom and dancing with every girl or boy (choose one, the other, or both; who am I to judge?). When it's over, you're tired, but you know their names and their favorite color/ or pet/ or rock band. As in life, you gotta kiss a lot of toads before you find your Prince/ or Princess Charming. This chapter introduces you to all the components that make up Enterprise Manager so you can try each one out a little.

Introducing Enterprise Manager

You are about to go exploring where no nerd has gone before. Well, hardly any. You are about to enter into a bunch of individual software modules that together make up Enterprise Manager. Enterprise Manager is a standard part of your Oracle9i installation. You can add extra components, called Packs, to the basic configuration for extra cost. The basic configuration alone is a valuable part of your DBA arsenal and worth your time to explore.

You can follow many different paths to open the door to the Enterprise Manager's tools. You can use Console to launch any individual tool to set up jobs that monitor events in one or more databases. You can launch individual toolsets, such as Performance Monitor, from your desktop. If, like me, you want to get to in there and work with tables, data, and security, your best bet is to begin with Console.

Console, as the name implies, is a visual workshop in which you can explore your database's makeup, from what files store the data to what users are allowed to change their own password. Console gives you an easy pick list of the most commonly used DBA applications on your desktop. You begin by selecting the database you want to explore, and then you select which tool to open. To start Console, follow these steps.

1. **Start Console.**

   On Windows platforms, choose Start➪Programs➪Oracle HOME2➪ Enterprise Manager Console. Note that the Oracle HOME2 label may have a different name, such as ORAHOME81, on your computer. The person who installed the software on your machine designates the name.

   On UNIX, Linux, or any other platform, type **oemapp console** at the operating-system command line.

   You see the logo screen for Oracle Enterprise Manager, and then the Oracle Enterprise Manager Console login window appears.

2. **Make sure the Launch Standalone option is selected, and then click OK.**

   Console's initial screen appears.

3. **Double-click the Databases folder.**

   All available databases are listed.

4. **Double-click the name of the database that you want to work on.**

   If this is the first time you have used Console or if you have not saved your login settings, you see a login screen. Otherwise, you see a list of Managers (including Instance, Schema, Security, and Storage), as shown in Figure 5-1.

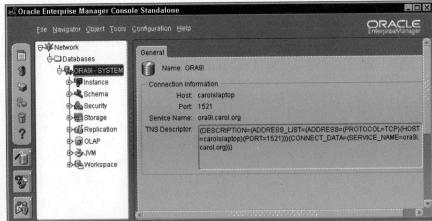

Figure 5-1: Give Console a try — you'll love it.

5. **If you see a login screen, follow these steps to log in:**

    a. **For the Username, type** SYSTEM.

    b. **For the Password, type** MANAGER **or whatever the current password is for SYSTEM on your database.**

    c. **For the Connect As option, select Normal.**

    d. **Click to add a check mark to the Save As Local Preferred Credentials option.**

    e. **Click OK.**

    Console asks whether it's okay to save your credentials in a local encrypted file.

    f. **Click OK to continue.**

    The list of Managers (including Instance, Schema, Security, and Storage) appears (see Figure 5-1).

Now that you have started Console, you are ready to dive in! Put on your Speedos and get started. I begin with the top view and snorkel my way in from there.

Exploring Four Console Tools

This section covers four standard, major tools in Enterprise Manager Console: Storage Manager, Security Manager, Schema Manager, and Instance Manager. For this section, I assume that you have already started Console, as described in the preceding section, so you can reach all four tools quickly.

Storage Manager: The external viewpoint

The first stop on your round-the-world cruise of Console is Storage Manager. Here you can get a good view floating above your Oracle world. This manager is concerned with the outermost layer of Oracle9i — where the rain meets the sea, you might say. Where logic meets physics.

Fire up Storage Manager by following these simple instructions:

1. **In Console's main window, double-click the Storage icon.**

    The next window you see is Storage Manager's introduction page.

2. **In the left window, double-click the Tablespaces folder.**

3. **In the right window, scroll to the right until you see a graph showing each tablespace and what portion is currently in use.**

   This graph is handy for monitoring the storage space used (and unused) by the database. In Figure 5-2, you can see that the main focus of Storage Manager is your files. The buttons and menus are the same as most of Enterprise Manager tools and are described in detail in Chapter 1.

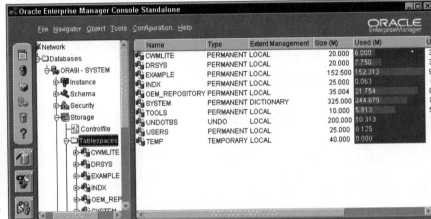

Figure 5-2: The space usage table shows remaining and used space.

4. **Below the Tablespaces folder, click one of the tablespaces.**

   A two-tabbed window shows up in the right frame, as you see in Figure 5-3. Under the General tab, you can look at the datafiles that make up this tablespace. You can add a new datafile by typing in the blank row in the Datafiles area. You can take a tablespace offline, put it online, or change it to read-only using the buttons and check boxes in the Status area.

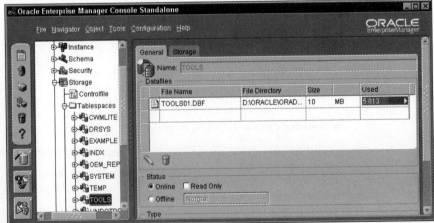

Figure 5-3: A tablespace gets at least one datafile allocated exclusively for its use.

5. **Right-click the file name and choose Edit.**

   Make a megabyte out of a kilobyte right here. Adjusting the size of a tablespace could not get any easier.

6. **Click Cancel to close the edit window.**

   Moving along to the next stop on the tour, I want to direct your attention to the unassuming list on the left side of that coral reef. Look below your list of tablespaces and find the next folder, labeled Datafiles.

7. **In the left window, double-click the Datafiles folder.**

   A list of the same type as the one for the tablespaces shows up. This one lists each of your datafiles and tells you how much room is left in each one. Good data at a glance! Monitoring this list over a period of time can help you determine which of your datafiles is growing.

8. **In the left window, click one of the datafiles.**

   You have before you the inner secrets of the chosen datafile. Work with your datafiles here. Change a file name, adjust its size, take it offline, or take it out for a date!

   The big green cube icon on the left side of your window creates something: It changes its meaning to match your area of focus. In other words, when you are here, looking at datafiles, the green cube creates a new datafile. When you are there, looking at tablespaces, the clever beast creates a new tablespace.

   Next stop: rollback segments, the underbelly of the inner workings of Oracle9i.

9. **In the left window, scroll down until you see the Rollback Segments folder, and then double-click it.**

   A list of your rollback segments appears below the folder on the left, and the same list, showing the current state of affairs, appears on the right. Here you can see at a glance if any of your rollback segments are filling up.

10. **In the left window, click one of the rollback segments.**

    The window on the right shows you the control panel for this rollback segment. Here you can take the rollback segment online or offline, shrink it, expand it, or copy it.

    Rollback segments are happiest when left alone. The care and feeding of rollback segments is beyond the scope of this book. Read up on them in the *Oracle Server Administrator's Guide* before you make any changes to rollback segments.

11. **In the left window, scroll up to the Storage folder and double-click it.**

    Storage Manager closes.

Congratulations! You have explored two parsecs of the Oracle9i galaxy and returned unharmed. You are ready to refuel and head into another domain: Security Manager. Engage!

Security Manager: The keeper of the gate

Using Security Manager is like becoming a Klingon Security Officer. Nothing gets past you. You check IDs; ask, "What's the password?"; and boot aliens out if they don't have the right answer. You stamp everyone's passport with access rights to various areas on your Oracle9i ship. Sometimes you change a guy's password just so he has to come by and visit you.

Chapter 8 tells much more about users. It shows you how to use Security Manager to create a user and change a password. Chapter 11 has hands-on instructions on how to create roles and privileges.

Rev up Security Manager (affectionately known as "S&M" to the tinfoil hat crowd) and follow the instructions as I take you through a wild mouse ride into the realm of security.

1. **In Console's main window, double-click the Security icon.**

   Security Manager's introduction page appears.

2. **In the left window, click the plus sign next to the Users folder.**

   The left window shows the gender of every user (just kidding!). Actually, Oracle9i appears to be nongender specific; all these users are wearing wet suits and have oversized heads. What is Oracle9i trying to tell us?

3. **Below the Users folder, click one of the users.**

   A tabbed window appears in the right window, as you see in Figure 5-4. Under the General tab, you can look up a user's profile. You can change the password. You can assign default tablespaces, which tell Oracle9i where to put tables created by this user. The Quota tab lets you set limits on the amount of space available for this user's tables.

4. **Click the Role tab.**

   Here you can add a role or remove a role. The available roles are on the top of the screen, and already assigned roles are on the lower part of the screen. The System Privileges tab is similar, except that it contains privileges, such as CREATE USER, and other useful capabilities.

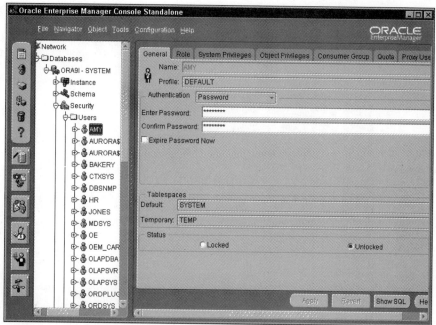

Figure 5-4:
Users have
names,
passwords,
privileges,
and quotas.

5. **Click the Object Privileges tab.**

   I love this. It's like looking at a miniversion of Schema Manager. This is where you can add special privileges to a user, such as, oh, maybe, let this user view a table owned by the BAKERY user.

6. **In the top part of the screen, double-click a Schema name.**

   A list of object types (Table, Index, and so on) appears below the Schema name.

7. **Double-click the Tables folder.**

   As you expect, a list of tables appears.

8. **Click a table.**

   Finally, you see something new! Here you see a list of object privileges that are available to the user for this object. Assign the privilege by selecting it and then clicking the down arrow, which moves the privilege to the Granted Privilege list. As you see in Figure 5-5, the Apply button is now available for you to complete the task.

9. **Click the Revert button to undo the change.**

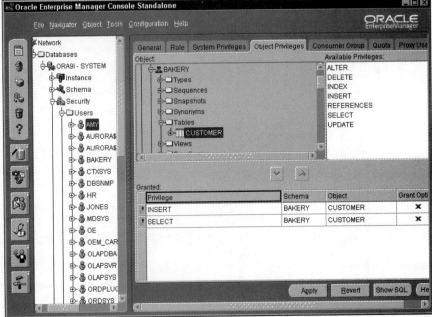

Figure 5-5:
Use the
Object
Privileges
feature to
give a user
the ability to
query a
table.

10. In the left window, scroll down and click the Roles folder.

Roles, like users, can be created and assigned privileges or even roles. For example, you can create a single role called NEPTUNE and then give it all the roles you defined previously (SEASNAKE, MERMAID, WHALE) so that NEPTUNE has the privileges of all these roles combined.

If you remove the CONNECT role, Oracle9i will not allow the user to log in to the database. Also, SYS and SYSTEM are special users created to manage internal data dictionary tables and views. Do not change the roles or privileges of these two users.

Our final stop in the Security Manager dive: Profiles.

11. In the left window, below the list of roles, click the plus sign next to the Profiles folder.

The Profiles folder appears below the Roles folder. Many times, all you see is the default profile.

12. In the left window, double-click the DEFAULT profile.

The window that appears on the right lets you set parameters for this profile and limit users to a maximum amount of CPU time or storage space. Another cool feature is the password settings.

13. Click the Password tab.

You can adjust the password behavior for all users that belong to this profile. For example, you can make all passwords expire every 30 days. You can even prevent the user from reusing old passwords for a year if you feel especially secure that way.

14. **In the left window, below the DEFAULT profile, double-click the Users Assigned folder.**

     A list of users assigned to this profile appears. To add a user to a profile, you must go back to the Users folder, select the user, and then modify the assigned profile.

15. **In the left window, scroll up to the Security icon and click its minus sign.**

     Security Manager closes.

If you happen to have more than one database to manage, you can switch from one database to another inside Console by clicking another database name. Each database name contains its own list of the Security, Instance, Schema, and Storage icons. In addition, if you click a database and want to change the user you have logged in with, choose Navigator⇨Connect, which opens a new login window. After logging in, you return to the windows of Console.

When you are all safe and securely sound, you can turn the corner and cruise on down Main Street to Schema Manager.

Schema Manager: The builder of tables

Finally, you're in the thick of things. Schema Manager shows you all your tables, lets you add referential integrity (relationships between two tables), and gives you an easy way to copy tables.

You can generate a report of your database's configuration, a list of all the tables or other objects in your database, and a host of other interesting reports. Simply right-click the area of interest, such as the Tables folder in Schema Manager, and choose Save List. Presto, a window appears to generate the report. You can then select the format (such as HTML) and save or just view a report.

In Schema Manager, you can even create a printed report of your data that can be automatically formatted in HTML — ready for the Web!

Chapters 9 and 10 cover how to use Schema Manager to create a table or object. Right now, it's time for a quick tour of Schema Manager's highlights. Just follow the instructions, relax, and adjust your helmet for a whirlwind tour.

1. **In Console's main window, double-click the Schema icon.**

   Schema Manager's introduction page appears. Schema Manager handles objects, including tables, views, synonyms, constraints on tables, relationships between tables, and packages. In the left window, you can see a complete list of items tracked by Schema Manager. Pay no attention to the big purple ball on the right. I can only guess what kind of crazed, tinfoil-crowned lunatic dreamed up this bizarre graphic. (I would hate to be a mouse in the corner of his or her virtual bedroom!) I guess users just have to live with it. It disappears after another few mouse clicks, thank goodness.

2. **From the menu bar, choose Navigator⇨View By Schema.**

   You see a list of all the users that own tables or other objects. You can browse through Schema Manager in either mode.

   A set of tables, views, and other objects that are all created by one user are collectively called a *schema*. You do not give a schema a name. It inherits the name of its creator. For example, if the user's Oracle name is AMY, the schema's name is AMY. This explains why you see user names listed in Schema Manager.

3. **Choose Navigator⇨View By Object.**

   You return to the default mode of Schema Manager. Next, you start moving through some of the more interesting features of Schema Manager.

4. **In the left window, double-click the Synonym folder.**

   You see a list of synonym owners in the left window and a full list of synonyms in the right window, as shown in Figure 5-6.

Figure 5-6:
Synonyms
are owned
by a
schema
and also
reference a
schema and
an object.

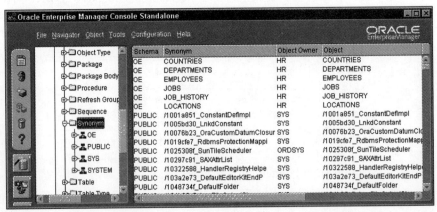

5. **In the right window, click the column heading labeled Synonym.**

Oracle9i sorts the list of synonyms by name. On the right side in Schema Manager, as in the other tools, you can sort by any listed column.

6. **In the left window, double-click the SYS schema.**

The left window expands to show a list of the synonyms owned by SYS. The right window lists only these synonyms rather than listing all of them. Don't you just adore the green sunglasses next to each synonym name?

7. **In the left window, below the Synonyms folder, click one of the synonyms.**

A property page shows up in the right window. You can't do much more than look at this particular page because you can't dynamically change the features of synonyms. To change a synonym, you must remove it and re-create it.

Grayed-out text in a box means that you can't change that feature. (You can barely read this kind of text — it's a feature, not a bug.)

8. **In the left window, double-click the Table folder.**

You may have to scroll down a bit to see the Table folder. Just as with the synonyms, you get a complete list of all the tables in the database.

9. **In the left window, below the Table folder, double-click the AMY schema.**

Just as you expected (it's becoming predictable), you see a list of all the tables created by AMY on the left and on the right.

10. **In the left window, click one of the tables.**

The window on the right shows details about the table. This property page is more involved than most of the property pages you see in Schema Manager.

11. **Expand the Name column so that you can read the full names listed below it.**

Click and drag the border between the Name and Schema column headings.

You can modify some features (such as the datatype and size) right in this window. To add a new column at the end of the list of columns, simply type the new column name in the first empty row and continue to fill in the datatype, size, and so on.

To remove a column from an existing table, select the column so its entire row is highlighted. Then right-click and choose Drop Column. Refer to Chapter 20 to find out about changing the name of a column in a table.

12. **Click the Constraints tab.**

    This window shows you all the constraints on the table. You can add or remove constraints here. This window is where you create primary keys and foreign keys, two of the most common table constraints. Chapter 9 details the steps for creating primary and foreign keys.

13. **Expand the list for the current table.**

    In the left window, click the plus sign next to the table name. Notice that you can list indexes, partitions, snapshot logs, and triggers for this table. Chapter 18 shows you how to add an index to a table. The other three items are not covered in this book because they are advanced features.

14. **View or edit the table data.**

    Do not edit data in any table owned by SYS or SYSTEM. These are controlled by the database itself. Changes to data in these tables can damage your database.

    If you have installed the sample schema, you can look at the data now as follows:

    a. **Under the Table folder, double-click AMY.**

    b. **In the left window, right-click the EMPLOYEE table name and choose Table Data Editor.**

       A spreadsheet of table data appears, as shown in Figure 5-7. You can find some really great new features here! Besides being able to edit the table's data, you can create a query using SQL or a Web-ready report.

       To create a query, click the SQL icon. You see a preformatted query that contains a list of all the columns. Add a WHERE clause (or whatever you want) and then view the results in the table. If you want to create a Web-ready report of the data, click the Report icon (found along the left border of the spreadsheet).

15. **Close the edit window by clicking the X in the top-right corner.**

16. **Expand the View folder and then expand the SYS schema under the View folder.**

    You may need to scroll down in the left window to find the View folder. As predictable as a Vulcan's brow, a list of SYS views appears on the left.

17. **In the left window, click one of the views.**

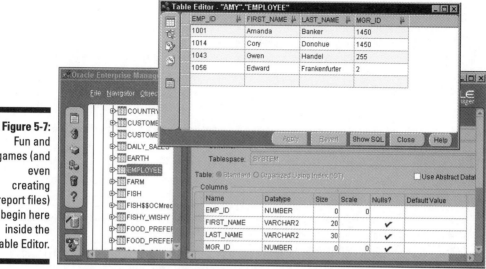

Figure 5-7:
Fun and
games (and
even
creating
report files)
begin here
inside the
Table Editor.

This feature is really cool. In the olden days, you had to wade your way through Martian mud to find the query that was behind a view (men are from Mars; women are from Venus; children are from Heaven; programmers are from Klathos the Wormworld). Now, it's a walk in the park. You can even make changes right in this text box and change the view by clicking the Apply button. Now that's cool.

18. **Scroll back up to the Schema icon and click its minus sign.**

    Schema Manager closes.

Now it's time to wrap it all up with the control tower of the managers: Instance Manager.

Instance Manager: The activity monitor

This final manager has a different point of view: It watches all the action as it happens inside the database and helps you keep tabs on your users and your databases. To get going:

1. **In Console's main window, double-click the Instance icon.**

    Instance Manager's introduction page appears.

2. **Click the Configuration icon.**

In the right window, you see the status of your database. In other chapters, you find out how to use Instance Manager to do these tasks:

- Save parameter settings
- Shut down the database
- Start the database

And now, a first-class tour of the coolest features of Instance Manager:

3. **At the bottom of the right window, click the All Initialization Parameters button.**

An alphabetical list of all the parameters available and their current settings for your database appears. Figure 5-8 shows the list for my database.

Notice the column headings that can help you later when you are tuning the database:

- **Default.** When this box has a check mark, it means that the parameter is set to its default setting at the moment.

- **Dynamic.** A check in this box means that you can use the ALTER SYSTEM SQL command to reset this parameter for your session, so you can tune that parameter for special cases (such as an overnight job) without shutting down the database to do it. If there's no check mark in this box, you must shut down and restart the database to adjust this parameter.

- **Category.** This column gives you a hint on how the parameter gets used in the database. For example, a parameter in the Cache and I/O category affects how the database interacts with memory and reading and writing data.

4. **Select a parameter and click the Description button.**

A box opens at the bottom of the screen showing a description of whatever parameter you click. This is great documentation to know about! Figure 5-8 shows the parameter list with the description of the blank_trimming parameter.

Try this: Click the Category column to sort all the parameters by category. Now you can quickly review the description of every parameter that affects the Optimizer, or memory, or whatever area you may need to tune.

5. **Click the Cancel button.**

Closing the parameter window brings you back to the main Instance Manager window.

6. **In the left window, double-click the Sessions folder.**

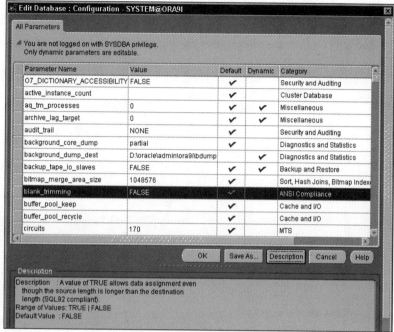

Now you see who is logged into your database. Use the Refresh button in the left window to refresh your view of sessions. You see user names as well as the process they are running.

7. In the left window, click a user (other than one called Background).

The right window shows activity, terminal, time logged in, and so on. Figure 5-9 shows this window.

You can disconnect a user's session here with the Kill Session button. You can examine the SQL command that the user is currently executing by clicking the SQL tab. Disconnecting may be critical if you're trying to figure out which query is causing your system to slow down to a crawl — kill that session!

8. In the left window, scroll up to the Instance icon and click its minus sign.

Instance Manager closes.

What a joy ride. You can see lots more of the Storage, Security, Schema, and Instance Managers in later chapters. I need a nap. Call me in the morning.

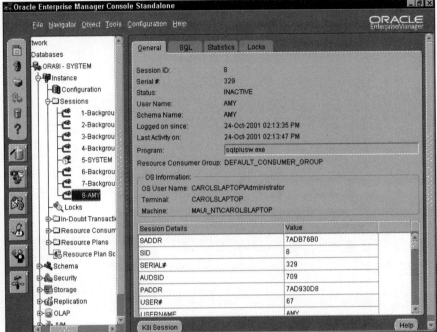

Figure 5-9:
User
sessions are
revealed
right down
to the SQL
command
they
execute.

Part II
Getting Started

In this part . . .

Databases don't grow on trees. They are carefully (or carelessly) grown from an idea hatched in the mind of some crazed genius, namely you. Perhaps you don't actually do the creating, but instead you're at the mercy of the whims of some other crazed genius. This part is your mini-lesson on database design and the inner workings of Oracle9i. It helps you answer these burning questions:

- ✔ If I put data into these tables, should I buy another hard drive?
- ✔ Who am I and what is my role in the world?
- ✔ What the heck did Joe Programmer/Analyst do six months ago?

After you discover that there is some method to the madness, I show you step-by-step how to create a new Oracle9i user. Enough theory — now get down to business and do something!

Chapter 6

The Relational Model and You

This chapter gives you the information and the confidence that you need to create terrific tables and join them into a relational database. While you're playing matchmaker and creating relationships among these tables, keep in mind how you're really going to use this stuff when you're on your own. The last sections in the chapter discuss what to do with those newfangled thingies — objects — and how Oracle9i works with objects.

Redundant Relational Database Redundancy

Imagine that you're at your doctor's office with a sprained wrist. The receptionist gives you a clipboard holding a long yellow form. You dutifully but sloppily begin to fill out the form, using your left hand because your right wrist is sprained. You fill in your name, last name first, and address; then you fill it in again in the next section of the form. By the time you reach the third section in which you read, "Patient's name and address," your right wrist is throbbing and your left hand is cramped. You leap up and yell, "I hate repeating myself! I hate repeating myself! I hate repeating myself!" The receptionist calmly replies, "Perhaps you would like to file a complaint. Please fill in your name and address on this form in triplicate."

Most likely, the database that stores the information on that yellow form is not a relational database. Relational databases are famous for saving time, space, and wrists by minimizing repeated data. Data lives in one table and has a key. Other tables retrieve that data with the key. Here's how relational databases minimize repeated data.

The database has one table for both name and address. The operator types it once, and the database assigns a *key* — a column or set of columns that identifies rows in a table. Another table tracks the doctor visit and contains a column for the key of the row with the patient's name and address. Another column gets the key for the billing name and address. A third column has the key for the insured's name and address. Relational databases have many advantages:

- ✔ The patient writes the name and address only once. (Saves your wrist!)

- ✔ The name and address are entered into the database only once. (Saves file space!)

- ✔ Any time the same patient returns, the same name and address can be used without any repeated typing. (Saves form-filling and filing time!)

- ✔ Changes in the name and address are entered once and affect all three tables automatically. (Are we in love yet?)

- ✔ If the names and addresses are different for the patient, billing party, or insured person, the database handles the differences without making special exceptions. Very simply, the second address is a new row in, for example, the PATIENT_NAME_&_ADDRESS table, and this new ID goes in the appropriate column of the DOCTOR_VISIT table.

Keys Rule

When you think of a key, you probably picture your house key or perhaps the key to your Jaguar. Without that key, you can admire your Jaguar like all the other poor schmucks on your block, but you can't drive it. If you lose your key, you have to get a new one made. If you get a totally new key, you have to change the locks because the old key no longer works. Database keys have similar attributes:

- ✔ Keys are important in locating a particular row in a table.

- ✔ Keys get you inside a table quickly and directly.

- ✔ If you change the key, all the copies of that key must be replaced with copies of the new key.

- ✔ If you remove the key completely from a table, you lose the fastest method of retrieving the information — kind of like a PT Cruiser that you have to roll down the driveway to start. Not a pretty sight.

Considering types of keys

Three kinds of keys are used in relational databases:

- ✔ **Primary key.** This key is the kingpin of all keys. The primary key may be one column or a set of columns. In all cases, the primary key contains a value that is unique across all the rows in that table. If you know the primary-key value, you can single out one row in a table, regardless of how many rows the table contains. A primary key for tables is like a Social Security number for U.S. citizens. A single column that contains an ID number is the best kind of primary key for fast retrieval of data.

- ✔ **Foreign key.** A key that resides in one table but is the key to a different table is called a *foreign key.* The primary key of the connected table is kept in the foreign-key column in the other table. Perfectly clear, right? Well, I told you it was foreign! The next section, "Importing foreign keys," has the details.

- ✔ **Unique key.** The primary key identifies each row in a table. Sometimes you have a second way to identify a unique row. This second way is called a *unique key, or alternate key,* and it is a column or set of columns, just like the primary key.

Importing foreign keys

A foreign key lives in a table for only one reason: to connect the table to another table. Like a foreign country's diplomat, a foreign key represents its entire country — that is, its entire table. By plugging a foreign key into a table, you make a link to all the information stored in the other table. Strategic and careful use of foreign keys requires logic and common sense — and sometimes experimentation. Be sure to declare all contraband when you pass through Customs. Search and detention can be unpleasant.

Imagine that you're a baker and you make ten kinds of bread. Each kind has a price and many different ingredients. Your database administrator (every baker has one) designed two tables for you: one for the bread and one for the ingredients. Each of these tables has a primary key. The BREAD table's primary key is BREAD_NO, and the INGREDIENT table's primary key is INGREDIENT_NO. To calculate the cost of a loaf of bread, you ask your database administrator to create a third table: the RECIPE table, where you have your head baker enter the ingredients and the amount of each ingredient used for the bread.

The three tables are diagrammed in Figure 6-1. The diagram shown in the figure is a classic type of diagram used in designing relational databases; it's called an Entity Relationship Diagram (or ERD).

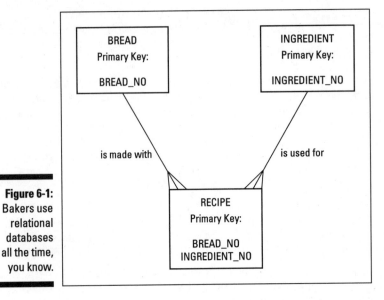

Figure 6-1:
Bakers use relational databases all the time, you know.

After dusting flour off the keyboard and the computer screen, you discover that your head baker left some data that you can use in the tables. Figure 6-2 shows you the three tables in Oracle9i.

```
Oracle SQL*Plus                                              _ □ ×
File  Edit  Search  Options  Help
SQL> SELECT * FROM BREAD;

  BREAD_NO BREAD_NAME      SELLING_PRICE
---------- --------------- -------------
         1 Cinnamon Swirl           2.95
         3 Plain White              2.05
         2 Nutty Banana             3.25
SQL> SELECT * FROM INGREDIENT;

INGREDIENT_NO INGREDIENT_NAME PRICE_PER_OUNCE
------------- --------------- ---------------
          101 Cinnamon                      2
          102 Flour                       .04
          103 Bananas                     .06
          104 Nuts                        .22
          105 Yeast                        .2
          106 Salt                        .03
SQL> SELECT * FROM RECIPE;

  BREAD_NO INGREDIENT_NO     OUNCES
---------- ------------- ----------
         1           101          2
         1           102         64
         1           105          2
         1           106         .3
         2           102         72
         2           103          4
         2           105          2
         2           106         .5
         3           102         72
         3           105          2
         3           106         .5
SQL>
```

Figure 6-2:
Bread has ingredients, as you can clearly see in the recipe table.

Now you're probably wondering how to calculate the profit (selling price minus cost) of each kind of bread. By reading each table's foreign-key connections, you can determine that it costs $3.54 to make Nutty Banana bread. You're selling the bread for $3.25, so it must be your loss leader. Go ahead. Break out your calculator. Do the math. I show you the calculations here. Follow along with me by looking at Figure 6-2:

1. **At the top of Figure 6-2, look at the** BREAD **table query results.**

   Nutty Banana bread has a primary key of 2.

2. **At the bottom of the figure, look at the** RECIPE **table query results.**

   Four rows have 2 as the foreign key in the BREAD_NO column.

3. **Read across the four rows.**

   You find numbers in the foreign-key column called INGREDIENT_NO.

4. **Go to the** INGREDIENT **table query results in the middle of the figure.**

   You see that the numbers are primary keys representing the following ingredients in Nutty Banana bread:

   102 = Flour

   103 = Bananas

   105 = Yeast

   106 = Salt

5. **Reading across the rows, find the cost of each ingredient.**

6. **Multiply the cost of each ingredient by the amount in the** RECIPE **table.**

   You can calculate the cost of a loaf of Nutty Banana bread as follows:

   72 oz. Flour × .04 = 2.88

   4 oz. Bananas × .06 = .24

   2 oz. Yeast × .2 = .40

   .5 oz. Salt × .03 = .015

   Total cost = 3.535

For more foreign-key goodies, refer to Chapter 9, where you find out how to create foreign keys for yourself.

Giving the foreign-key columns the same names as the corresponding primary-key columns, which I illustrate in the baker example, clearly defines the relationships. In fact, many software tools generate SQL match tables by looking for identical column names. This is known as the "Baldwin Brothers" convention, and you probably want to adhere to it.

The Key, the Whole Key, and Nothing but the Key

The heading of this section is the database designer's battle cry. The heading is also a cute summary of the most common style of relational databases — the so-called, much-maligned, often-imitated, never-duplicated *third normal form*.

The gurus who dreamed up relational database theory were strange. Their idea of normal does not fit in with the average guy's dream date. They have many definitions of normal, starting with the first normal form and ending somewhere around the forty-ninth normal form. Even the nerds in the software-development department gave up after the third or fourth one. So that's how you get the third normal form. They never even touched my personal definition of normal, which involves solar-flare-reduction hats and turkey dogs.

Here's a breakdown of the third normal form (the normalization rules for primary keys):

- ✔ **First, the key.** Every column in a table and all the data in that column must relate to the key of the table.

- ✔ **Second, the whole key.** Each column and its data must apply to the entire key, not just part of it.

- ✔ **Third, nothing but the key.** Every column and its data must relate to the key and not to any other columns in the table.

Here are some real-life database examples.

Old MacDonald's farm

"Old MacDonald had a farm, E-I-E-I-O. And on that farm he had some cows, E-I-E-I-O." The table that you see in Figure 6-3 breaks the first rule — the FARM_ADDRESS and OWNER columns do not directly relate to the BAD_COW primary key, which is COW_ID_NO.

You can move FARM_ADDRESS and OWNER to a table called FARM, as shown in Figure 6-4. This approach solves the problem that you run into when you have a change of address or owner for one of the farms in the FARM table. If you leave the address in this BAD_COW table, you have many rows to change. If you keep the address in a separate table, FARM, you have only one row to change.

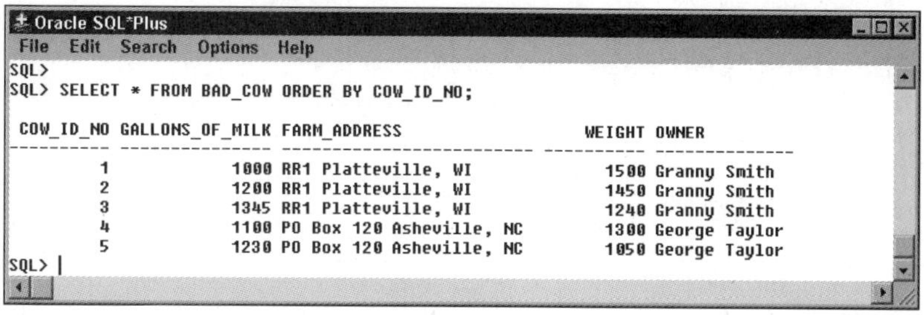

Figure 6-3:
The
BAD_COW
table
knowingly
breaks the
first
normaliza-
tion rule:
the key.

```
± Oracle SQL*Plus                                                    _ □ ×
 File   Edit   Search   Options   Help
SQL>
SQL> SELECT * FROM BAD_COW ORDER BY COW_ID_NO;

 COW_ID_NO GALLONS_OF_MILK FARM_ADDRESS                    WEIGHT OWNER
---------- --------------- ------------------------------ ------ ---------------
         1            1000 RR1 Platteville, WI               1500 Granny Smith
         2            1200 RR1 Platteville, WI               1450 Granny Smith
         3            1345 RR1 Platteville, WI               1240 Granny Smith
         4            1100 PO Box 120 Asheville, NC          1300 George Taylor
         5            1230 PO Box 120 Asheville, NC          1050 George Taylor
SQL> |
```

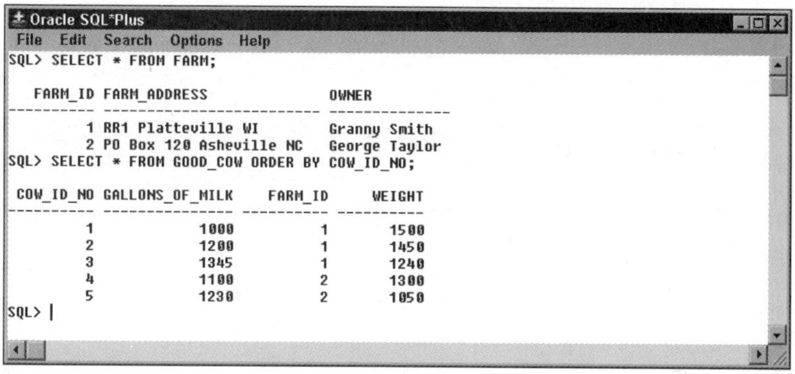

Figure 6-4:
The
GOOD_COW
and FARM
tables
comply with
the first
normaliza-
tion rule:
the key.

```
± Oracle SQL*Plus                                                    _ □ ×
 File   Edit   Search   Options   Help
SQL> SELECT * FROM FARM;

  FARM_ID FARM_ADDRESS               OWNER
--------- -------------------------- --------------
        1 RR1 Platteville WI         Granny Smith
        2 PO Box 120 Asheville NC    George Taylor
SQL> SELECT * FROM GOOD_COW ORDER BY COW_ID_NO;

 COW_ID_NO GALLONS_OF_MILK      FARM_ID      WEIGHT
---------- --------------- ----------- -----------
         1            1000           1        1500
         2            1200           1        1450
         3            1345           1        1240
         4            1100           2        1300
         5            1230           2        1050
SQL> |
```

Figure 6-4 shows you how to make BAD_COW into GOOD_COW and FARM, two relational tables connected by a key. The primary key in GOOD_COW meets the first rule of normalization — every column in the GOOD_COW table relates to a cow! Awesome.

By the way, the FARM table also complies with the second normalization rule — every column in the FARM table relates to a farm. Plowing ahead, look at the second rule.

Porridge for everyone

"Pease porridge hot, pease porridge cold, pease porridge in the pot, nine days old." The table in Figure 6-5 violates the second rule: the whole key. In this case, the key is two columns: FIRST_NAME and FOOD. The TEMPERATURE and FOOD_AGE columns relate to both columns in the key, but the PERSON_AGE column relates to only the first column in the key.

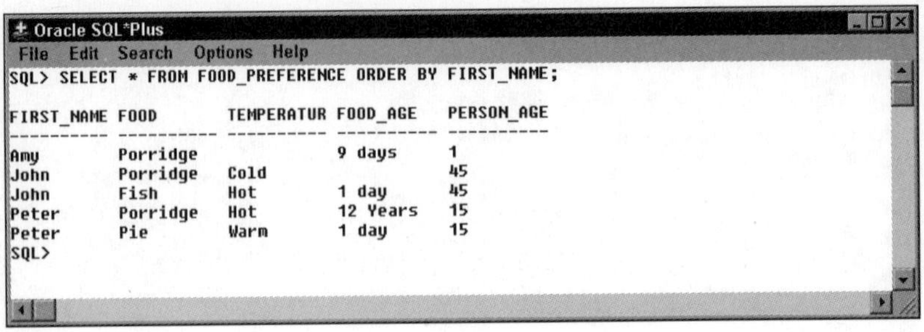

Figure 6-5:
FOOD_
PREFER-
ENCE is out
of alignment
with the
second nor-
malization
rule: the
whole key.

Figure 6-6 shows you how to correct this problem. PERSON_AGE moves to a table called PERSON in which FIRST_NAME is the primary key.

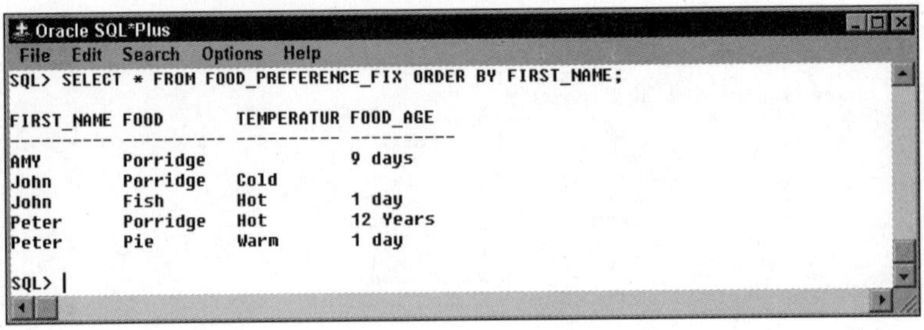

Figure 6-6:
FOOD_
PREFER-
ENCE_FIX
now has no
out-of-place
columns.

This prevents you from having to repeat data in the FOOD_PREFERENCE table that really belongs in the PERSON table. If a person's age changes, you need to change it only in the PERSON table. Otherwise, you chase around in the FOOD_PREFERENCE table to update the data there, too.

Back on the farm

"Baa-baa, black sheep, have you any wool?"

"Yes, sir, yes, sir, three bags full. One for my master and one for my dame, and one for the little lad who lives down the lane."

The table in Figure 6-7 violates the third rule: nothing but the key. The OWNER_OF_BAGS column refers to the sheep's bags of wool rather than to the sheep. This column does not belong in the SHEEP table. Because you put the column in the wrong table, the data inside is confusing. The column contains three owners: Master, Dame, and Little Lad.

Figure 6-7:
The black
sheep of the
family
breaks the
third rule:
nothing but
the key.

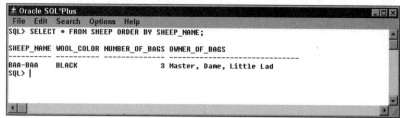

Common sense says that a column called OWNER in a table called SHEEP has
the owner of the sheep in it. To correct the problem, create a new table that
relates to the SHEEP table but is especially for bags of wool. Call the table
WOOL_BAG. As you can see in Figure 6-8, I removed the OWNER_OF_BAGS
column from the SHEEP table. In the new table, WOOL_BAG, I added a foreign
key (SHEEP_NAME) that relates each wool bag row in the WOOL_BAG table to a
sheep in the SHEEP table.

Figure 6-8:
Now the
information
is in a
related
table.

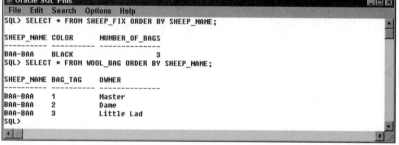

One Too Many: The Bread and Butter of Relational Databases

The one-too-many concept is delightfully simple: Don't repeat the same
column inside one row; move it to a new table. Or else.

For example, suppose that you're tracking all the recycled materials collected
in your community by two recycling companies. You create a table (see Figure 6-9) that has columns such as MATERIAL_1, MATERIAL_2, and MATERIAL_3.

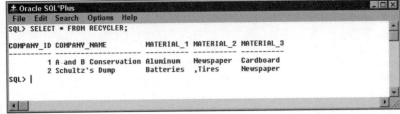

Figure 6-9:
Recyclers
recycle
recyclable
materials.

You may already see a problem brewing. What if A and B Conservation starts recycling glass, for example? You have to make big changes whenever the data changes. Maybe you can get extra pay for working overtime.

A better way to handle this problem is to use a single column for all the recycled material. This column moves to a separate table so that each new material gets a new row. Figure 6-10 shows the two tables that evolve from this revolutionary change.

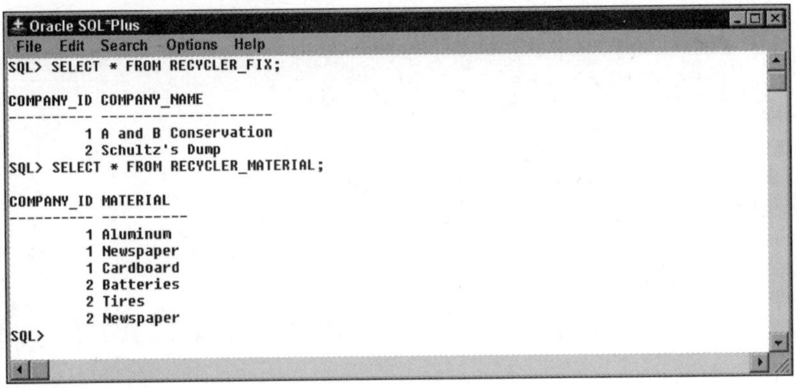

Figure 6-10:
Recyclers
and their
materials,
redesigned
for
flexibility.

This setup makes adding an endless list of recycled materials to either company's repertoire possible. Now you have many rows instead of many columns. You have moved repetitive columns out of one table and into their own table so that you have a constant, rather than an increasing, number of columns and an ever-increasing number of rows. This setup works much better because you are not required to make any changes in your table's design as new information is added. It's flexible. It's the backbone of every relational database. Maybe you can get extra pay for saving on overtime. If you are working as a civil servant, just ignore my last suggestion and continue what you were doing. Just kidding!

Objects and the Oracle9i Database

Are you ready? This section covers something that's new to Oracle: the object. Oracle9i technically can be called an *object-relational database*. This term means that Oracle9i contains all the features of a relational database combined with some of the features of an object-oriented database. The program is a *hybrid,* which means that you have some choices about how to set up your database design.

This section covers the basic definitions of Oracle9i's world of objects. Chapter 10 shows you how to create objects in your object-relational database if you choose to use them.

Defining an object

An object can be anything, sort of. In terms of Oracle9i, an *object* is a framework that defines

- How data is stored
- Where data is stored
- What kind of data is stored
- How to put data together into logical whole parts

That last item is the part that's really interesting and unique to objects. In fact, if you prefer, Oracle9i allows you to define the first three items in the traditional relational database style and then gives you a way to map these relational tables into objects.

Objects — a life of their own

Think of an *object* as a holistic set of concepts. Your object contains data about a real-world thing, such as a car part. In addition to the data, your object contains information about what you can do with the data. It's like having the car-parts data and the assembly instructions for the car.

An object can contain other objects. For example, you might define one object called PERSONAL_ADDRESS that contains up to three lines of a person's address. Another object, called PERSONAL_INFO, contains a person's name, Social Security number, and the PERSONAL_ADDRESS object for that person.

The scoop on types

Types are Oracle9i's way of defining the format of an object column, an object table, a nested table, or an array. Types are like wrappers around an object, the data, the methods, and even relational tables or views. The basic syntax for defining a type is similar to the syntax for defining a table. Table 6-1 shows a list of the types of types that you can define with Oracle9i. I have mentioned the term *method* several times. The following section defines the term more clearly.

Table 6-1	Object-Relational Types
Name	*Purpose*
BODY	An object component that contains definitions of the methods (or functions) that can be performed on an object.
OBJECT	A collection of data, tables, and methods defined and manipulated as a unit.
TABLE	A table mapped to an object.
ARRAY	A variable-length array, similar to a nested table but referenced and accessed as a set rather than as individual rows of data. This is also called VARRAY in some parts of Oracle's documentation.
NESTED TABLE	A table within a table or within some object. Oracle9i stores this type as though it were a relational table, but it can be used only in the context of the object.

Methods to their madness

Methods are self-contained bits of programming code that travel with an object, delivering parts or modifying data according to the method code. Methods are the heart of object-oriented technology.

Suppose that you are working with an object-relational database schema that contains information about making a model airplane. A model airplane has several subassemblies, such as the engine and the instrument panel, which are made up of individual parts. A change in any individual part may affect the assembly of the entire plane. If the fuel gauge in the cockpit is changed to a different diameter, for example, the hole drilled in the instrument panel must also be changed.

You can use object *types* to define the individual parts, the subassemblies, and the entire airplane. Object *methods* define how these object types interact. One program uses the object types and methods to handle changes in the data. Another program can use the objects and their associated methods to extract a complete instruction booklet for the plane.

Connecting relational tables with objects

Oracle9i is a hybrid of both relational and object-oriented databases. To allow you to combine the two to get the best of both worlds, Oracle9i provides two bridges between relational tables and objects:

- ✔ **Object view.** An *object view* maps relational tables to an object. Like relational views, the object view does not have data of its own; it is merely a way of looking at the underlying tables. The object view allows you to use existing relational tables in an object-oriented way.

- ✔ **Object table.** An *object table* is a table made up of rows that are themselves objects, or a table that has one or more columns with objects types as their datatype. An object table is a way to collect groups of like objects and manipulate them with more traditional relational-table techniques. Object tables can have primary keys and indexes.

If you use object views, the underlying data resides in relational tables that can be updated with the usual SQL commands.

When you use object tables, the underlying data resides in objects. You must maintain data through those objects, usually by using a programming language such as Java or PL/SQL.

SQL has been extended to handle more object queries, inserts, updates, and deletions. Expect even more convenient extensions for objects in the future.

Chapter 7

Getting Familiar with Data-Dictionary Views

*W*ho are users in the Oracle9i database, and what have they created? How does Oracle9i know which tables a user can see and which tables a user can't touch? Where is the off switch? You can find the answers to all these questions — except the last — with data-dictionary views.

Data-dictionary views are actually views based on underlying tables called system tables. *System tables* gather information about tables, rows, views, columns, security, users, and even the files allocated to store the Oracle9i database itself. System tables keep track of all the users, as well as what each user can and can't do. Oracle9i has lots more views than previous versions of Oracle.

The Oracle9i Optimizer or other internal processes use most of these views internally. Some of them, however, can be useful to you. Rather than deciphering a 900-plus list of data-dictionary views, you can read this chapter to find out about the important views that help you see information about database. You also see how to access that information.

Using Data-Dictionary Views

Table 7-1 shows you the best-kept secrets in the Oracle9i database, including info about what resides in data-dictionary views. The views help you interpret the internal workings of Oracle9i easily.

Table 7-1	The Ultimate Table of Views	
View	*Who Needs It*	*What the View Shows You*
ALL_CATALOG	DBA, table owner, user	Every table, view, object, and synonym that you can look at. You may or may not be allowed to update these items. This view helps you determine what resources the database has, including objects that you, a role you have, or PUBLIC has been granted privileges to use. PUBLIC is Oracle's special user that all Oracle users share; refer to Chapter 11 for information about using PUBLIC with table privileges (grants).
ALL_OBJECT_TABLES	DBA, object owner	List of all object-oriented tables in the database.
ALL_USERS	Anyone	The names and creation dates for all other users in the database.
DBA_FREE_SPACE	DBA	The remaining free space in each datafile.
PRODUCT_COMPONENT_ VERSION	Anyone	Shows all installed products (such as SQL*Plus and PL/SQL) and their complete version numbers, which is useful if you're reporting errors to Oracle.
USER_INDEXES	Table owner	All the indexes that you create.
USER_TAB_PRIVS_ MADE	Table owner	The privileges that you have given (with the GRANT command) on tables you own.
USER_TABLES	Table owner	Your tables, as well as statistics about them.
USER_VIEWS	Table owner	Your views, complete with the SQL code that you use to create them. Here's a great opportunity to share your views with a captive audience.

All these views adjust their data to fit the currently logged-in user. So, when I say "you" in Table 7-1, *you* refers to the Oracle user who is currently logged into the database.

In the data-dictionary views, you can find much of the information that's displayed graphically in the Enterprise Manager tools. You can use the data-dictionary views to write SQL queries to gather information about your database. You may want to create a report on the status of your database by using other report-writing tools. The data-dictionary views give you a great source of information on which to base reports. (Writing queries on data-dictionary views is no different than writing queries on any table or view in your database.)

Looking at Data-Dictionary Views with SQL*Plus

This section deals with two useful commands that you can use to take a quick look around in the data-dictionary views. To run these commands, follow these steps:

1. **Start SQL*Plus.**

   On Windows platforms, choose Start⇨Programs⇨Oracle HOME⇨ Application Development⇨SQL*Plus.

   On UNIX, Linux, or any other platform, type **sqlplus** at the operating-system prompt to start the command-line version of SQL*Plus.

2. **Log in as the Oracle user.**

   If you see a login window, follow these steps:

   a. **Type the user name and password. If you installed the sample schema, type** AMY **for the name and** AMY123 **for the password.**

   b. **In the Host String box, type the Oracle Net name of the Oracle9i instance on your local computer or on your network.**

   For a local database, you can usually leave this blank. For a database on a network, ask your administrator to provide you with a valid host string.

   c. **Click OK.**

If you see a prompt instead of a login window, follow these steps:

a. In the Username box, type AMY@*XXXX*, **replacing** *XXXX* **with the Oracle Net name of the Oracle9i instance on your local computer or on your network.**

For example, if you want to log into the ORCL database as AMY, you would type **AMY@ORCL**.

b. Press Enter.

c. Type the password.

If you log in as AMY, type **AMY123** for the password.

d. Press Enter.

The SQL prompt line appears. Your session may or may not have the Windows-like screen, but all the commands work the same.

3. **Type the following SQL command and then press Enter:**

```
DESC USER_TABLES;
```

DESC is short for DESCRIBE, which is a special SQL*Plus environment command that lets you see the list of columns or attributes of a table, view, or object table, as you see in Figure 7-1. You can use this for any table, view, or object table. You can use it also for object types to see a list of the type's attributes.

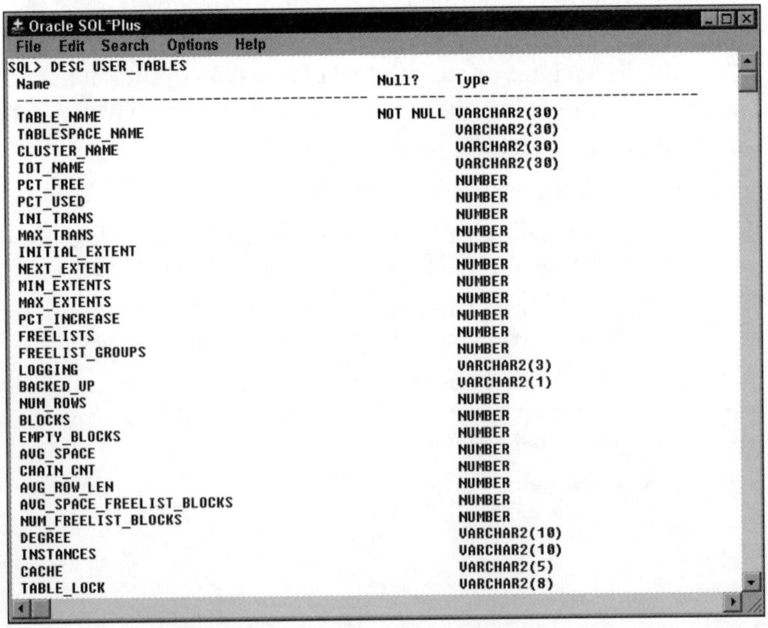

Figure 7-1:
A description of all the columns available in this view appears with the DESC command.

4. Type the following SQL command and then press Enter:

```
SELECT TABLE_NAME, NUM_ROWS, BLOCKS, AVG_ROW_LEN
FROM USER_TABLES
/
```

Oracle9i lists the results of your query. Figure 7-2 shows a partial listing.

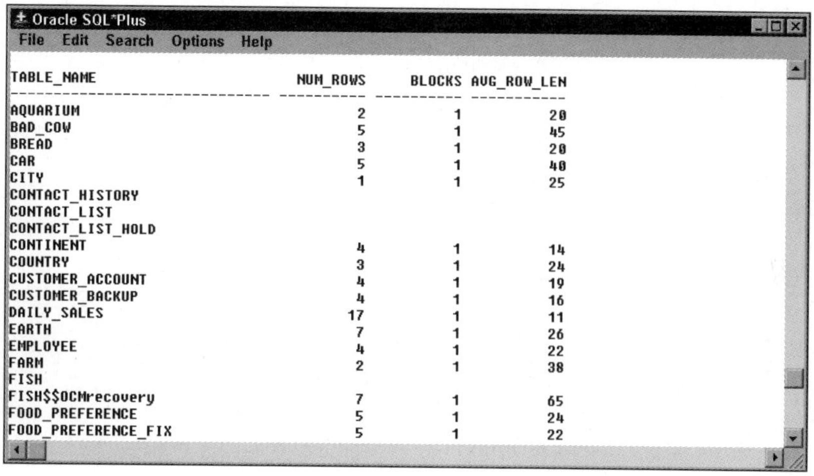

Figure 7-2:
Look over
table
statistics by
querying the
USER_
TABLES
view.

TABLE_NAME	NUM_ROWS	BLOCKS	AVG_ROW_LEN
AQUARIUM	2	1	20
BAD_COW	5	1	45
BREAD	3	1	20
CAR	5	1	40
CITY	1	1	25
CONTACT_HISTORY			
CONTACT_LIST			
CONTACT_LIST_HOLD			
CONTINENT	4	1	14
COUNTRY	3	1	24
CUSTOMER_ACCOUNT	4	1	19
CUSTOMER_BACKUP	4	1	16
DAILY_SALES	17	1	11
EARTH	7	1	26
EMPLOYEE	4	1	22
FARM	2	1	38
FISH			
FISH$$0CMrecovery	7	1	65
FOOD_PREFERENCE	5	1	24
FOOD_PREFERENCE_FIX	5	1	22

5. Type EXIT **and then press Enter.**

SQL*Plus closes.

The data-dictionary views give you a great deal of useful information about your database. Use these views well. Use them often. Enjoy their companionship. Make them some little tinfoil hats, too, so that they feel like part of the group. Well, at least keep in mind that you can use the views later without too much trouble.

Chapter 8

Oracle's User

- -

- -

I'm not saying that this is true for you, but for me, having a strong sense of who I am really helps me get through life. This chapter is all about you and your identity.

In Oracle9i, you log in with a user name and a password — your Oracle9i identity. Your database administrator (DBA) assigns one or more roles (a collection of capabilities) to your Oracle9i user name. This chapter covers how you create your Oracle9i identity and how you can create other identities if you're the DBA. Even if you're not the DBA, you can use the information in this chapter to understand how you, as an Oracle9i user, fit into the picture.

Playing a Role

Here's a fun fact about Oracle9i: An Oracle9i user creates every table in Oracle9i. A group of tables created by the same user is called a *schema*. You call the Oracle9i user name that creates the table (or object) the table's *owner*. The owner can do anything to the table, including dropping it from a (virtual) moving train.

Every Oracle9i user has the potential to create tables because the database administrator (DBA) can assign any user the *role* (group of capabilities) that allows the user to do so. The DBA stratifies users into roles that limit or expand their capabilities and, with infinite wisdom, decrees which users are also owners and which are merely tourists who can look around but can't vote in a local election.

My point is that being an Oracle9i user is not bad. In fact, being an Oracle9i user can be pretty cool. Perhaps you work in an office and share accounting database tables with 20 other staff members. You and your coworkers have individual Oracle9i user names, and one Oracle9i user name creates (and thus owns) all the tables you use. Typically, the table owner is someone in the MIS department. It is a sign that your company trusts your integrity when you are assigned an Oracle user name. Armed with your Oracle name and password, you have access to information found nowhere else.

Oracle9i allows owners to share their tables with users like you, by giving you permission to do various activities with the tables. The owner may allow you to only look at the data in one table and not change anything, for example. In a different table, the owner may allow your Oracle9i user name to add new rows or modify the data in existing rows. Each of these actions has a specific privilege that the table owner grants to you. To understand how your role affects what you can do with Oracle9i, you first have to understand the kinds of users in Oracle9i.

Note: When a user creates something in the database, the item can be a table, an object table, an object view, an index, a synonym, or a view. Throughout this chapter, I refer to *tables, table owners,* and *table privileges* for convenience. However, the item can be a table or any other kind of database feature that stores or looks at data. The concepts I discuss in this chapter apply to these other kinds of database features as well.

What kinds of users are there?

In a database context, asking the age-old question "Who am I, and what is my role in life?" brings you to Oracle9i roles. Oracle9i comes loaded with a set of roles. Five of these roles are important for you to know about. The others are pretty much behind-the-scenes roles. In addition to these basic roles, the DBA can create as many other roles as necessary. (Chapter 11 tells you all about how programmer types use custom-made roles.) Roles become time-saving tools for the table owner because the table owner can assign a set of privileges once to a role instead of assigning the privileges to each individual Oracle9i user name.

Here are the five standard roles in Oracle9i:

✔ **DBA.** The Grand Poobah of all roles. In the Oracle9i world, more than one DBA can exist. Incredible, but true. The Oracle9i DBA can create new Oracle9i user names, add disk space to the database, start and stop the database, and create roles and synonyms for all other Oracle9i users. The DBA can export tables that belong to any user. The DBA can also create more DBAs. It's a form of cloning, but totally legal.

✔ **EXP_FULL_DATABASE and IMP_FULL_DATABASE.** The Romulus and Remus of the Oracle9i realm, these two can make a copy of the entire universe and duplicate it elsewhere by using the Oracle9i suite of export and import tools. What power! Few are chosen for these honored positions. Usually, the DBA adds these roles to his or her own plate.

✔ **RESOURCE.** This role makes you an owner (that is, as soon as you create a table). All the movers and shakers in the database have this role, which allows you to do the following:

- Make tables, indexes, views, and synonyms

- Export and import your own tables

- Drop, modify, recreate, adjust, bend, and create relationships for your own tables

- Grant privileges — such as the capability to read or modify your table's data — to other users

Even though you can do all this to your own tables, you can't do anything to another user's tables unless that table's owner gives you privileges.

✔ **CONNECT.** The people who use the database for any reason whatsoever are in this role. The CONNECT role gets you in the door, and very little else. You can look at tables or views that have been granted privileges to PUBLIC. Typically, these tables are general lookup tables, such as a list of state abbreviations. You aren't allowed to create any tables. The only way that you can do more is if owners give you additional privileges to look at their tables and add, modify, and delete data in those tables.

The DBA can give you more privileges by assigning additional roles or system privileges to you. These roles are created for the purpose of giving a set of privileges to any user who is a member of that role. For example, the DBA can assign the CREATE ANY SYNONYM privilege to a user so that the user can create a synonym.

What kind of user are you?

If you share Oracle9i at your workplace and you wear a pocket protector, you may have the authority to create tables. If you're not sure, ask the DBA this question: "I just created this table with ten million rows. Now how do I get rid of the pesky thing?" Then see how fast the DBA runs over to your desk. If the DBA is at your desk in less than ten seconds, you have the power to create tables; otherwise, you probably don't.

If the DBA doesn't give you an indication of what your user role is, how can you find out? By using SQL*Plus or Enterprise Manager Console.

Everything in this chapter is performed with Console. To see the SQL commands that you can use to do the same tasks, download the sample files from this book's special Web site. See the For Dummies Web site at www.dummies.com/extras/oracle9i.html. You can find all the examples in the Samples/Chapter08 directory. Check the Readme.html file for more details.

Here's how you can find out what your user role is by using Enterprise Manager Console:

1. **Start Console.**

   On Windows platforms, choose Start⇔Programs⇔Oracle HOME2⇔ Enterprise Manager Console. Note that the Oracle HOME2 label may have a different name, such as ORAHOME81, on your computer. The person who installed the software on your machine designates the name.

   On UNIX, Linux, or any other platform, type **oemapp console** at the operating-system command line.

   You see the logo screen for Oracle Enterprise Manager, and then the Oracle Enterprise Manager Console login window appears.

2. **Make sure the Launch Standalone option is selected, and then click OK.**

   Console's initial screen appears.

3. **Double-click the Databases folder.**

   All available databases are listed.

4. **Double-click the name of the database that you want to work on.**

   If this is the first time you have used Console or if you have not saved your login settings, you see a login screen. Otherwise, you see a list of Managers (including Instance, Schema, Security, and Storage).

5. **If you see a login screen, follow these steps to log in:**

   a. **For the Username, type** SYSTEM.

   b. **For the Password, type** MANAGER **or whatever the current password is for SYSTEM on your database.**

   c. **For the Connect As option, select Normal.**

   d. **Click to add a check mark to the Save As Local Preferred Credentials option.**

   e. **Click OK.**

   Console asks whether it's okay to save your credentials in a local encrypted file.

f. Click OK to continue.

The list of Managers (including Instance, Schema, Security, and Storage) appears.

6. Double-click the Security icon.

Security Manager's introduction page appears.

7. In the left window, double-click the Users folder.

This action displays a list of users on the right and on the left. The list on the right shows a few important details about all the users. The list on the left is used to zoom in on each user so that details are displayed on the right.

8. In the left window, double-click the user name that interests you.

You see a property sheet on the right with page tabs across the top.

9. Click the Role tab to see what roles this user does and doesn't have.

Oracle9i lists both the available roles and the granted (assigned) roles. As you can see in Figure 8-1, the roles that this user currently has appear at the bottom.

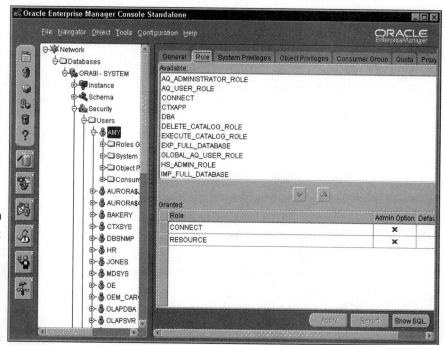

Figure 8-1:
Available roles are on the top, and assigned roles are on the bottom.

In this example, you have two roles: the CONNECT role and the RESOURCE role. Having these roles means that you can log in to Oracle9i and have fun creating your own tables and performing other tasks. Refer to the list in the preceding section for a more detailed explanation of roles.

If you see other roles, they're probably associated with jobs you do that require you to log in to Oracle9i screens. As long as you have the RESOURCE role, which allows you to create tables, you're in business.

The Role tab is where you can add or remove roles. Refer to Chapter 11 for complete instructions. Because you logged into Security Manager as a DBA, you can click any of the user names, look at their roles, and even change them.

Creating a New User from Scratch

Creating a new life is a big responsibility — you have to feed it and change it every day for years. Creating a new user in Oracle9i also carries some responsibilities, but generally the user won't wake you up in the middle of the night and send you stumbling for a bottle and a burp cloth.

Console makes quick work of creating a user and assigning it a few roles.

All right, then. Here's an easy way to create a new user life in Oracle9i by using Security Manager. If you have Security Manager open already, skip Step 1.

1. **Start Console in stand-alone mode, double-click the Databases folder, double-click the database you want to work on, and log in as the DBA user (if necessary).**

   For details, refer to Steps 1 through 6 in the "What kind of user are you?" section.

2. **Choose Object⇨Create.**

   You see the Create On window, where you decide what kind of thing you are creating.

3. **Choose User and then click Create.**

   The Create User dialog box appears, as shown in Figure 8-2. This is not really a wizard, but it should be, because creating new life definitely is in the realm of wizards.

4. **In the Name box, type a name for the new user.**

   Oracle has rules about what you use for a user name. Refer to the "Choosing a name for your new baby" sidebar for details and advice on user names and passwords.

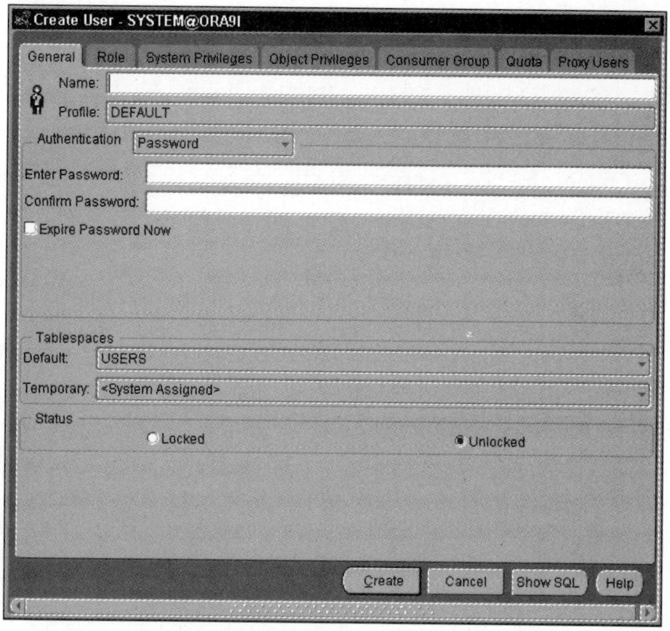

Figure 8-2:
Creating a
new user is
a snap with
the Create
User dialog
box.

5. **Choose the type of authentication.**

For the example, choose Password authentication. You can click the
arrow in the Authentication box to see the three choices:

- **Password.** Probably the most common selection. This is the traditional method of authentication, which requires the user to type a
password before he or she enters a database transaction.

- **External.** This method of authentication allows users to pass into
the database using their identities from the operating system. For
example, if you log in to your NT network as HOMER, the Oracle9i
user name for you is OPS$HOMER. (OPS$ is the default value of the
prefix assigned by the DBA for all externally authenticated users.)
To log in to SQL*Plus or some application, you simply type a slash
where you normally enter your Oracle9i user name and password.
This feature is convenient because the user doesn't need to know a
second name and password.

- **Global.** This method of authentication was new in Version 8 of
Oracle. Intended for use across distributed database systems, this
method requires authentication to take place outside the database
using Oracle Advanced Security (OAS). This method lets you validate a common user name and password with a variety of methods,
such as SSL or Kerberos, before the user can reach any database in
your distributed network of databases.

6. **In both the Enter Password box and the Confirm Password box, type the password.**

   The password appears on the screen as a line of asterisks (*).

7. **Select or don't select the Expire Password Now check box.**

   If you select the box, users must enter a new password the first time they log in to the database.

8. **Select a default tablespace.**

   Click the arrow in the Default box to see your choices. Normally, you select USERS as the default tablespace. This is the tablespace Oracle9i puts the user's tables in if the user creates a table and doesn't explicitly assign it to a different tablespace.

9. **Select a temporary tablespace.**

   Click the arrow in the Temporary box to see your choices. Normally, you select TEMP as the temporary tablespace, which is the tablespace that Oracle9i puts data in while it is generating query results or preparing a view — grabbing some space and releasing it when the job is finished.

10. **Select the status for the new user.**

    The default setting is Unlocked. This setting means that the user may log in to the database as soon as you have finished creating the user. If you want to wait and unlock the user name at some other time, select Locked, which prevents the user from logging in to the database.

11. **Assign roles to the new user.**

    Click the Role tab in the Create User dialog box. The list of available roles appears, as shown in Figure 8-3. To allow the new user to create tables, you must double-click the RESOURCE role. By default, all users are assigned the CONNECT role, which is required for logging in to the database.

12. **Click the Create button.**

    Your work is finished. Oracle9i creates the new user name and returns you to the main window of Security Manager.

Remember to write down the name and password that you create and keep them in a secure and hidden place (not taped to your monitor).

Choosing a name for your new baby

What's in a name? Don't ask me; I named my kid Blue. But I got more conventional and gave him the middle name Skyler. Then I got psychic and gave him another middle name: Mercury. Worked for me.

As the DBA, you have the responsibility of creating all the new users for your Oracle9i database. When setting up a name for a new user, you have

to follow the rules. You can use up to 30 characters. A letter and single-digit number each count as one character. The same rules apply to setting up passwords. My advice is to use a single word or acronym for a new user name. You will appreciate this later when you have to type the name as the identifier in front of every table you create.

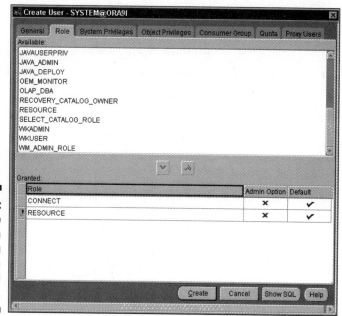

Figure 8-3:
While creating a user, you can assign the initial roles.

Changing Your Password

Whether you are a DBA or not, Oracle9i may require you to select a password for your Oracle9i user name. The password, like the user name, can be up to 30 characters long. Here are my recommendations:

✔ Choose a password that you can easily remember *and* that has a number in it. Take your middle name (Skyler, for example), and then add a number or two (Skyler11). A password that contains both numbers and letters is hundreds of times more difficult for a hacker to crack!

✔ Change your password as often as your DBA tells you to. If no one tells you anything, tell yourself to change your password every two months.

If you are the DBA, you can change the password of any user in the database. Here are the steps, which are similar to the steps for creating a new user. If you have Security Manager open already, skip to Step 3.

1. **Start Console in stand-alone mode, double-click the Databases folder, double-click the database you want to work on, and log in as the DBA user (if necessary).**

   For details, refer to the "What kind of user are you?" section.

2. **Double-click the Security icon.**

   The Security Manager's introduction page appears.

3. **In the left window, double-click the Users folder.**

   This action displays a list of users on the left and on the right.

4. **In the left window, click the user whose password you are changing.**

   The user's profile window appears in the right window.

5. **In the Enter Password box and again in the Confirm Password box, type the new password.**

   Write down the name and password you just changed and keep them in a secure and hidden place.

6. **Click the Apply button to complete the job.**

   Security Manager accepts the change and returns you to the main window.

You're finished. Easy, wasn't it? Chapter 11 covers another aspect of passwords: setting a time limit for a password so it expires automatically. The next part of the book puts you in the driver's seat, showing you how to make your own tables.

Part III
Putting Oracle9i to Work

In this part . . .

This part is kind of like puberty. You have a brand-new body of knowledge, and now you're trying to put it all into practice.

You get revved up in the first chapter in this section by creating your very own tables. You even get to play with objects. Find out how the experts do it! Next, read about all of your choices for creating a secure working environment for your database tables. I give you some common-sense guidelines to help you make wise decisions about security using Oracle9i roles and privileges.

Have you ever considered using your database from a distance, such as from across the Internet or across the room? Find out what you can do with Java and Oracle9i in Chapter 13.

Have a grand tour of the newest toy in the Oracle9i playroom: XML Developer's Kit. Try creating a Web page from your data.

All this work deserves tender loving care and protection. How would you feel if you lost it all and had to start over? Don't get caught with your data showing. As Chapter 15 explains, back up now or lose sleep later.

Chapter 9

Defining Tables, Tablespaces, and Columns

. . . .

In This Chapter

▶ Pondering the possibilities of tablespaces

▶ Talking the technical talk about columns

▶ Discovering special SQL words for when you bang your thumb

▶ Wizarding a table with Enterprise Manager Console

▶ Creating a table with SQL

. . . .

*T*his chapter is full of good stuff, so fasten your seat belt. You're about to discover where to put tables, how to name your columns, and what datatypes to assign to them. You also see how to make tables with SQL code or Enterprise Manager Console. Get ready: You're flying now!

Tablespace: The Final Frontier

Tablespaces are the portions of the database that Oracle9i reserves for your tables. Your database administrator (DBA) may not have told you a thing about tablespaces. On the other hand, this same DBA may come whining to your desk, saying that you just brought the database to its knees by using all the space in the SYSTEM tablespace. Read on to find out what you actually did.

If the DBA allows you to create tables or other objects, he or she assigns a *default tablespace,* which is where all your objects go. This default tablespace is sort of like your own private science lab. If your DBA did a good job, your default tablespace is tucked away in a safe corner. That way, your incredible genius can blossom without disturbing anyone.

If you are the DBA, you will find this section important because your duties include assigning storage amounts and areas for all the users of your database.

You may, however, have to lower yourself to paying attention to where your tables go and even create new tablespaces before you have a good home for your new tables or objects. The rest of this section describes your choices in tablespace creation. After you have a tablespace to use, you can tell Oracle9i where to put the tables as you make them. You see how to do so in the sections on creating tables later in this chapter.

If you are working with Personal Oracle9i or on your own PC, you can skip the rest of this section and jump right to the section called "Console's Spreadsheet for Tables" because Oracle9i can take care of the structure for you. Oracle9i can place all the tables in the default tablespace and arrange them in the files already assigned to your tablespace. The exact placement of tables in the files is up to Oracle9i and has no bearing on how you use the tables.

Oracle Managed Files: The real world meets the virtual world

How do you decide the size of the datafiles that support your tablespaces? How do you choose what size each tablespace is going to be? A new feature, Oracle Managed Files, makes these kinds of decisions easier.

Before Oracle9i, your database came with a set of standard files. Whenever your database size grew beyond the storage capacity of those initial files, you — as the DBA — had to add new datafiles. Now, Oracle9i provides an automated way to handle the files. Using Oracle Managed Files, you allow the database to automatically add or delete data files as needed to fit your growing or shrinking database storage requirements. Set it and forget it!

Even with the Oracle Managed Files, you must do some planning for the tablespaces that your database uses. The next section describes new features that make tablespaces more efficient for storage.

Locally managed versus dictionary managed tablespaces

A *dictionary managed tablespace* uses the database data dictionary to keep track of space usage. This information is stored in data-dictionary tables, which also keep track of other data-dictionary information such as users, roles, and a table's column names. Older Oracle databases use this traditional method to track information about tablespaces.

A *locally managed tablespace* stores information about its own storage in a special area of the tablespace itself. This is a new technique, introduced to help manage very large tablespaces or databases with a lot of user activity, such as those used by online e-commerce Web sites.

Note: Oracle now recommends that you create all your tablespaces as locally managed tablespaces.

Some of the advantages of using locally managed tablespaces follow:

> ✔ **Simplified space allocation in tablespaces.** The AUTOALLOCATE clause does this by allowing the tablespace to determine the best extent sizes itself.
>
> ✔ **Fewer calls to the database data dictionary.** If many users try to use the database at once, a traffic jam of requests to the data dictionary can occur. Locally managed tablespaces handle data insertions, updates, and deletions without calling the data dictionary.

Next, you see examples of the SQL commands to create each kind of tablespace. You can run these in SQL*Plus.

Suppose that you want a dictionary managed tablespace called AMYDDSPACE to start at 5MB in size and grow an additional 5MB whenever a new extent is needed to hold more data. Here is the SQL command to create the tablespace:

```
-- 01_dictionarytablespace
CREATE TABLESPACE AMYDDSPACE
DATAFILE '/ORACLE9i/data/amyddspace01.dbf' SIZE 50K
    DEFAULT STORAGE (
        INITIAL 5M
        NEXT 5M
        MINEXTENTS 2
        MAXEXTENTS 50
        PCTINCREASE 0);
```

The following statement creates a locally managed tablespace named AMYSPACE that starts as 5MB and automatically allocates new extents of the appropriate size as needed:

```
-- 02_localtablespace
CREATE TABLESPACE AMYSPACE
DATAFILE '/ORACLE9i/data/amyspace01.dbf' SIZE 5M
    EXTENT MANAGEMENT LOCAL AUTOALLOCATE;
```

You can see just by looking at the commands that the second one is easier. You are simply allowing Oracle to do more of the work for you.

If you are responsible for planning the table structure for the database or your part of the database, you can create a single large tablespace for an entire set of tables rather than many small tablespaces. I recommend being conservative about the number of tablespaces that you create. Every tablespace you add increases your work in managing the database. When you have many tablespaces, you may run into a problem: The overall database has enough space to hold all your data but cannot use all the space because you placed a table in a tablespace that is out of room. Tables cannot span multiple table-spaces. (One exception that allows a table to span multiple tablespaces is the partitioned table, which is appropriate only for large tables — tables that take up more than 1GB of space.) Remember — always consult your DBA about table placement.

A Word or Two about Columns

Oracle9i needs tables, and tables need columns. Even if a table contains no rows, it must have at least one column. When creating columns, you want to consider names, datatypes, and null values. This section goes into more detail about column datatypes and null values in your data. Chapter 2 covers the naming conventions used for columns, as well as for tables, indexes, and other database items.

Defining columns in Oracle9i

You define columns when you create a table in the database. You must name the column; then you tell Oracle9i what kind of data goes into the column by specifying the datatype of the column. In a nutshell, Table 9-1 shows all your choices when you define columns in Oracle9i. You may want to mark the table for later reference.

Table 9-1	The Complete Guide to Datatypes		
Datatype	*Parameters*	*Example*	*Description*
VARCHAR2(n)	n=1 to 4,000	VARCHAR2(25)	Text string with a variable length. Specify the maximum length (n) when defining the column. This datatype holds letters, numbers, and symbols in the standard ASCII text set (or EBCDIC, or whatever set is standard for your database). If your data is shorter than the maximum size, Oracle9i adjusts the length of the column to the size of the data, which is a great space-saver. If your data has trailing blanks, Oracle9i removes the trailing blanks. VARCHAR2 is the most commonly used datatype.

Datatype	Parameters	Example	Description
NUMBER(p,s)	p=1 to 38, s=−84 to 127	NUMBER(10,2)	Use this datatype only for numbers. Specify the precision (p), which is the number of digits, and the scale (e), which is the number of digits to the right of the decimal place. For example, to define a number with a maximum of 999.99, use NUMBER (5,2). Oracle9i truncates data that doesn't fit into the scale. You define a column as NUMBER(5,2), for example, and then add a new row to the table, telling Oracle9i to put the number 575.316 in this column. The number that is actually stored in the column is 575.32 because Oracle9i automatically truncates the decimals at the hundredths, which is the scale that Oracle9i defined for that column. If you define a column as NUMBER(3,0) and then add a row with data 575.316 in that column, the actual number stored is 575.
DATE	none	DATE	Valid dates range from January 1, 4712 B.C. to A.D. December 31, 9999. Oracle9i stores DATE internally as a 7-byte number and, by definition, also includes the time in hours, minutes, and seconds.

(continued)

Table 9-1 *(continued)*

Datatype	Parameters	Example	Description
CHAR(n)	n=1 to 2000	CHAR(14)	Text string with a fixed length. The default length is 1. You can specify the maximum length (n) when defining the column. If you add data to this kind of column and the data is shorter than (n), Oracle9i adds blanks to the end of the data to make it a fixed length. Suppose that your column is datatype CHAR(10), and you insert a row with HENRY in the column. HENRY is five characters long. Oracle9i takes HENRY, adds five blanks to the end of it, and then stores it in the database that way. The main difference between CHAR and VARCHAR2 is that CHAR pads the data with blank spaces and VARCHAR2 strips blank spaces, making VARCHAR2 more compact and efficient than CHAR for storing data.
NCHAR(n)	n=1 to 2,000	NCHAR(30)	See CHAR, which is the same except that the characters stored depend on a national character set (Chinese characters, for example). Oracle9i supports many languages this way.
NVARCHAR2(n)	n=1 to 4,000	NVARCHAR2(65)	*See* VARCHAR2. NVARCHAR2 has the same attributes, except that it stores characters for any language (national character set) supported by Oracle9i.

Datatype	Parameters	Example	Description
LONG (obsolete soon)	none	LONG	Maximum size is 2GB. Used for large chunks of data that don't need to be available for text searching. Use VARCHAR2 when you need to do text searching. The large object datatypes — BLOB, CLOB, NCLOB, and BFILE — will soon replace LONG.
RAW(n) (obsolete soon)	n=1 to 2000	RAW(500)	Raw binary data of a variable length. You must specify the maximum length (*n*) when defining the column. Oracle9i uses the RAW datatype for small graphics or formatted text files, such as Microsoft Word documents. RAW is an older datatype that will eventually disappear and be replaced by the large object datatypes: BLOB, CLOB, NCLOB, and **BFILE**.
LONG RAW (obsolete soon)	none	LONG RAW	Raw binary data of a variable length. The maximum length is 2GB. Oracle9i uses the LONG RAW datatype for larger graphics; formatted text files, such as Word documents; audio; video; and other nontext data. You can't have both a LONG and a LONG RAW column in the same table. LONG RAW is an older datatype that will eventually disappear and be replaced by the large object datatypes: BLOB, CLOB, NCLOB, and BFILE.

(continued)

Table 9-1 *(continued)*

Datatype	Parameters	Example	Description
BLOB, CLOB, NCLOB	none	BLOB	Three kinds of large objects (LOBs) used for larger graphics; formatted text files, such as Word documents; audio; video; and other nontext data. Maximum size is 4GB. LOBs come in several flavors, depending on the kind of bytes that you use. Oracle9i stores these internal LOBs in the database. (*See also* BFILE.) Special functions for reading, storing, and writing LOBs are available, but I don't cover them in this book. If you want to use this datatype, refer to your Oracle9i manual.
BFILE	none	BFILE	Large binary object (LOB) stored outside the database. Maximum size is 4GB. This external LOB type is tracked in the database but actually stores data in a datafile outside the database. Oracle9i can read and query BFILEs but can't write to them. Special functions for reading, storing, and writing LOBs are available, but I don't cover them in this book. If you want to use this datatype, refer to your Oracle9i manual.
REF	*schema. objectname*		Reference object identifier. This type of column is used in object tables to define a foreign key to another object.

Datatype	Parameters	Example	Description
ROWID (for internal use)	none	ROWID	Internal Oracle datatype that stores the physical locator string for a row of data. Generally speaking, you never create a column of this datatype. You can, however, query the ROWID of any table's rows by adding ROWID to the SELECT clause.
UROWID (for internal use)	none	UROWID	Universal ROWID. Hexadecimal string that shows the logical location of a row on an index-organized table, an object table, or a non-Oracle entity.

The most commonly used datatypes are VARCHAR2, DATE, and NUMBER. You commonly use the CHAR datatype for coded data of a constant length, such as state abbreviations.

The LOB datatypes (BLOB, CLOB, and BFILE) are becoming more popular now that more and more multimedia data is stored in Oracle databases. For example, you definitely need LOB datatypes when you create a database with delivery-on-demand music-CD selections or something fun like that.

Remember that whenever you define a column, you choose to allow or disallow null values in the column by leaving out or including, respectively, the NOT NULL parameter. See the "What is a null?" sidebar for examples of how null values differs from zeros or blanks when Oracle9i evaluates your queries.

Allowing nulls or not

When designing columns, you need to consider whether to allow nulls in the columns. Here's the rule: Primary keys (the unique identifier for a table) can't contain nulls, and this requirement is added automatically when you create the primary-key constraint. Otherwise, anything goes. I advise allowing nulls everywhere except in primary keys. Even if your brain knows that the column will always contain data, exceptions to rules always exist. If you define the column to not allow nulls, you may be in a bind if you are adding a new row that really has no value for that column.

Suppose that you do choose to define the column so that you don't allow nulls. You can do so by adding the NOT NULL constraint to the column in the CREATE TABLE statement (see the next section).

Refer to Chapter 19 for information on how to change a column's null value setting (from nulls allowed to nulls not allowed, and vice versa).

TECHNICAL STUFF

What is a null?

When the column of a row has no data, Oracle9i describes the column as being *null* or having a null value. Use null when you do not know the value of the data. If I put together a table for the fish in my aquarium, for example, I may have a null value (no data) in the DEATH_DATE column of the row for Wesley. This value means that Wesley is alive or that I don't know when he died.

Oracle9i allows null values in columns of all datatypes. Oracle9i doesn't allow null values in only two instances:

✔ Primary-key columns

✔ Any column defined with the NOT NULL constraint

As another example of the definition of a null value, imagine that you are filling out a questionnaire at your local pizza parlor. One question is, "What is your favorite topping on pizza: cheese or mushrooms?" You like both so much, you cannot decide, and you leave the answer blank. The lack of data indicates that you have not selected your favorite topping. The pizza parlor's database has a null value in the FAVORITE_TOPPING column when your questionnaire is added to the table. In other words, your favorite topping is unknown.

Do not use null to represent zero. Zero is a known quantity. You can add, subtract, and generally use zero in calculations. You cannot add, subtract, or use null values in calculations. When you add a null to 10, the result equals null. To say the same thing in a different way: Add some unknown quantity to 10, and you get another unknown quantity.

Nulls do not equal nulls or any other value. Oracle9i evaluates the following statement as false, for example, even when a null value is in the SELLING_PRICE column:

SELLING_PRICE = NULL

The correct way to write this phrase is

SELLING_PRICE IS NULL

If you want the opposite evaluation, use

SELLING_PRICE IS NOT NULL

The preceding phrase is true when any value is in the SELLING_PRICE column and false when a null value is in the column.

Console's Spreadsheet for Tables

So you want to create a table of your very own, eh? You've come to the right place. When you want to create a brand-new table, use Console. This section shows you how.

To practice creating tables in general, follow the steps in this section and create a sample table — in this example, a table for the fish in my aquarium. My aquarium has grown since the first edition of the book. My first pet fish, Wesley, who ate all the other fish that I had, is now in fishy heaven, and my tank has a new bunch of fish with less cannibalistic tendencies.

I can track all kinds of information about my fish with this table. The pieces of information that I want to track for each fish are

✔ The fish's given name

✔ The name of the aquarium I have the fish in (just in case I get several aquariums)

✔ The approximate date my fish was hatched

✔ The date of death on my fish's death certificate (if it has died)

✔ The fish's color

✔ The breed of fish

✔ The gender, if I can figure it out (male, female, or unknown)

✔ Any comment about my fish, such as where I bought it or its favorite food

Each of these items becomes a column in the `FISHY_WISHY` table.

The following three sections describe how to create a table using Console. The steps are creating the column definitions, defining primary-key constraints, and setting the storage allocations. You perform all these in a single session in Console.

Step 1: Defining the columns

Here are the steps for using Enterprise Manager Console to create this table. (If Console is already open, skip to Step 6.)

1. **Start Console.**

   On Windows platforms, choose Start➪Programs➪Oracle HOME2➪ Enterprise Manager Console. Note that the Oracle HOME2 label may have a different name, such as ORAHOME81, on your computer. The person who installed the software on your machine designates the name.

On UNIX, Linux, or any other platform, type **oemapp console** at the operating-system command line.

You see the logo screen for Oracle Enterprise Manager, and then the Oracle Enterprise Manager Console login window appears.

2. **Make sure the Launch Standalone option is selected, and then click OK.**

Console's initial screen appears.

3. **Double-click the Databases folder.**

All available databases are listed.

4. **Double-click the name of the database that you want to work on.**

If this is the first time you have used Console or if you have not saved your login settings, you see a login screen. Otherwise, you see a list of Managers (including Instance, Schema, Security, and Storage).

5. **If you see a login screen, follow these steps to log in:**

   a. **For the Username, type** SYSTEM.

   b. **For the Password, type** MANAGER **or whatever the current password is for SYSTEM on your database.**

   c. **For the Connect As option, select Normal.**

   d. **Click to add a check mark to the Save As Local Preferred Credentials option.**

   e. **Click OK.**

   Console asks whether it's okay to save your credentials in a local encrypted file.

   f. **Click OK to continue.**

   The list of Managers (including Instance, Schema, Security, and Storage) appear.

6. **Choose Object⇨Create.**

The Create dialog box appears, so you can decide what kind of thing you are creating.

7. **Choose Table, click to uncheck the Use Wizard check box, and click Create.**

The Create Table dialog box appears. It looks like the table information box you see for existing tables, except the spreadsheet portion and most of the boxes are empty, ready for you to fill in all the details.

8. **Click the first box and then type the name of the table.**

Chapter 2 has a list of naming standards for tables. For the example, type **FISHY_WISHY.**

9. **Click the arrow in the Schema box and select one of the available schema.**

    The schema is the table owner. For the example, select AMY.

10. **Leave the tablespace as the default.**

    Console selects the default tablespace for the schema that you selected, which is usually the appropriate choice.

11. **Leave the Define Columns option selected.**

    This creates a relational table. The other choices allow you to create an object table or a table based on a query. Your screen should look like Figure 9-1.

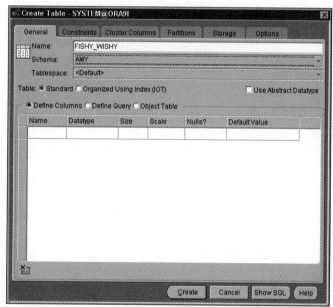

Figure 9-1:
Begin creating a table by giving it a name and a schema.

12. **In the Name box in the lower half of the window, type a column name.**

    For the example, type **NAME_OF_FISH**.

13. **In the Datatype drop-down list, choose a datatype.**

    For the first example column, use VARCHAR2, which is the default datatype. When you want a different datatype, simply click once in the Datatype box, and the box changes to a drop-down list. Click again to open the list and scroll to the datatype you want to use.

    See the list of datatypes in Table 9-1 for descriptions of all the choices. VARCHAR2 is the most commonly used datatype for text information. You can type the first letter of the datatype to select it faster.

14. **Adjust the size of the column, if necessary, by typing the maximum size you want in the Size and Scale boxes.**

   For the first column in the FISHY_WISHY example, accept the default of 10 for the length. Console doesn't allow you to type in the Size or Scale boxes if you don't need them for the selected datatype. Remember, Oracle9i measures size in number of characters or digits. If your column holds a person's last name, for example, you may adjust the size to 30 because you estimated that last names could never be longer than 30 letters.

   The Scale box defines decimal places for numbers. In this example, leave it blank.

15. **For the Nulls? box, accept the default (nulls are not allowed).**

   If this is a column that allows null values, you can click the box and change the blank box to a blue check mark. The blue check mark means yes. In this box, it means that null values are allowed.

16. **Fill in the default value. (This step is optional.)**

   The default value is the data that goes in the column when you add new rows to this table that haven't specified a value for this column. The default value can be a phrase, word, letter, number, date, or whatever fits the datatype of this column.

   You assign a default value of YES to the ADD_TO_MAILING_LIST column in your NAME_AND_ADDRESS table, for example. Unless you specifically put in a value of NO (or MAYBE, or something else) in the ADD_TO_MAILING_LIST column when you insert new rows, every new row gets a YES in the ADD_TO_MAILING_LIST column.

   Figure 9-2 shows the FISHY_WISHY table's first column, which is called NAME_OF_FISH.

17. **Add more columns as needed.**

   Each time you start typing the name of another column, a blank line is added so that you can define another new column below it. Repeat Steps 12 through 16 until you've defined all your columns to your satisfaction. For the example, add the following columns:

   - AQUARIUM_NAME, datatype VARCHAR2, length 20, nulls allowed, default value is 'TANK1'. (Be sure that you type the single quotation marks around the default value.)

   - BIRTH_DATE, datatype DATE, nulls allowed, no default value.

   - DEATH_DATE, datatype DATE, nulls allowed, no default value.

   - COLORS, datatype VARCHAR2, length 15, nulls allowed, no default value.

   - BREED, datatype VARCHAR2, length 10, nulls allowed, no default value.

- SEX, datatype CHAR, length 1, no nulls, default value of 'M' (including the single quotation marks).

- COMMENT_TEXT, datatype VARCHAR2, length 100, nulls allowed, no default value.

18. **Adjust the order of the columns, insert new columns, and remove unwanted columns.**

    After defining all the columns, you may find that you want to move a column up or down in the list. To do this, right-click in the box to the right of the column. This highlights the entire row of boxes for the particular column and displays a menu, as shown in Figure 9-3. Select the appropriate item from the menu.

Although you could create the table right now by clicking the Create button, go on to the next section instead to add a primary-key constraint to the table. Adding the constraint at the same time that you create the table will save you time in the long run.

Some designers like to arrange columns in alphabetical order; others like to arrange them in a logical order (name, address, city, state, and so on). Arranging columns the latter way is better if you use Oracle Forms or other tools that generate data-entry screens by using the order of your columns as a guide. These tools set up the data-entry screen so that the user enters each column in the order in which it appears in the database table. The closer your columns match the order in which you want people to enter data, the easier it will be to modify the data-entry screen.

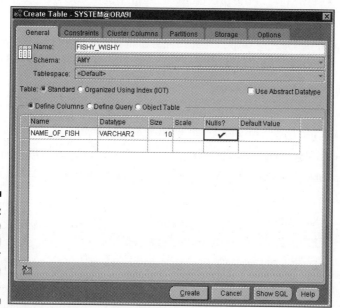

Figure 9-2:
The Create Table dialog box after you add the first column.

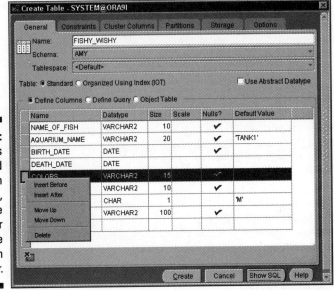

Figure 9-3:
Use this
menu to add
columns in
the middle,
remove
columns, or
change the
column
order.

Step 2: Defining the constraints

This section shows you how to add a primary-key constraint to a table. (For a description of primary keys, see Chapter 6.) You can use this section for existing tables as well as for new tables. The example in this section is a continuation of the one in the preceding section, where you created a table called FISHY_WISHY.

You should be looking at the Create Table dialog box, as shown in Figure 9-3. Now, continuing with the example, define the primary-key constraint as follows:

1. **Click the Constraints tab.**

   This is where you define the key.

2. **Click the Name box to begin defining the constraint.**

   For the example, type **FISHY_WISHY_PK** as the constraint name.

3. **Double-click the Type box and make a selection.**

   You have four choices:

   - UNIQUE creates an alternate

   - PRIMARY creates a primary-key constraint

   - FOREIGN creates a foreign-key constraint

- CHECK creates a constraint that checks for specific values in a column

For the example, choose PRIMARY.

4. **Accept the default in the Disable? box.**

   The blank box means "No, this constraint is not disabled."

5. **Skip the rest of the boxes in the top section.**

   These are used mainly for foreign-key constraint definitions. For the example, you are defining a primary key, so these are not required.

6. **Double-click Table Columns.**

   This displays the list of columns in the Constraint Definition (lower) section of the window.

7. **Select the column you want to use as the primary key.**

   In the example, choose NAME_OF_FISH.

8. **Skip the Referenced Columns box.**

   This is used for foreign-key constraints.

Figure 9-4 shows the Constraints tab with a completed primary-key constraint for the sample table.

Although you could click the Create button to create the table, continue to the next section and define the storage space assigned to the table when you create it.

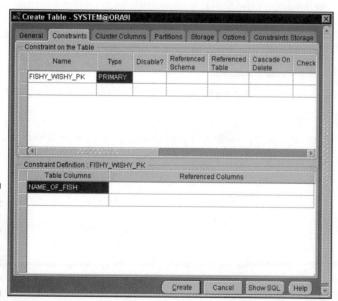

Figure 9-4:
Define a
primary key
on the
Constraint
tab.

Step 3: Defining the storage

The final step for defining and creating a new table involves calculating storage space. Console contains an automatic storage calculator.

You are already in Console, looking at the Create Table dialog box. You have already defined the columns and the constraints. Now, follow along to define the storage requirements for the table:

1. **In the Create Table dialog box, click the Storage tab.**

   This displays a storage definition dialog box.

2. **Click the Auto Calculation option.**

   The boxes change so that you can enter information about the use of your table.

3. **Fill in each box.**

   For the example, fill in this information:

   - For Initial # Rows, type **1000**.

   - For Growth Rate: type **100** and select **month**, for 100 rows per month.

   - In the Update Activity area, select the option labeled Low or None option.

   - In the Insert Activity area, select High and then select Including Deletes.

   Figure 9-5 shows the Storage dialog box with all the information filled in. Notice that in the SQL Text box, this information has been translated to storage parameters, such as PCTFREE (free space left for updates) and STORAGE (initial space allocated).

4. **Click the Create button.**

   This saves your work to the database, creating the FISHY_WISHY table.

Congratulations — you finished your table definition. Console generates the table and returns to the main window. You can see your table in place with the rest of AMY's tables by opening the folders in the left window.

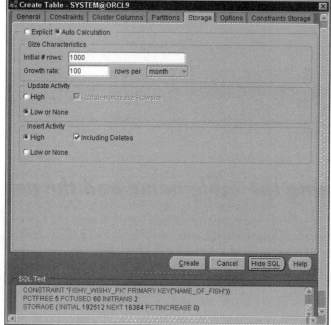

Figure 9-5:
Storage
parameters
are
calculated
for you
using
Console's
Auto
Calculation
button.

A Table of Your Own with SQL

This section shows you how to use SQL to create your own table. You use the same sample table (FISHY_WISHY) that you used in the previous sections, to help you see the similarities and differences in the two table creation methods.

Here is the complete SQL command for creating the FISHY_WISHY table:

```
-- 03_createtable
CREATE TABLE FISHY_WISHY
(NAME_OF_FISH VARCHAR2(10) NOT NULL,
AQUARIUM_NAME VARCHAR2(20) DEFAULT 'TANK1',
BIRTH_DATE DATE,
DEATH_DATE DATE,
COLORS VARCHAR2(15),
BREED VARCHAR2(10),
SEX CHAR(1) DEFAULT 'M' NOT NULL,
COMMENT_TEXT VARCHAR2(100),
PRIMARY KEY(NAME_OF_FISH))
TABLESPACE USERS
STORAGE(INITIAL 200K NEXT 20K MAXEXTENTS 200);
```

Next, you walk through the different parts of this command. The next three sections describe the following:

 ✔ Defining the table name and columns
 ✔ Defining the primary-key constraint
 ✔ Defining the storage parameters

The last section ends with you creating the table in SQL*Plus. Come on in; the water's fine.

Defining the table name and the columns

The CREATE TABLE code creates a table for the fish in my aquarium. I can track all kinds of information about my fish with this table. Following are the pieces of information that I want to track for each fish:

 ✔ The name of the fish
 ✔ The name of the aquarium that the fish are in (just in case I get several aquariums)
 ✔ The birthday of my fish
 ✔ When the poor thing died (if it has died)
 ✔ Its color
 ✔ The breed of fish
 ✔ Male, female, or unknown gender
 ✔ A comment about why the fish died or any other comments, such as where I bought it or its favorite color

Each of these items becomes a column in the FISHY_WISHY table.

The SQL code for creating the table name (the first portion of the complete command) looks like this:

```
CREATE TABLE FISHY_WISHY
```

If you want, you can add the schema name to the command, so it looks like this:

```
CREATE TABLE AMY.FISHY_WISHY
```

When you don't include the schema, the user who issues the command owns the table automatically. If you are logged in as AMY, for example, the schema becomes AMY.

Next, you add definitions for each column. The entire definition of columns is enclosed in parentheses. Each column has the following parameters defined:

✔ **Name.** The column name.

✔ **Datatype.** The datatype, such as `VARCHAR2` or `DATE`.

✔ **Length.** Specify the number of characters or numerals. For numbers, a second value can define the number of numerals to the right of the decimal place. This is not needed for dates.

✔ **Nulls.** You need to specify `NOT NULL` only to restrict the column from containing null values. The default is `NULL`, meaning the column can contain null values.

✔ **Default value.** This value is inserted into new records if no value is specifically assigned to the column.

The first column is the `NAME_OF_FISH` column. It has a datatype of `VARCHAR2` and a length of 10. It can't have nulls and has no default value. The SQL code for this column looks like this:

```
(NAME_OF_FISH VARCHAR2(10) NOT NULL,
```

The opening parenthesis is needed because this is the first column defined. The comma at the end means that more columns will be defined.

Here is a list of the columns that follow the `NAME_OF_FISH` column in the sample `FISHY_WISHY` table:

✔ `AQUARIUM_NAME`, datatype `VARCHAR2`, length 20, nulls allowed, default value is `'TANK1'`. (Be sure that you type the single quotation marks around the default value.)

✔ `BIRTH_DATE`, datatype `DATE`, nulls allowed, no default value.

✔ `DEATH_DATE`, datatype `DATE`, nulls allowed, no default value.

✔ `COLORS`, datatype `VARCHAR2`, length 15, nulls allowed, no default value.

✔ `BREED`, datatype `VARCHAR2`, length 10, nulls allowed, no default value.

✔ `SEX`, datatype `CHAR`, length 1, no nulls, default value of `'M'`.

✔ `COMMENT_TEXT`, datatype `VARCHAR2`, length 100, nulls allowed, no default value.

The SQL command up to this point, including the table name and all the columns, looks like this:

```
CREATE TABLE FISHY_WISHY
(NAME_OF_FISH VARCHAR2(10) NOT NULL,
AQUARIUM_NAME VARCHAR2(20) DEFAULT 'TANK1',
BIRTH_DATE DATE,
DEATH_DATE DATE,
COLORS VARCHAR2(15),
BREED VARCHAR2(10),
SEX CHAR(1) DEFAULT 'M' NOT NULL,
COMMENT_TEXT VARCHAR2(100))
```

Note: The command contains all the required elements to create a table. You could run the command in SQL*Plus to create the table. However, for the example, you extend the SQL code to include a primary-key constraint and storage information.

In the next section, you add the primary-key constraint.

Defining the primary-key constraint

A *primary-key constraint* defines the primary key for the table and automatically restricts the columns in the primary key so that they can't contain null values. Most tables you create will contain primary keys.

In the example, the FISHY_WISHY table's primary key contains a single column — the NAME_OF_FISH column. The SQL code for its primary key looks like this:

```
PRIMARY KEY(NAME_OF_FISH)
```

If the table's primary key has two or more columns, they are listed in the parentheses. For example, suppose that the ADDRESS_BOOK table has a primary key of three columns: PERSON_ID, ADDRESS_TYPE, and ADDRESS_SEQUENCE_NO. The SQL code for this primary key would be

```
PRIMARY KEY(PERSON_ID, ADDRESS_TYPE, ADDRESS_SEQUENCE_NO)
```

Add the primary-key constraint at the end of the column definition section. It is placed before the closing parenthesis for the list of columns.

The SQL code for the FISHY_WISHY table, with the primary-key constraint added, looks like this:

```
CREATE TABLE FISHY_WISHY
(NAME_OF_FISH VARCHAR2(10) NOT NULL,
AQUARIUM_NAME VARCHAR2(20) DEFAULT 'TANK1',
BIRTH_DATE DATE,
DEATH_DATE DATE,
COLORS VARCHAR2(15),
```

```
BREED VARCHAR2(10),
SEX CHAR(1) DEFAULT 'M' NOT NULL,
COMMENT_TEXT VARCHAR2(100),
PRIMARY KEY(NAME_OF_FISH))
```

Here is another point at which you can run the SQL code and create the table. If you did so, Oracle9i would use default values for the storage location and size for the table. However, your job is not complete! The sample table needs storage parameters that are not the default ones, so you must add them.

Adding storage parameters and creating the table

There are many storage parameters, and you could spend hours reviewing how they interact. To simplify this task, I focus on the three most commonly specified storage parameters. They are

✔ INITIAL. The size of the table at the time it is created. This makes room for your initial group of records and ensures that the records are stored together, making retrieval more efficient.

✔ NEXT. The size of the next chunk of space (*extent*) that the table grabs after it uses its initial allocation of space. This lets your table grow at a controlled rate.

✔ MAXEXTENTS. The maximum number of times the table is allowed to grab another chunk of space. This sets a cap on the maximum size of the table.

For the example table, you create the table with 200K of initial storage space, and allow for up to 200 extents with 20K of space in each extent. The table will be stored in the USERS tablespace. The SQL code for the storage parameters follows:

```
TABLESPACE USERS
STORAGE(INITIAL 200K NEXT 20K MAXEXTENTS 200)
```

The storage parameters are added to the end of the CREATE TABLE command.

You've completed the main steps in writing the SQL command for creating a table. Here are the steps for using SQL*Plus to create this table:

1. **Start SQL*Plus.**

   On Windows platforms, choose Start⇨Programs⇨Oracle HOME⇨Application Development⇨SQL*Plus.

   On UNIX, Linux, or any other platform, type **sqlplus** at the operating-system prompt to start the command-line version of SQL*Plus.

2. **Log in as the Oracle user.**

   a. **Type the user name and password. If you installed the sample schema, type AMY for the name and AMY123 for the password.**

   b. **In the Host String box, type the Oracle Net name of the Oracle9i instance on your local computer or on your network.**

   For a local database, you can usually leave this blank. For a database on a network, ask your administrator to provide you with a valid host string.

   c. **Click OK.**

   The SQL*Plus window appears.

3. **Type the SQL code to create the table.**

   If you're using the sample schema (from the Oracle9i extras you get at www.dummies.com/extras/Oracle9i.html), type the following code in the top part of the window:

```
CREATE TABLE FISHY_WISHY
(NAME_OF_FISH VARCHAR2(10) NOT NULL,
AQUARIUM_NAME VARCHAR2(20) DEFAULT 'TANK1',
BIRTH_DATE DATE,
DEATH_DATE DATE,
COLORS VARCHAR2(15),
BREED VARCHAR2(10),
SEX CHAR(1) DEFAULT 'M' NOT NULL,
COMMENT_TEXT VARCHAR2(100),
PRIMARY KEY(NAME_OF_FISH))
TABLESPACE USERS
STORAGE(INITIAL 200K NEXT 20K MAXEXTENTS 200);
```

   If you are not using the sample schema, use the preceding SQL command as a model for your own CREATE TABLE statement.

4. **Press Enter to run the command.**

   After SQL*Plus runs the command., it replies in the top window as follows:

```
Table created.
```

Now that you've created your own table, can you get it out of your life? No problem! Just drop it. This command works better on databases than it does with my dog ("Drop it, boy, drop it!"). Here's the SQL code to remove a table:

```
DROP TABLE tablename;
```

tablename is (naturally) the name of the table that you want to remove.

Use the DROP command only when you are certain that you can't fix the table and you don't need the data because you can't restore the table by using ROLLBACK after you drop it. The only way to restore the table is from a backup copy. See Chapter 3 for a discussion of the ROLLBACK command.

DROP and DELETE are very different commands. DROP removes the table definition from your database, without a trace. DELETE removes the rows from a table but leaves the table itself intact. Refer to Chapter 4 for instructions on how to delete rows by using SQL.

As in life, the only constant in Oracle9i is change. After you create a table, its structure can change. To see how to change columns or their attributes using Console, see Chapter 19. Chapter 19 also shows you how to add or change primary and foreign keys.

Chapter 10

Creating Object Types, Objects, and References

- -

- -

*T*his chapter provides some easy examples to help you get acquainted with your new best friend: the object. You create a simple set of objects that are related to one another. You also see where methods may be added to the set of objects, but you don't actually create methods because you would need to use PL/SQL, a subject that is beyond the scope of this book. If you aren't clear on what an object is, you may want to head to Chapter 6 and read the sections on objects before reading this chapter.

An Overview of Creating Objects

Enterprise Manager Console is smart enough to handle object types, object tables, and other related items, making it easy to figure out what you're doing. No tinfoil hat required!

To really get into this chapter, grab your baker's hat and a white apron. Okay, you can substitute a baseball cap for the baker's hat. Then imagine that you're a bread baker and want your Oracle9i database to keep track of your excellent recipes, the inventory of ingredients in your bakery, and a bit of information about your customers. Figure 10-1 shows a static type diagram of the Perfect Bakery.

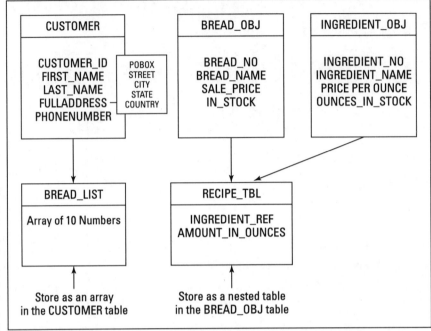

Figure 10-1:
Being
a baker,
you buy
ingredients,
bake bread,
and sell it to
customers.

Does that diagram look familiar? In Chapter 4, you use these same object tables to experiment with queries, inserts, and updates. You probably already have the BAKERY schema in your database. If so, here is what you should do so that you can create a clone of the BAKERY schema while working through the examples in this chapter:

1. **Create a user named BAKERY1.**

2. **Give this user the CONNECT and RESOURCE roles.**

When following along with the examples, make sure you use the BAKERY1 user.

Get all the SQL commands used to create the schema in this chapter from www.dummies.com/extras/Oracle9i.html. After you download and unzip the file, you can find the examples in the Samples/Chapter10 directory.

In a nutshell, here are the steps you perform during this chapter to create a set of related objects:

1. **Create an object type to define one row or part of a row for each object.**

2. **Create a table type for each nested table and array.**

3. **Create object tables using the types created.**

4. **Create object-relational tables using the types created.**

In the sample bakery schema, you create the following items, in this order:

- INGREDIENT_TYPE object type
- RECIPE_TYPE object type
- ADDRESS_TYPE object type
- RECIPE_NEST nested table object (uses RECIPE_TYPE)
- BREAD_TYPE object type (uses RECIPE_NEST)
- BREAD_ARRAY array type
- BREAD_OBJ object table (uses BREAD_TYPE)
- INGREDIENT_OBJ object table (uses INGREDIENT_TYPE)
- CUSTOMER object-relational table (uses ADDRESS_TYPE and BREAD_ARRAY)

The first step toward creating the Perfect Bakery database schema is to design the object types for each object that you need.

Types Need No Space

Unlike your new roommates, types need no space in your closet. That is, defining a type doesn't gobble up space in your database. Defining a type is more like defining a datatype than defining a table. In fact, Oracle sometimes refers to types as *user-defined datatypes.* The type itself never holds any data, whereas the table usually doesn't hold data when it's defined but grows as data is added to the table rows. Types are used while defining the kind of data that a table contains, which is the same way that datatypes are used in tables.

You can create these three kinds of types in Oracle9i:

- **Object type.** This type defines a row in an object table. An object type can also be used in another object type, so it may contain only part of an object table row. In fact, after it's defined, an object type can be used as the datatype of a column in an object table.

- **Array type.** This type defines a limited set of repeating rows, where each row is a single attribute. The attribute can be a regular datatype (such as a number or date) or can be defined as an object type. This is also called the varrying array or varray type.

- **Table type.** This type defines a nested table. A nested table can contain multiple attributes. Like the array type, an attribute in the table type can be a regular datatype (such as a number or date), an object type, or a combination of both.

✔ **SQLJ object type.** This object type creates a list of attributes that appear on the outside like regular SQL column attributes but are handled on the inside (using methods) as Java attributes.

✔ **Incomplete object type.** This object type is defined in name only. It allows you to build other object types that are interrelated. An incomplete object type must be completed before you can use it in the definition of an object table.

In the bakery example, you define four object types, one array type, and one table type.

Defining an object type

Defining an object type is similar to defining a table, except you don't define space requirements for an object type. (The space definition comes later in this chapter, when you define an object table that uses the object type.)

If you want to create the objects yourself as you read this chapter, first create a user named BAKERY1, with CONNECT and RESOURCE roles. Then follow the examples.

Follow these steps to create an object type:

1. **Start Console.**

   On Windows platforms, choose Start➪Programs➪Oracle HOME2➪Enterprise Manager Console. Note that the Oracle HOME2 label may have a different name, such as ORAHOME81, on your computer. The person who installed the software on your machine designates the name.

   On UNIX, Linux, or any other platform, type **oemapp console** at the operating-system command line.

   You see the logo screen for Oracle Enterprise Manager, and then the Oracle Enterprise Manager Console login window appears.

2. **Make sure the Launch Standalone option is selected, and then click OK.**

   Console's initial screen appears.

3. **Double-click the Databases folder.**

   All available databases are listed.

4. **Double-click the name of the database that you want to work on.**

   If this is the first time you have used Console or if you have not saved your login settings, you see a login screen. Otherwise, you see a list of Managers (including Instance, Schema, Security, and Storage).

5. **If you see a login screen, follow these steps to log in:**

    a. **For the Username, type** SYSTEM.

    b. **For the Password, type** MANAGER **or whatever the current password is for SYSTEM on your database.**

    c. **For the Connect As option, select Normal.**

    d. **Click to add a check mark to the Save As Local Preferred Credentials option.**

    e. **Click OK.**

    Console asks whether it's okay to save your credentials in a local encrypted file.

    f. **Click OK to continue.**

    The list of Managers (including Instance, Schema, Security, and Storage) appears.

6. **Choose Object⇨Create.**

    A menu appears, listing all the possible objects that you can create.

7. **Select Object Type, and then click Create.**

    You see the Create Object Type dialog box, where you define the object type.

8. **Type a name and select a schema for the object.**

    For the bakery example, you create the INGREDIENT_TYPE object type first, so type **INGREDIENT_TYPE** in the name box and select BAKERY1 as the schema. Figure 10-2 shows the Create Object Type dialog box at this point.

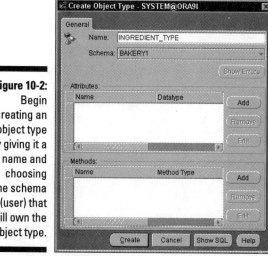

Figure 10-2:
Begin creating an object type by giving it a name and choosing the schema (user) that will own the object type.

9. **In the Attributes area, click the Add button.**

The Create Attribute dialog box appears.

10. **Define one attribute.**

Here you add each attribute one at a time to this object type. For the example object type, the first attribute is named INGREDIENT_NO and is the NUMBER datatype. Choose NUMBER for the Type, and then type a Length of **5** and a Precision of **0**. Figure 10-3 shows the filled-in fields for this attribute.

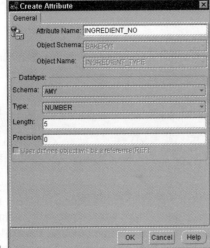

Figure 10-3:
You reach this attribute definition dialog box by clicking the Add button.

Note: The initial release has a small glitch, so that you see the AMY schema in Figure 10-3 where you should see the word *None*. Even so, the screen creates the attribute correctly. No doubt, this error will be corrected in future releases.

The Schema box in the Datatype area allows you to use another object type as the datatype of this attribute. When you choose a schema, all the object types owned by that schema appear in the datatype list.

Figure 10-4 shows the dialog box filled in for an attribute that uses another object type as its datatype.

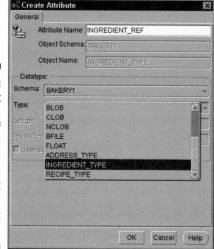

Figure 10-4:
If you select
a schema,
the list of
datatypes
in the Type
box includes
that
schema's
object
types.

To define a referenced object (similar to a foreign key), you must do two things: Select the schema and object type that defines the referenced object and then click the check box labeled User Defined Object Will Be a Reference (REF). By activating this check box, you tell the Oracle9i database to create a column of the REF datatype. After an object table is created and a row is added, the REF column contains an object ID (OID) belonging to one row of the referenced object.

After you select a datatype, fill in the proper length and precision if needed. The boxes for length and precision are open for editing if you've chosen a datatype that requires their definition. Refer to the table in Chapter 9 for all the gory details.

11. **Click OK to complete the attribute definition.**

    You return to the main Create Object Type dialog box.

12. **Repeat Steps 9 through 11 for all attributes.**

13. **Click the Create button to save the object type to the database.**

    The database thinks for a moment and then gives you a pop-up window saying Object type created successfully. Oracle9i returns you to the main window of Schema Manager.

For the example schema, create all the object types by following the preceding steps. Refer to Table 10-1 for the elements of each object type in the example. First, create the objects that aren't dependent on other objects — INGREDIENT_TYPE, ADDRESS_TYPE. Then create the RECIPE_TYPE object type. Don't create the BREAD_TYPE object type now; you create that later in this chapter, when you need to define the array type.

Table 10-1	Object Type Definitions			
Object Type Name	**Attribute Name**	**Datatype**	**Length**	**Precision**
INGREDIENT_TYPE	INGREDIENT_NO	NUMBER	5	0
	INGREDIENT_NAME	VARCHAR2	30	
	PRICE_PER_OUNCE	NUMBER	8	4
	OUNCES_IN_STOCK	NUMBER	10	1
RECIPE_TYPE	INGREDIENT_REF REF INGREDIENT_TYPE,			
AMOUNT_IN_ OUNCES	NUMBER	10	1	
ADDRESS_TYPE	POBOX	VARCHAR2	20	
	STREET	VARCHAR2	50	
	CITY	VARCHAR2	35	
	STATE	VARCHAR2	20	
	COUNTRY	VARCHAR2	25	

If you would rather not create the object types yourself in Console, you can continue with the example by running the BAKERY_STEP1_OBJECT_TYPE.sql SQL script, which is with the Oracle9i files on the For Dummies Web site (www.dummies.com/extras/Oracle9i.html). This script creates all the object types for you. Start SQL*Plus, log in as BAKERY1, and type the following command (adjusting the path to match the location of the file on your computer):

```
START C:\Samples\chapter10\BAKERY_STEP1_OBJECT_TYPE
```

Sure, take the easy way out!

Making a table type

Although most migratory birds build their nests from sticks, the rare Ootypee bird builds its nest with old Formica tables and always builds inside another bird's nest, taking up so much room that it sometimes overflows onto another part of the tree. And so, the story of the nested table begins.

A *nested table* stores a table of data in a single column within another table. Sometimes the nested table takes up more room than the original table and must be moved to its own location in the database.

Creating a nested table within an object type requires that you first define a table type. A table type is like an array type but can store an unlimited number of rows.

I am too good to you! You can skip all the following steps by running the BAKERY_STEP2_TABLE_TYPE.sql script (on the For Dummies Web site at www.dummies.com/extras/Oracle9i.html), creating the RECIPE_NEST table type, and adding it to the BREAD object type. Just log into SQL*Plus as BAKERY1 and type this command (adjusting the path for your computer):

```
START C:\Samples\chapter10\BAKERY_STEP2_TABLE_TYPE
```

Follow these steps to create a table type using Console:

1. **Start Console in stand-alone mode, double-click the Databases folder, double-click the database you want to work on, and log in as the DBA user (if necessary).**

   For details, refer to Steps 1 through 5 in the "Defining an object type" section.

2. **Choose Object⇨Create.**

   A menu appears, listing all the possible objects that you can create.

3. **Select Table Type, and then click Create.**

   You see the Create Table Type dialog box, where you define the table type.

4. **Type a name and select a schema for the table type.**

   For the example, you create the RECIPE_NEST table type first, so type **RECIPE_NEST** in the Name box and select BAKERY1 as the schema. See Figure 10-5.

5. **In the Datatype area, select a schema (if needed) and a datatype.**

   If you're using a regular datatype, such as NUMBER, leave the schema set to the default, None. If you're using an object type, select the schema of the object type that you need.

   If you're diligently building the sample schema, select BAKERY1 as the schema and select RECIPE_TYPE as the datatype. Leave the check box blank.

6. **Click the Create button.**

   The database ponders for a moment and then displays Table type created successfully. Oracle9i returns you to the main window of Schema Manager.

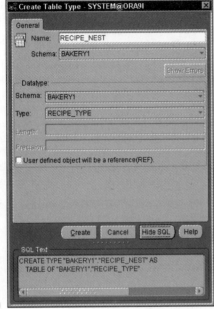

Figure 10-5:
A table type
eventually
becomes a
nested table
in another
object type
or a table.

Now that you have a table type, you'll want to use it. The next set of steps shows you how to add a nested table to an object type definition. In the example, you want to add the RECIPE_NEST table type to the BREAD_TYPE object type as the RECIPE_TBL attribute. Follow the bouncing ball. . . .

1. Begin creating the object type that will contain the nested table.

Choose Object➪Create➪Object Type from the main menu and define all the other attributes for the object type. In the example, you create the BREAD_TYPE object type in the BAKERY1 schema up to the point where you are ready to add the RECIPE_TBL nested table attribute. Add the following attributes as you did for the INGREDIENT_TYPE (see the steps in the previous section called "Defining an object type" for details):

- BREAD_NO with datatype of NUMBER, length of 5 and precision of 0

- BREAD_NAME with datatype of VARCHAR2, length of 20

- SALE_PRICE with datatype of NUMBER, length of 5 and precision of 2

- IN_STOCK with datatype of NUMBER, length of 10 and precision of 0

2. Click the Add button to create a new attribute.

You see the Create Attribute dialog box, where you define the nested table attribute in this object.

3. **Type a name, and then select the schema and the table type in the Datatype area.**

   In the example, you're adding the RECIPE_NEST table type to the BREAD object type, so name the attribute **RECIPE_TBL**. Type this attribute name, select BAKERY1 as the schema, and select RECIPE_NEST as the datatype. Your screen should look like Figure 10-6.

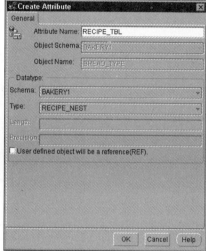

Figure 10-6: Add the nested table type to an object type just as you add any other attribute.

4. **Click OK to return to the main definition window.**

   You see the attribute added to your object type.

5. **Click Create to save the object type to the database.**

   The database ponders for a moment and then displays Object type created successfully. The object type is created with the nested table included, and Oracle9i returns you to the main window of Console.

Even if you have your entire schema laid out in a diagram, determining which object type to create first takes some planning. Just remember to start creating the objects with the fewest associations and work your way to the objects with the most associations.

Creating an array type

An *array* consists of a single attribute that can be repeated a finite number of times. It's like storing a miniature table inside your object. You create an array by defining an array type and then using the array type as the attribute within an object type.

The first step toward creating an array is to decide what kind of attribute will be repeated. The attribute can be a regular datatype, such as NUMBER, or an object type.

If you choose to create an array with a regular datatype, you can immediately define the array type. If you want to use an object type in your array, you must first create that object type and then define the array type, similar to the sequence used in a nested table.

In the example schema, you create an array that is a list of the last ten breads your customer bought, listing the BREAD_NO only.

To create an array type, follow these steps:

1. **Start Console in stand-alone mode, double-click the Databases folder, double-click the database you want to work on, and log in as the DBA user (if necessary).**

   For details, refer to the "Defining an object type" section.

2. **Choose Object⇨Create.**

   A menu appears, listing all the possible objects that you can create.

3. **Select Array Type, and then click Create.**

   You see the Create Array Type dialog box, where you define the table type.

4. **Type a name, and then select a schema for the table type.**

   For the example, you create the BREAD_ARRAY table type first, so type **BREAD_ARRAY** in the Name box and select BAKERY1 as the schema.

5. **Type the size of the array.**

   This defines the maximum number of records stored in the array. For this example, type the number 10.

6. **In the Datatype area, select a schema (if needed) and a datatype.**

   If you're using a regular datatype, such as NUMBER, leave the schema set to the default, which is None. If you're using an object type, select the schema of the object type that you need.

   For this example, leave the Schema box default as None and select NUMBER for the datatype. Specify 5 as the length and 0 as the precision. Figure 10-7 shows the Create Array Type dialog box filled in for BREAD_ARRAY.

7. **Click the Create button.**

   The database ponders for a moment and then displays Array type created successfully.

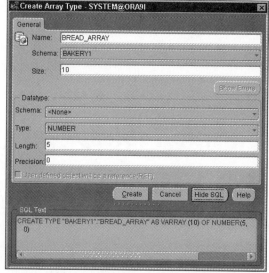

Figure 10-7:
An array type can be used in another object or in an object-relational table.

Once again, I bail you out. You can opt out of creating the array type in the sample schema by running the script named `BAKERY_STEP3_ARRAY.sql` (see the For Dummies Web site at `www.dummies.com/extras/Oracle9i.html`). This script creates the array type for you.

Built-in types for multimedia

Oracle9i has some cool object types you can use. These are especially created to help you handle multimedia in the database and, as a unit, are called interMedia. Their capabilities are especially tuned for audio, video, and imagery data. All these object types take advantage of Oracle's LOB storage techniques.

Each specific type of media (audio, video, and so on) has specific methods designed for that media type. For example, you can store all the songs for a CD in the database and retrieve these to burn your CD. Methods in the audio object (ORDAUDIO) determine the number of channels used in recording, the encoding type, and the play time of the song.

As another example, imagine that you want to store an art gallery full of pictures. You can use the image object (ORDIMAGE) for this. ORDIMAGE lets you find out the height, width, total size, and format type of an image. In addition, the image object can translate an image from one format to another.

Go to the Oracle Web site and look at all the examples of how to use *inter*Media with Java, PL/SQL, and the Web. You can find tools to download, sample programs to run, and lots of extra documentation. Start at this location:

```
technet.oracle.com/products/
           intermedia
```

You can add the array type as an attribute's datatype to any of your objects.

In the sample schema, the CUSTOMER object table can use BREAD_ARRAY as one of its columns. You create the CUSTOMER object table in the "Making an object table with mixed columns" section later in this chapter, after you create the framework for the schema. The next step is to instantiate some objects!

Objects Still Sit inside Tablespaces

After you have the complete set of object types, array types, and table types, you can create the object tables needed to store data. When defining object tables, as with relational tables, you must define the amount of space that is required as well as which tablespace the object table is stored in.

Another kind of table that uses object types is the object-relational table, or hybrid table. You define this table as if it were a relational table, except one or more of the columns has an object type, array type, or table type as its datatype. So you end up with a relational table with objects embedded in a few of its columns. You create both kinds of tables in the following two sections.

Making an object table

Using Console to create an object table is easy. If you want to continue with the sample schema (refer to Figure 10-1), follow the steps in this section to create the BREAD and INGREDIENT object tables.

In the previous sections of this chapter, you create an object type for each of these objects. Here you create the object tables.

You can create the two object tables for the sample schema by running the BAKERY_STEP4_OBJECT_TABLE.sql script included with the Oracle9i sample files and scripts at the For Dummies Web site at www.dummies.com/extras/Oracle9i.html. (Just remember that making your own mistakes can help you figure out how this stuff works.)

You may notice that the following steps for creating an object table are very much like creating a normal table (if you're already in Console, skip Step 1):

1. **Start Console in stand-alone mode, double-click the Databases folder, double-click the database you want to work on, and log in as the DBA user (if necessary).**

   For details, refer to the "Defining an object type" section.

2. **Choose Object⇨Create.**

A pop-up menu appears, listing all the possible objects that you can create.

3. **Select Table, remove the check from the Use Wizard check box, and click Create.**

   The wizard isn't educated in the ways of object tables and only guides you in creating relational tables. Instead, you see the Create Table dialog box, where you define the object table.

4. **Type a name and then select a schema for the object table.**

   For the example, create the BREAD_OBJ object table first. Select BAKERY1 as the schema.

5. **Click the Object Table option.**

   The lower part of the window changes its format to help you define the object table.

6. **Select the schema and object type that the object table uses.**

   In the example, first select BAKERY1 as the schema and BREAD_TYPE as the object type. After you do this, the lower portion of the window displays all the attributes contained in the object type.

7. **Define the nested table storage name and then click OK.**

   Because your object type contains a nested table, another window pops up for defining the name of the table that will physically store the nested table. For the example, type **RECIPE_NT_STORAGE**. Figure 10-8 shows the Nested Tables window at this point in the example.

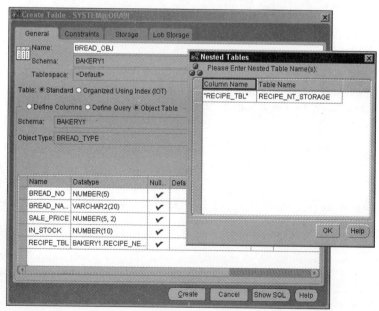

Figure 10-8:
If you have a nested table, give it a name for the physical storage table here.

8. **Define default values, constraints, and storage if needed. (This step is optional.)**

   Someday in the not-too-distant future (like at the end of this chapter), you may find that you need these options and that you're ready to explore. For now, leave these options in their default modes. Figure 10-9 shows the Create Table dialog box after I clicked the Show SQL button so that you can also view the SQL command generated.

9. **Click Create to complete the definition and commit it to the database.**

   The database evaluates your humble request and grants it, saying, `Table created successfully`. That was so easy!

Next, to continue with the example, follow the same steps to create the `INGREDIENT_OBJ` object table.

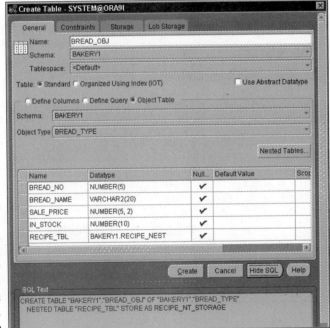

Figure 10-9: The attributes appear automatically in this window.

Making an object table with mixed columns

A second variety of object table contains regular relational columns and one or more columns that use an object type, array type, or table type as the column's datatype. Your understanding of this kind of object table will become clearer when you try an example.

Go ahead and take a peek at the SQL for the hybrid table. You can find it in the file called BAKERY_STEP5_OBJ_REL_TABLE.sql in the Samples/chapter10 directory of the downloaded files from the For Dummies Web site (www.dummies.com/extras/Oracle9i.html).

Follow these steps to create an object table with a mixture of regular and object-type columns (if Console is already started, skip to Step 2):

1. **Start Console in stand-alone mode, double-click the Databases folder, double-click the database you want to work on, and log in as the DBA user (if necessary).**

   For details, refer to the "Defining an object type" section.

2. **Choose Object⇨Create.**

3. **Select Table, remove the check mark from the Use Wizard check box, and click Create.**

4. **Type a name and select a schema for the object table.**

   For the example, create the CUSTOMER object table and select BAKERY1 as the schema.

5. **Define the relational columns as usual.**

   The sample table has three relational columns. Define these columns as usual by typing the column names, datatypes, sizes, and so on in the appropriate boxes. Here are the details:

   - CUSTOMER_ID with datatype of NUMBER, length of 5 and precision of 0
   - FIRST_NAME with datatype of VARCHAR2, length of 15
   - LAST_NAME with datatype of VARCHAR2, length of 20

6. **Define the first object column.**

   Click the Use Abstract Datatype check box. This reveals the Schema and Ref boxes for the column definitions. Begin as if you're creating a normal column by typing the column name; then select a schema for the column and select the appropriate type as the datatype.

   For the example, the column name is FULLADDRESS, the schema is BAKERY1, and the type is ADDRESS_TYPE.

7. **Define another relational column.**

   In this example, PHONENUMBER is a VARCHAR2 datatype with a length of 25 column.

8. **Define the second object column.**

   In the example, this column is named BREAD_LIST and is of the type BREAD_ARRAY owned in the BAKERY1 schema. Figure 10-10 shows the Create Table dialog box with all the columns defined.

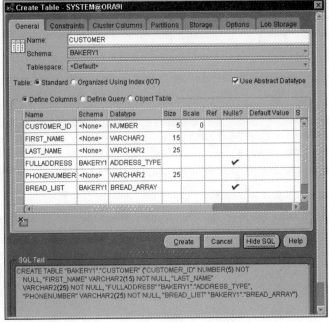

Figure 10-10:
This object
table
contains
four
relational
columns
and two
object type
columns.

9. **Click Create to complete the process.**

The Oracle9i engine grumbles and then says, `Table created suc-cessfully.`

Creating constraints on object tables

When you make object tables, you probably need to define some of these types of constraints:

- ✔ A primary key
- ✔ One or more attribute as not null
- ✔ A default value for one or more attribute

How will you do that? Well, you can use Console to help you. Follow along with this example to add all three of these constraints to the `BREAD_OBJ` table.

The SQL commands to create all three constraints are in the sample files on the For Dummies Web site at `www.dummies.com/extras/Oracle9i.html`. Look at the file called `Samples/chapter10/BAKERY_STEP5_CONSTRAINTS.sql`.

1. **Start Console in stand-alone mode, double-click the Databases folder, double-click the database you want to work on, and log in as the DBA user (if necessary).**

   For details, refer to the "Defining an object type" section.

2. **Double-click the Schema icon.**

   This expands to a list of object types (such as tables, procedures, and so on).

3. **Double-click the Tables folder.**

   Now you see a list of schemas that contain tables.

4. **Double-click the BAKERY1 schema.**

   Now you see a list of the object tables you created in this chapter.

5. **Click the BREAD_OBJ table.**

   The General tab of the Create Table dialog box appears.

6. **Add** `NOT NULL` **or** `DEFAULT VALUE` **constraints.**

   Under the Nulls? and Default Value columns, each attribute has a box. To set an attribute to `NOT NULL`, simply click in the Nulls? box so that the check mark disappears from the box for that attribute.

   To set a default value for any attribute, type the value in the box in the Default Value column for that attribute. In Figure 10-11, the `BREAD_NAME` attribute has been changed to `NOT NULL`, and the `IN_STOCK` column has a default value of 0.

7. **Click the Constraints tab.**

   The constraints list for the object table are displayed.

8. **Add a primary-key constraint.**

   When you define an object table, it contains an OID (object identifier) automatically. You can use the Constraints tab to add your own primary key so that your object table is more like the relational tables. For this example, type the **BREAD_OBJ_PK** constraint name. Then select PRIMARY as the constraint type. Finally, in the lower area under Table Columns, select BREAD_NO. Figure 10-12 shows the constraints at this point.

   Note: The first release in Windows 2000 was unable to complete the primary key constraint, so I had to resort to SQL*Plus. This problem should be resolved in the next release of the software.

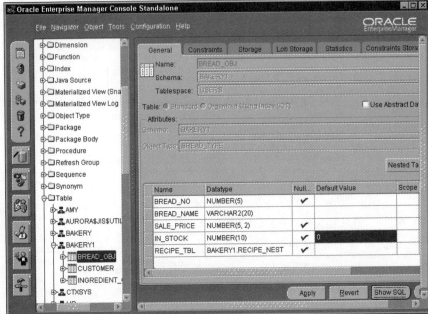

Figure 10-11:
Add default values and NOT NULL constraints to an object table here.

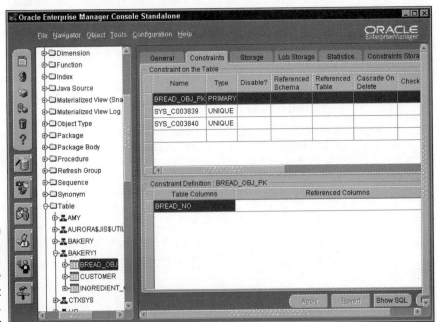

Figure 10-12:
Add a primary-key constraint now.

9. **Click Create to complete the definition and commit it to the database.**

   Console executes your command and displays the revisions on the screen.

Creating the constraints for the BREAD_OBJ table is covered in the file called Samples/chapter10/BAKERY_STEP6_ADD_CONSTRAINT.sql. Made you look!

You're finished with the entire sample schema. Fantastic! Did you find out a thing or two? I sure did.

Chapter 4 covers all kinds of interesting details on how to add data and query these kinds of object tables. Check it out. Chapter 11 looks into users, roles, and other mysteries of life.

Chapter 11

Security Options: Roles and Grants

● ●

In This Chapter

▶ Finding your built-in security blankets (the Nankie Phenomenon)

▶ Playing roles

▶ Designing roles in Security Manager

▶ Using Oracle Internet Directory system

● ●

Database designers can get bogged down in security. The concern about safety often starts innocently enough. Somebody in your office reads about a hacker in Australia who figured out the password to a protected file and ended up printing a love note in the newspaper. What you don't find out until much later is that the kid is the son of the office's vice president, who talks in his sleep.

Anyway, I devote this chapter to showing off the Oracle9i security features that are at your disposal. You can't control what the office vice president says in his sleep, unless he neglects to wear his little tinfoil nightcap. You can control what role he is assigned and the table privileges assigned to that role.

Security Blanket Included

Here's what you get as standard security in the Oracle9i database world:

✔ All tables and objects have an owner — the user who created the tables and objects.

✔ If you're the owner, the DBA, you are allowed to

- View data

- View and modify the structure (column names and so on) of tables and objects

- Add and delete data rows

- Add, change, and remove data in any table or object row or column

- Modify structures (add, change, and remove columns)
- Remove entire tables or objects
- Create synonyms, views, indexes, primary keys, relationships, and references
- Grant and revoke privilege to any user or role to perform the preceding tasks

The security measures that you have are kind of like the relationship Dr. Frankenstein had with his little creation — they can get out of hand. Here's an interesting fact about security: If you query a table that you don't have privilege to see, you get this error message:

```
ORA-00942: table or view does not exist
```

This message has panicked many an innocent database user and designer. Just remember, if you're logged into the database as any user besides the table owner, the table is still there, and the cause of the misleading error message is that the table owner has not granted you the privilege needed to see the table.

You must prefix table names with the owner's name when querying or modifying data in a table not owned by you. For example, when logged in as HARRY, you must add the owner prefix to query the AQUARIUM table owned by AMY:

```
SELECT * FROM AMY.AQUARIUM;
```

The only exception to the owner-prefix rule is when a synonym that points to the table is created. Refer to Chapter 12 for details.

This chapter contains a wealth of information about creating a reasonable security scheme for your Oracle9i database and deciphering the meanings of terms such as *role* and *privilege*.

Roles Meet the Real World

Roles help you keep track of who can do what in the database. To illustrate, I can show you how roles existed in the olden days — back when I was your age. This example sounds a lot like a story-problem I had in math class.

Suppose that you are in charge of an office that has 35 employees, 15 of whom are salaried and 20 of whom are hourly. Of the 5 office managers, 2 are hourly and the rest are salaried. You want all hourly employees to enter their time-card information in the TIMECARD table; then you want all managers to review and adjust the pay rates in the PAY_RATE table. Figure 11-1 shows how you grant table privileges directly to each employee in the prerole era of Oracle Version 6 and earlier.

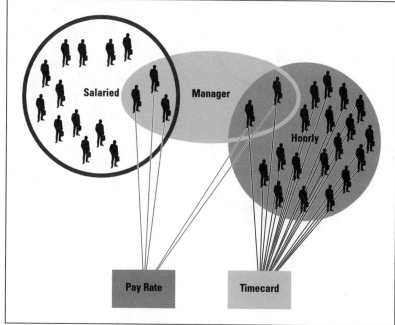

Figure 11-1:
Ancient
Oracle
practices
included
granting
table
privileges
directly to
each user.

Beginning as early as Oracle 7, you have an alternative to granting table privileges to each user individually: roles. For our example, you can create two roles:

- ✔ The MANAGER role can view and change pay rates.
- ✔ The HOURLY employee role can enter time-card data.

The two roles overlap, as shown in Figure 11-2, because managers can also be hourly employees. Using Oracle9i, you can grant table privileges to two roles instead of to each employee.

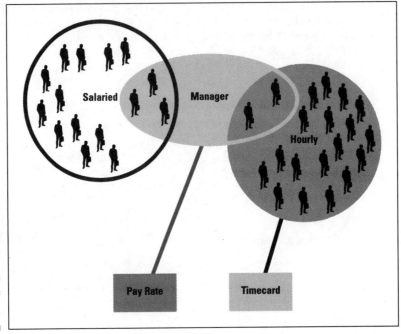

Figure 11-2:
The modern streamlining of Oracle9i lets you grant privileges to a few roles instead of tons of users.

At first glance, a clever person may exclaim, "Wait just a darned minute! Oracle has increased my workload! Now I assign the employees roles and grant table privileges to roles." This observation is clever — but inaccurate in the long run. You may not notice the advantages of the role system until you start making changes. Without roles, when you add a new table that is used along with the TIMECARD table, you give table privileges to each of 20 individual employees. With roles, you need only one privilege. Get the idea?

Roles and Privileges with Security Manager

Creating and assigning roles is so simple, it's scary! Only the DBA can create roles, unless the DBA grants this privilege to another user or role. Only the table owner can grant privileges (unless the table owner gives this right to another user or role, or unless someone bribes the headwaiter).

Armed guards versus open arms

You may spend more time designing and implementing the security system than you do building the rest of the database system. A broad spectrum of security approaches exists. In the strictest approach, users have multiple passwords. In the most lackadaisical approach, every user logs on as the DBA, and you conveniently post the user name and the password on the Internet.

Here's a typical security approach:

✔ One common user name (and no additional password) is required for read-only access to the database.

✔ Roles for designers allow them to create and remove tables.

✔ Roles for users allow them to update certain tables or allow them access to groups of tables for each functional area.

Roles, grants, and profiles are for Oracle9i databases that many users share. You don't need roles if you work with your own private database, unless you have multiple personalities.

You can go totally overboard devising roles for every conceivable situation, mixing and matching the roles like my family's socks — which usually doesn't work. A little common sense and intuition go a long way when you're devising roles. Remember, simpler is usually better.

This section shows you how to create roles and assign the roles to users. To help illustrate the steps, imagine that you want to create two roles for your employees. One role, called HOURLY, gives employees access to the TIMECARD table, where they can log hours worked. Only hourly employees need this role. The other role, called MANAGER, lets a manager review and change the pay rate for an employee, which is stored in the PAY_RATE table.

Begin by creating the two new roles you have in mind.

Creating a role and assigning object privileges

When creating a role, you can simultaneously add the privileges associated with that role, provided your SYSTEM user has the correct privileges before you start.

The first time you try to assign object privileges to roles, you may get this error message:

```
Ora-01031: insufficient privileges
```

If you do, this means that SYSTEM (or whatever DBA user you are currently using when you receive the message) is missing some system privileges needed to grant privileges on tables owned by other users. Cancel your current operation by clicking the Cancel button. Go into SQL*Plus as the owner of the tables on which you will grant privileges. For each table, issue this command:

```
GRANT SELECT, INSERT, UPDATE, DELETE ON tablename
TO SYSTEM WITH GRANT OPTION;
```

After doing this once for each table, you can return to Security Manager and do the job. For this example, log into SQL*Plus as AMY (password AMY123) and execute these two commands before following the next steps:

```
-- 01_granttosystem
GRANT SELECT, INSERT, UPDATE, DELETE ON PAY_RATE
TO SYSTEM WITH GRANT OPTION;
GRANT SELECT, INSERT, UPDATE, DELETE ON TIMECARD
TO SYSTEM WITH GRANT OPTION;
```

Here are the steps using Security Manager to create a role:

1. **Start Console.**

   On Windows platforms, choose Start⇨Programs⇨Oracle HOME2⇨Enterprise Manager Console. Note that the Oracle HOME2 label may have a different name, such as ORAHOME81, on your computer. The person who installed the software on your machine designates the name.

   On UNIX, Linux, or any other platform, type **oemapp console** at the operating-system command line.

   You see the logo screen for Oracle Enterprise Manager, and then the Oracle Enterprise Manager Console login window appears.

2. **Make sure the Launch Standalone option is selected, and then click OK.**

   Console's initial screen appears.

3. **Double-click the Databases folder.**

   All available databases are listed.

4. **Double-click the name of the database that you want to work on.**

   If this is the first time you have used Console or if you have not saved your login settings, you see a login screen. Otherwise, you see a list of Managers (including Instance, Schema, Security, and Storage).

5. **If you see a login screen, follow these steps to log in:**

   a. **For the Username, type** SYSTEM.

   b. **For the Password, type** MANAGER **or whatever the current password is for SYSTEM on your database.**

    c. For the Connect As option, select Normal.

    d. Click to add a check mark to the Save As Local Preferred Credentials option.

    e. Click OK.

    Console asks whether it's okay to save your credentials in a local encrypted file.

    f. Click OK to continue.

    The list of Managers (including Instance, Schema, Security, and Storage) appears.

6. **Choose Object⇨Create⇨Role, and then click the Create button.**

    The Create Role dialog box appears.

7. **In the Name box, type the new role name.**

    Follow the Oracle9i naming rules listed in Chapter 2. For the example, type **MANAGER**.

8. **Select the authentication that you prefer.**

    Usually, you select None, indicating that you need no role-specific authentication. Figure 11-3 shows the Create Role dialog box at this point.

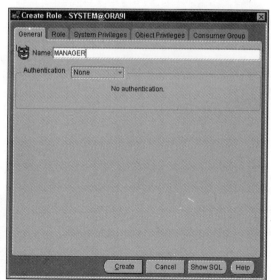

Figure 11-3:
A new role in the making.

9. **Click the Object Privileges tab.**

    A list of schemas appears.

10. In the Object area, navigate to the appropriate schema and table.

Do this by clicking the plus sign next to the schema you want to use. For the example, open the AMY schema. Next, open the Tables folder by clicking the plus sign. Then select the PAY_RATE table.

You see a list of privileges in the Available Privileges area.

11. Select each privilege and click the down arrow to assign it.

In our example, select the SELECT privilege and click the down arrow. The privilege appears in the lower area, labeled Granted. Next, select the UPDATE privilege and click the down arrow. Figure 11-4 shows the Create Role dialog box at this point, including the generated SQL script.

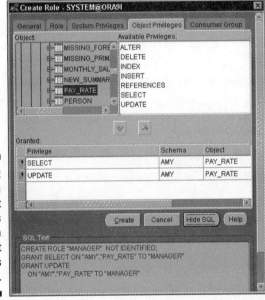

Figure 11-4: Assign object privileges to a role in the Object Privileges tab.

12. Click the Create button to complete the process.

Security Manager responds with `Role created successfully`.

13. Repeat Steps 6 through 12 to create another role.

For the example, create a second role called HOURLY that has SELECT, INSERT, and UPDATE privileges on the `TIMECARD` table in the AMY schema.

You have two new roles, complete with privileges. Next, you assign the appropriate users to the new roles.

Assigning users to a role

After you create a role, you, as the DBA, can assign this new role to users. Table owners can add more table privileges for the tables they created to this role also.

Continuing with the example from the preceding section, you created two new roles, HOURLY and MANAGER, to define two groups of employees. You now assign some users to their respective roles. One user, JONES, is both a manager and an hourly employee. Another user, SMITH, is an hourly employee.

Here are the steps for assigning these roles. If you are already in the Console, skip to Step 2.

1. **Start Console in stand-alone mode, double-click the Databases folder, double-click the database you want to work on, and log in as the DBA user (if necessary).**

   For details, refer to Steps 1 through 5 in the preceding section.

2. **Double-click the Security icon.**

   Security Manager's introduction page appears.

3. **In the left window, double-click the User folder.**

   A list of all user names in the database appears.

4. **Click the user name that will receive the new role.**

   For the example, click JONES. The user's properties appear, as shown in Figure 11-5.

5. **Click the Role tab.**

   The list of roles for the user appears, with all available roles on the top and granted roles on the bottom.

6. **Select a new role and then click the down arrow in the middle of the screen to grant the role.**

   For this example, select and grant the HOURLY role. Oracle9i copies the chosen role (the HOURLY role in this case) to the lower list, indicating that the role is now assigned to the user (JONES).

7. **Repeat Step 6 for the MANAGER role.**

   You have assigned both roles to JONES.

8. **Click the Show SQL button to view the SQL commands generated by your actions. (This step is optional.)**

   Oracle9i generates SQL commands as you work. Then it executes them when you click the Apply (or Create) button. After the commands are executed, they disappear from the SQL window. Figure 11-6 shows the commands in the SQL window.

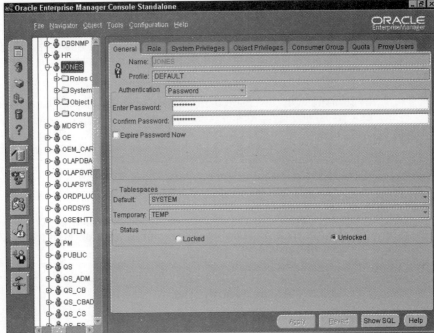

Figure 11-5:
Users are listed on the left, and the selected user's properties are shown on the right.

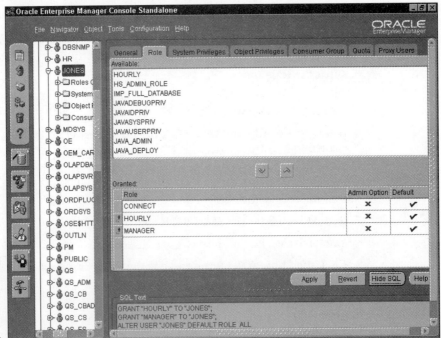

Figure 11-6:
Assign a role to a user here.

9. **Click the Apply button to save your work to the database.**

   Console remains in the Role tab but removes the plus signs in front of the new roles, indicating that they are currently assigned.

10. **Finish the example.**

    Assign SMITH the role of HOURLY by following Steps 4 through 6, selecting SMITH in Step 4 and HOURLY in Step 6, and then clicking the Apply button.

When you want to remove a role, simply go to the Role tab and move granted roles (in the bottom window) up to available roles (in the top window).

A role can have an assigned password, which means that a user must enter an additional password to access the role. Use this password-protected role only for high-security areas, such as the recipe tables for your famous banana bread.

Roles can sometimes be confusing, but they are a great way to enforce security. After you set up the roles and get the appropriate table privileges granted, adding users to and removing users from the roles is easy. Using roles instead of granting table privileges directly to each user name saves time in the long run.

Oracle Internet Directory

One of the complaints I hear about databases is that you put things in and it's hard to get them out again without bringing gifts to the DBA. Apparently, I was not the only DBA getting complaints! The new feature called Oracle Internet Directory is one of several new choices that allows you to display your data as if it were stored in regular data files in a familiar directory structure.

Oracle Internet Directory can be installed on the machine that contains your Oracle9i Enterprise Edition database. The Oracle Web site has a tutorial on how to install and use Oracle Internet Directory. I link the site from the Web site set up for this book at www.dummies.com/extras/oracle9i.html.

Note: The Oracle Internet Directory feature is not available for Personal Oracle9i.

Looking at a virtual private database on the Web

You can use Enterprise Manager to set up and manage Oracle Internet Directory. All you need is a database, some users, and a plan describing which of your users are allowed to view or modify one or more of your tables.

Here's an example of something you can do using Oracle Internet Directory. Suppose you have a database service over the Web. You just signed up three companies that want to store private tables in your database service. Naturally, each company wants to see and maintain only its own tables. As far as each company knows, it owns the entire database.

Creating the illusion of privately owned databases within a single database is called creating a *virtual private database*. Give yourself the title of Super-DBA and prepare yourself for an epic adventure.

Suppose that your new dot-com enterprise has three clients:

- **Goth's House of Fashion.** Three tables display all the latest styles for sale: ACCESSORIES, CLOTHES, and PHOTOS. You assign the user name of GOTH.

- **Samantha's Cleaning Service.** She has one table, called CLIENTLIST where she maintains a mailing list of customers and prospects. Her user name is SAM.

- **Blue's Weapon Museum.** His arsenal is documented in two tables: WEAPON and WEAPONHISTORY. Blue's user name is BLUE.

You use Enterprise Manager's Directory Manager to set up the three groups of tables (one for each user) and assign the users access to the tables.

Now you have three distinct and secure areas for each of your three users in Oracle Internet Directory. The next section shows you how to set up a Web-accessible utility in which your users can view data, make changes, and save their changes back to the database. Using this tool, you don't have to write any Java code to display and manipulate data.

Self-service data administration on the Web

The preceding section described an example of setting up three virtual private databases. If your three clients were able to link to your network without an Internet connection, they would already have access to the directory structure and their data. Your enterprise is located on a Web site, however, and you want your clients to use the Web to reach their data. This is where the self-service tool provided with Oracle9i comes in.

The Self-Serve Administration servlet gives your users a window into their data using a Java servlet that connects them to the Oracle database in a secure, password-protected window.

If you use Oracle9i Application Server (a product you can buy from Oracle to manage a Web site), the servlet is automatically installed for you. If you use another Web server, you can download the servlet from Oracle's Technet Web site at `technet.oracle.com`.

Chapter 12

Views and Synonyms: Do You See What I See?

*I*n this chapter, you find out about alternative ways to view tables in Oracle9i. You also discover how to make tables look as though they have different names or fewer columns and rows. You see how to combine tables into single larger tables without actually duplicating data. Then you discover how to use synonyms and grants to give users specialized security settings.

The features in this chapter are kind of like sunglasses at the beach: They're not essential but using them makes viewing swimsuits (or the lack thereof) much easier. Sunglasses also allow you to block out the glare from the white Maui sand (which keeps blowing onto your keyboard) and the glares from the people you're staring at.

Oracle Console has a window for creating views, and you can also create views using SQL in SQL*Plus. The best way to create a view is to use SQL commands in SQL*Plus. After you install the sample schema for this book found at the For Dummies Web site (www.dummies.com/extras/oracle9i.html), you can run all the SQL examples in this chapter in SQL*Plus. (Check out the Web site for instructions on how to install the samples in an Oracle9i database, too.)

You'll find that creating views is just like creating queries, which I discuss in Chapter 3. Views can be based on queries that range from the simple to the complex. Dive right in and give views a try.

Views: Like a Table — Almost

Views have one primary purpose: They rearrange the way you see a table, a portion of a table, or a group of tables without creating copies of the underlying data. A *view* is a window into the underlying table. A view changes the outward appearance of the table without changing the data in the table.

Imagine that you have a great comprehensive table called NAME_AND_ADDRESS, which contains the name and address of every customer you ever did business with as well as every potential customer who filled out a questionnaire at your store.

Your sales department uses the NAME_AND_ADDRESS table to go after new leads and drum up new business. In fact, salespeople are frustrated because they have to weed through all the hundreds of current and past customers' names to find all the hundreds of prospects' names.

Your accounting department uses the NAME_AND_ADDRESS table as its master mailing list. People in accounting send Christmas cards to all your current and past clients. The accounting department also gets tired of having to separate the rows of current and past clients from the rows of potential clients.

Views help you solve the dilemma of having two interest groups sharing one table. You can create two views of the NAME_AND_ADDRESS table: a PROSPECT view that shows only potential clients and a CLIENT view, which you limit to current and past customers. Your sales department can use the PROSPECT view instead of the NAME_AND_ADDRESS table. From the salespeople's point of view (pardon my pun), you have given them a customized table for their own special needs, and they decide that you really love them. And after your accountants begin using the CLIENT view in lieu of the NAME_AND_ADDRESS table, they buy you a new desktop pen set to show their appreciation.

The two views that you just created each contain a subset of the data in the underlying table. Refer to the next section for a look at different ways to create views that contain subsets of a table's data. You can also create views that span several tables and make them appear to be a single table. You can explore these kinds of views in subsequent sections of this chapter.

You can use views just as you use tables in queries, reports, and online forms. Here are the restrictions that apply to using views:

✔ If the view combines multiple tables, you can view the table data, but sometimes you can't update the data.

✔ In general, the user who creates a view should own all the referenced tables. If some of the tables belong to other users, complex rules regarding updates through the view exist. Views that are for query only aren't a problem as long as you have permission (the SELECT privilege) to query the table.

Views that narrow

The basic command for creating a new view looks like this:

```
CREATE [or REPLACE] VIEW viewname as
SELECT columnname1, columnname2, ...
FROM tablename
WHERE where-clause;
```

Replace *viewname* with the name of your view. Replace *columnname1*, *columnname2*, and so on with valid column names. Replace *tablename* with a valid table name. Replace *where-clause* with a valid WHERE clause. Actually, you can replace everything from the word SELECT through the end of the command with just about any valid query. After you create the command, Oracle9i replies with

```
View created.
```

You can change a view by revising the query and adding the or REPLACE phrase (in brackets in the preceding code) to the command. Oracle9i replaces the existing view or simply creates a new view if one doesn't already exist.

To remove a view, drop it as follows:

```
drop view viewname;
```

Oracle9i tells you that it took care of it:

```
View dropped.
```

Sometimes, a view becomes invalid because you made changes in the underlying table. In these cases, the next time you use the view, you receive an error message indicating that the view is invalid. If you dropped the underlying table, for example, Oracle9i says

```
ORA-04063: View "owner.viewname" has errors.
```

where *owner* is the view owner, and *viewname* is the name of the view.

This chapter includes lots of examples to give you a good idea of the versatility of views. Enjoy yourself.

Suppose that your top-secret spy agency has a table called SPY_MASTER that contains the names of counter-intelligence agents. You want your secretary to run a report that lists these agents and their code names, sorted by country. You also want to be the only person who can view or change the agents' actual names in the table.

You create a view called UNCLASSIFIED_AGENT that includes the agents' code names and the countries to which you have currently assigned them. You grant permission for your secretary to see this view. Figure 12-1 shows the table and the view, which contains only two of the three columns. The view is like a window that allows you to see into one part of the table. You'd better be nice to your secretary!

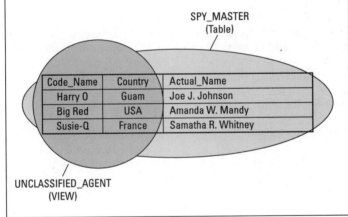

Figure 12-1: The spy table must be protected.

The code for creating the UNCLASSIFIED_AGENT view goes like this:

```
-- 01_basicjoin
CREATE OR REPLACE VIEW UNCLASSIFIED_AGENT AS
SELECT CODE_NAME, COUNTRY
FROM SPY_MASTER;
```

Note: All the examples in this chapter are based on tables owned by AMY in the sample schema. Before you begin, be sure you have created the AMY schema and have logged in as the AMY user (password AMY123) when you start SQL*Plus.

Suppose that your company payroll table contains the pay rate for each employee. You want to give managers the capability to view and modify only their subordinates' pay rates. The table, PAY_RATE, includes each employee's ID number and pay rate and the manager's ID number. You set up a view that customizes the PAY_RATE table so that each manager sees only his or her own employees, as shown in Figure 12-2. You call the view PAY_RATE_BY_ MANAGER_VIEW and give the MANAGER role permission to see and change data in this view.

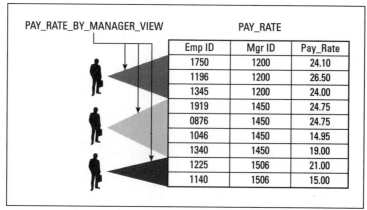

Figure 12-2: The view for your managers looks like this.

You can set up the code for creating this view in two ways. The first way creates a set of views, one for each manager. The SQL code looks like this:

```
CREATE VIEW MGR_1450_PAY_RATE_VIEW AS
SELECT * FROM PAY_RATE
WHERE MGR_ID = 1450;
```

The second way to set up the code requires a little more preparation. This way requires another table — the MANAGER table, which connects the manager's ID with the Oracle9i user ID. The SQL for the view looks like this:

```
-- 02_viewsubquery
CREATE OR REPLACE VIEW PAY_RATE_BY_MANAGER_VIEW AS
SELECT * FROM PAY_RATE
WHERE MGR_ID = (SELECT MGR_ID FROM MANAGER
    WHERE USER = MANAGER.ORACLE_ID);
```

The preceding example code contains the USER pseudocolumn in the last line. This column automatically contains the Oracle user name of the person running the query. For example, if the sales manager logs in as HARRYK, the USER pseudocolumn equals HARRYK and the row in the MANAGER table that contains HARRYK in the ORACLE_ID column matches the USER column. This way, each manager sees only his or her underlings.

On a similar note, Oracle9i has a small table called DUAL owned by the SYSTEM user and accessible to all Oracle users. DUAL always has one row and one column. (Now that I think about it, I wonder why Oracle called the table DUAL — I would call it SINGLE!) Refer to the "Pseudocolumns and the DUAL table" sidebar for a discussion on pseudocolumns and the proper use of the DUAL table.

Pseudocolumns and the DUAL table

A *pseudocolumn* is a column that Oracle9i defines for convenience. You can treat pseudo-columns just as you do any other column in queries, but you can't change pseudocolumn values.

DUAL is a real table in Oracle9i that you can use any time you want to retrieve a single row of pseudocolumns or a single row of literal values that require no table access.

Here's a list of some of the pseudocolumns that are available to you:

✔ **USER.** Oracle ID of the user who is currently logged in. USER is useful for security validation because if you forget what user ID you used, you can type

```
select USER from DUAL;
```

✔ **SYSDATE.** Current date and time. SYSDATE is in the standard date format for Oracle9i. You can use SYSDATE to datestamp rows or add today's date to a report. Here's how:

```
select to_char(sysdate,'mm/dd/yyyy hh:mi:ss') from dual;
```

The results show the current date and time in the specified format:

```
TO_CHAR(SYSDATE,'MM/DD/YYYYHH24:MI:SS')
---------------------------------------
09/09/2001 17:09:59
```

✔ **ROWID.** Unique location of a row. ROWID contains a hexadecimal number for the block, row, and file where the row is stored. ROWID is the fastest path for retrieving a row, but you can't use ROWID as the table's primary key because it can change if you relocate the table.

✔ **ROWNUM.** A number assigned sequentially to rows retrieved from a query. The first row returned is assigned ROWNUM 1, the second row is assigned ROWNUM 2, and so on. This pseudocolumn is useful for limiting the total rows returned in a query in which ROWNUM is less than 100.

✔ **NESTED_TABLE_ID.** A unique identifier assigned to each row in a nested table. This identifier is similar to a ROWID on a relational table.

Views that tie everything together

This section shows you how to use views to expand and combine multiple tables. You can use views to group common information from several tables in a single table without duplicating data. You retrieve the underlying data from the original tables when you use the view, which means that the views automatically use any changes made in the original tables.

The general syntax follows:

```
CREATE OR REPLACE VIEW viewname AS
SELECT columnname1, columnname2, ...
FROM tablename1, tablename2
WHERE tablename1.columnname3 = tablename2.columnname4;
```

Replace viewname with the name of your new view. Replace everything after SELECT with a valid query that joins multiple tables.

Suppose that you have created a table called COUNTRY in which each country has a number ID assigned, called COUNTRY_ID. The COUNTRY_ID appears as a foreign key in other tables, such as your CUSTOMER_ACCOUNT table. A *foreign key* connects one table to another.

The CUSTOMER_ACCOUNT table uses the COUNTRY_ID from the COUNTRY table for the customer's location. Figure 12-3 diagrams the table layout.

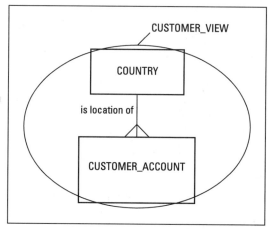

Figure 12-3: Customers live in countries, so the two tables are related.

You need a view that combines the COUNTRY_NAME and the CUSTOMER_ACCOUNT tables so that you have a simple and convenient way to create reports. This view allows you to create reports as though you had only one table with all the information in it. Writing a query on one table is easier and saves you time and effort. This view can be especially handy when other people need to write their own queries and are not experts like you on the subtleties of foreign keys. Figure 12-4 shows the data that appears in the tables and how it goes into the view.

COUNTRY

COUNTRY_ID	COUNTRY NAME
01	United States
02	Great Britain
03	Japan

CUSTOMER_ACCOUNT

CUST_ID	NAME	ADDRESS	COUNTRY_ID
001	Jane Smith	120 West	01
002	Harry Winters		01
003	Harry Owens	RR3 W. Vir	0?

CUSTOMER_VIEW

CUST_ID	NAME	ADDRESS	COUNTRY_ID
001	Jane Smith	120 West	United States
002	Harry Winters		United States
003	Harry Owens	RR3 W. Vir	Japan

Figure 12-4: Combining table data into a view allows easier access.

Here's the SQL code for creating this view:

```
-- 03_viewjoin
CREATE VIEW CUSTOMER_VIEW AS
SELECT CUST_ID, NAME, ADDRESS, COUNTRY_NAME
FROM CUSTOMER_ACCOUNT, COUNTRY
WHERE COUNTRY.COUNTRY_ID = CUSTOMER_ACCOUNT.COUNTRY_ID;
```

Views with Console

Console has a great little window for looking at the SQL command used to create a view. The following two sections show you how to look at the query that you used when creating a view and how to make changes in a view.

Creating views is easier using SQL than using Console. However, creating *object* views is easier using Console than using SQL. When creating a view, the Console doesn't save you much time. I recommend that you stick with the SQL method of creating views and then use Console to make small changes in the views. When it comes to creating object views, I recommend that you use Console. Refer to the "Object views with Console" section later in this chapter.

Looking at views with Console

Follow these steps to start Console and start looking at views:

1. Start Console.

On Windows platforms, choose Start⇨Programs⇨Oracle HOME2⇨ Enterprise Manager Console. Note that the Oracle HOME2 label may have a different name, such as ORAHOME81, on your computer. The person who installed the software on your machine designates the name.

On UNIX, Linux, or any other platform, type **oemapp console** at the operating-system command line.

You see the logo screen for Oracle Enterprise Manager, and then the Oracle Enterprise Manager Console login window appears.

2. Make sure the Launch Standalone option is selected, and then click OK.

Console's initial screen appears.

3. Double-click the Databases folder.

All available databases are listed.

4. Double-click the name of the database that you want to work on.

If this is the first time you have used Console or if you have not saved your login settings, you see a login screen. Otherwise, you see a list of Managers (including Instance, Schema, Security, and Storage).

5. If you see a login screen, follow these steps to log in:

    a. For the Username, type SYSTEM.

    b. For the Password, type MANAGER **or whatever the current password is for SYSTEM on your database.**

    c. For the Connect As option, select Normal.

    d. Click to add a check mark to the Save As Local Preferred Credentials option.

    e. Click OK.

    Console asks whether it's okay to save your credentials in a local encrypted file.

f. Click OK to continue.

The list of Managers (including Instance, Schema, Security, and Storage) appears.

6. **Double-click the Schema icon.**

Schema Manager's introduction page appears.

7. **In the left window, double-click the Views folder.**

A list of schemas appears below the Views folder. A list of all the views in the database appears in the right window. Notice the Status column in the right window. Each view is either Valid or Invalid.

8. **In the left window, double-click a schema.**

If you're using the example query, double-click AMY. You now see only AMY's views in the right window. You also get a list of AMY's views below the AMY schema in the right window.

9. **In the left window, click a view.**

For the example, click CUSTOMER_A_VIEW. The specifications for this view appear in the right window, as shown in Figure 12-5.

At this point, you can look at the SQL query that your view uses to retrieve data. If the view is invalid, you may want to make a correction in the SQL query: Refer to the next section to find out how.

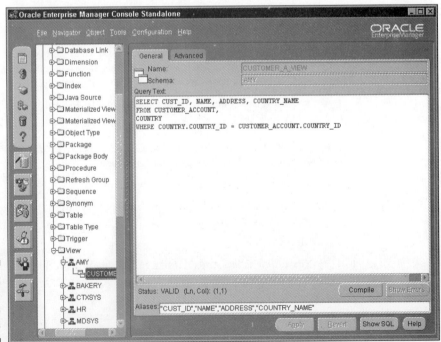

Figure 12-5: Console reveals AMY's view.

Changing a view with Console

Continuing the example in the preceding section, you should see a window showing the SQL code of the view that you want to change. If you're following the example from the preceding section, you see the SQL code of CUSTOMER_A_VIEW in the right window (refer to Figure 12-5). Okay, go ahead and make a change in your view by following these steps:

1. **Change the SQL code by adding, changing, or removing text.**

   For the example, delete ADDRESS to remove the ADDRESS column from the query. Delete the alias, "ADDRESS", from the list of column aliases found in the Aliases box (at the bottom of the screen).

2. **Apply the change by clicking the Apply button.**

   If your syntax is wrong, Oracle9i displays a pop-up window with an error message. In this case, review your changes and correct any syntax errors that you made. Then click the Apply button again. When your syntax is perfect, you receive no message from Oracle9i and the Apply button appears dimmed, meaning your changes have been applied.

3. **In the top-right corner of the Console window, click the minus sign to exit Console.**

Now you know how to look at a view and change your view. It's all a matter of your point of view, right?

Object views with Console

Object views — like the relational table views that are also covered in this chapter — are a method of transforming the way data appears to your users while keeping the data stored the way you prefer.

With an object view, you can store data in relational tables and still use the new features of Oracle9i. You can also interface with object-oriented programming languages more easily.

So how do you go about creating this thing called an object view? Follow these basic steps:

1. **Develop a query that reflects the data that you want to place in the object view.**

2. **Create an object type in Console that defines attributes corresponding to each column in the query.**

3. **Use the query and the object type to build the object view in Console.**

The following three sections show you how to complete these steps by using an example from the sample tables. Follow along!

First, create a query

The first step toward creating an object view is to develop a query. If you want to follow the example from the sample tables, use the following query:

```
-- 04_objectview
SELECT CUST_ID, NAME, ADDRESS, COUNTRY_NAME
FROM CUSTOMER_ACCOUNT,
COUNTRY
WHERE COUNTRY.COUNTRY_ID = CUSTOMER_ACCOUNT.COUNTRY_ID;
```

Check out Chapter 3 for all the basics of creating queries. It's there waiting for you anytime.

Second, create an object type

The second step is to create an object type that contains an attribute for each column in the query. For this example, I have already created an object type called CUSTOMER_TYPE in the AMY schema. The SQL command I used is

```
-- 05_objecttype
CREATE TYPE CUSTOMER_TYPE AS OBJECT
( CUST_ID NUMBER,
NAME VARCHAR2(30),
ADDRESS VARCHAR2(30),
COUNTRY_NAME VARCHAR2(15));
```

Refer to Chapter 10 if you want more information about object types. You can use Console or SQL*Plus to create the object view.

Third, create the object view

The final step is to create the object view itself. Console's Create View dialog box supports the creation of object views, making them quite easy to create.

1. **In Console's main window, choose Object⇨Create.**

   A list of objects that you can create appears.

2. **Choose View, uncheck the Use Wizard check box, and then click Create.**

   The Create View dialog box appears.

3. **Type the object view name.**

   If you're following the example from the previous two sections, type **CUSTOMER_OBJECT_VIEW**.

4. **Select the schema that owns the object view.**

   Use the arrow to the right of the Schema box to choose a schema. For the example, select AMY as the schema.

5. **In the Query Text box, type your query.**

   You can copy the query from a file opened in any text editor and paste the query into the Query Text box. Be sure that you do not include the semicolon at the end of the query because Console adds a semicolon automatically. Figure 12-6 shows the sample view up to this point.

6. **Click the Advanced tab.**

   This tab shows the extra parameters that you can specify for the view.

7. **Click the As Object check box.**

   Now you can edit the object definition section of the window.

8. **Select the schema that owns the object type you created.**

   Under normal circumstances, this schema is the same as the view schema. For the example, select AMY.

   Note: Due to a quirk in Console, you have to use your mouse to select AMY even if it appears automatically. This is the only way that AMY's object types will appear in the Object Type box.

9. **Select the object type you created that corresponds to the query of this view.**

   In the example from the preceding section, you created an object type with four attributes called CUSTOMER_TYPE. Select this object type.

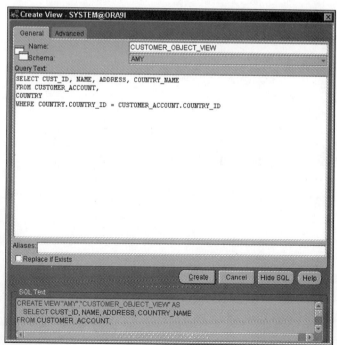

Figure 12-6:
Console starts off an object view as if it were a boring relational view.

10. **Click the Object Name check box, and then click Specify Attributes.**

    You must define the unique key field (object ID, also known as OID) for the object view using attributes of the object type. An OID is essential when creating object views.

11. **Click the attribute or attributes that make up the unique key field(s) for the object view.**

    As you click each attribute, a sequence number appears in the Order column. This column shows you the order in which the unique key will be built. For the example, click CUST_ID. Figure 12-7 shows the Advanced tab after you fill it in for an object view.

12. **Click Create to commit this *object d'art* to your repertoire.**

    Well done!

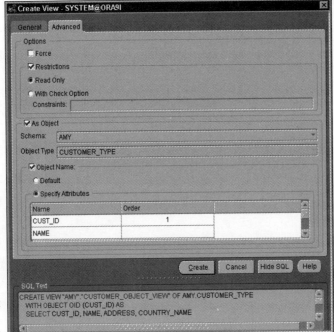

Figure 12-7: Console's Advanced tab contains all the details for object views.

The next section expands your mind with rose-colored glasses called synonyms.

Materialized views — pros and cons

Oracle views have had a bad reputation for slowing down performance. I have seen a lot of improvement in the performance of views over the years. But at times, you should still replace a view with a feature called a *materialized view,* which is a view stored as a table, complete with data. When you query a materialized view, it's just like querying a table. You can even put an index on the materialized view to speed up performance even more. Table 12-1 shows the pros and cons of using a materialized view.

Table 12-1	Pros and Cons of Materialized View
Advantages	**Disadvantages**
Speeds up queries using the view	Slows down inserts and updates to the underlying tables
Can be used to store data from remote databases	Increases database size by storing duplicate data
Can be used even when the view is not queried to speed up queries	Requires special system privileges

Note: Be sure that you grant the following two privileges to the owner of the materialized view before creating any materialized views. Here is the SQL command to grant the privileges you need:

```
GRANT CREATE ANY SNAPSHOT TO owner;
GRANT GLOBAL QUERY REWRITE TO owner;
```

Replace owner with the Oracle user who will own the materialized view.

To use Console to create a materialized view, follow these steps:

1. **In Console's main window, choose Object⇨Create.**

2. **Choose Materialized View (Snapshot), and then click Create.**

   The Create Materialized View dialog box appears.

3. **Type a name and select a schema for the view.**

   For the example, type **CUSTOMER_MATERIALIZED_VIEW** for the name and select AMY for the schema.

4. **Accept the default check mark on the Enable the Materialized View for Query Rewrite box.**

This allows the Optimizer to decide to use this materialized view when it finds other queries that use the same underlying tables as are found in the view. This gives the Optimizer an additional option to consider.

5. Fill in the query used for the view.

For this example, use the same query you've used in the other examples in this chapter:

```
SELECT CUST_ID, NAME, ADDRESS, COUNTRY_NAME
FROM AMY.CUSTOMER_ACCOUNT,
   AMY.COUNTRY
WHERE AMY.COUNTRY.COUNTRY ID =
AMY.CUSTOMER_ACCOUNT.COUNTRY_ID
```

Oracle recommends that you specify the schema in your query, so that in the case of query rewriting, there is no confusion about table names and aliases.

Figure 12-8 shows the window now that you have filled in the boxes.

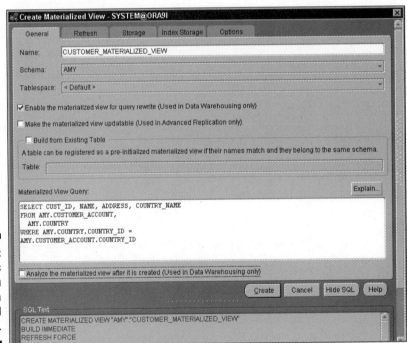

Figure 12-8: Here's where you create a materialized view.

6. Click the Refresh tab.

Here you have choices on how Oracle9i reloads the contents of the materialized view. All the data in the view is a copy of other data.

Synchronizing the copied data is called a *refresh* of the materialized view. You choose the timing of the data copying in this window. The choices are

- **On Demand.** Refresh the view only when you execute a command to do so.

- **On Each Commit.** Refresh the view every time the underlying tables change.

- **Automatically On.** Refresh the view at a certain date and time (usually right now) and then refresh the view after a certain period passes (such as a day or a week).

- **Never.** No refresh, ever.

For this example, you want the view as up-to-date as possible, so choose On Each Commit.

7. **Click Create to save your work.**

8. **Close Console.**

   Close Console by clicking the minus sign next to the Schema icon.

Do not overuse the materialized view. I recommend that you begin with regular views and wait to see how your system performance works out. Then, if you find a view that slows your performance, consider using a materialized view for that view alone.

Synonyms: Nicknames for Tables and Views

No, it's not that spice on sticky buns — a *synonym* is an alternate name. You can make a synonym for a table, a view, or even another synonym. After you create a synonym, you can use it as though it were a table. Like views, synonyms don't duplicate data — they're only a different route to the same data. Darn! Now I'm getting hungry!

You can create *public synonyms* for everyone to use. Usually only the database administrator (DBA) can make a public synonym. As with any other privilege in the database, however, your DBA can bequeath the capability to create public synonyms to you or to a role to which you belong.

If you prefer, you can create *private synonyms,* which only the synonym's owner can use.

Creating a synonym with Console

Here's how you use Console to create a synonym for an object:

1. **In Console's main window, choose Object⇨Create.**

   A list of objects that you can create appears in a pop-up window.

2. **Choose Synonym, and then click Create.**

   The Create Synonym dialog box appears. Check out those cool sunglasses! Retro to the max.

3. **Type the synonym name.**

   For this example, type **CUSTOMERS** to create a public synonym for the CUSTOMER_ACCOUNT table.

4. **In the Schema box, select PUBLIC or a schema name.**

   Selecting PUBLIC creates a public synonym. Selecting a schema name, such as AMY, creates a private synonym for that user. For the example, select PUBLIC. (PUBLIC is always at the end of the list of schemas.)

5. **Select the object type.**

   For the example, select TABLE. As you can see from the pull-down menu, you can create synonyms for many kinds of objects.

6. **Select the schema and object name of the object underlying the synonym.**

   For the example, select AMY as the schema and CUSTOMER_ACCOUNT as the object. Figure 12-9 shows the completed synonym window for the example.

7. **Click Create.**

The synonym name doesn't have to match the table's name. If you're creating a public synonym, it must be unique among all public synonyms.

When you create a *private synonym,* it has the same features as a public synonym, except that it's only for the use of the synonym creator and not for everyone else. I don't use private synonyms often, and you shouldn't either. Private synonyms can be confusing because they look like tables that you own yourself.

One good use of the private synonym is to create a shorthand name for a table. Suppose that you give a table some long name, such as CA_GRANT_STEP_ATTRIBUTE_TYPE. Later, you're experimenting with a query in SQL*Plus that uses this table. Your fingers get into wrestling matches as you type the table name over and over.

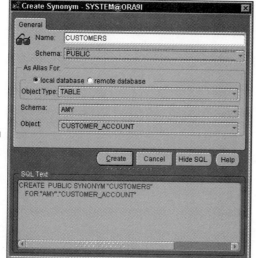

Figure 12-9:
Creating a public synonym is a simple task with Console.

Combining a grant and a synonym

A common mistake that Oracle9i users make in creating public synonyms is assuming that they can then share their tables with other Oracle9i users. Creating a public synonym for a table doesn't automatically allow other users to view or change the data in your table. You must assign the appropriate privileges using Security Manager, as described in Chapter 11. Generally speaking, you don't grant privileges on a synonym — you always grant privileges on the underlying table or view.

Chapter 13

Java and the Internet Database

*O*racle9i has its own Java Virtual Machine (JVM) that comes installed inside your Oracle9i database. JVM enables you to create, interpret, and execute Java applications. This chapter gives you information about what a JVM is and how to use it. Along the way, you find out how to create a Java stored procedure and then run it inside the database. Finally, you discover how to run a Java stored procedure from the Web.

You don't have to know how to program in Java to follow along with the examples in this chapter. However, if you want to find out more about Java, check out *Java For Dummies,* 3rd Edition, by Aaron E. Walsh (published by Hungry Minds, Inc.).

Discovering Java Virtual Machine

A Java Virtual Machine is like a miniature operating system. A Java Virtual Machine runs Java applications, which is why *Java* appears in its name. It's called a *virtual machine* because you can run programs inside it as if they were running on a separate computer. The great advantage of JVM is that it handles all operating-system-dependent commands for you. Commands that previously required special commands for each operating system can now be written exactly the same way, regardless of what kind of operating system the JVM interacts with. Java programs become totally portable, and Java programmers get big bucks.

Using Oracle9i's JVM — some benefits

If you've ever run Java applications on your computer, you have been using a Java Virtual Machine in your computer. For example, many Web sites use Java *applets* (miniapplications) for fun and interactive tasks, such as calculating a mortgage payment or playing tic-tac-toe. To run the applet, your Web browser contains a JVM of its own. Most developers who create Java applets and applications use the Java Virtual Machine from JavaSoft, which is called Java Run-time Environment (JRE). Oracle's JVM, which can do anything that JRE can do, runs within the framework of your Oracle9i database. In addition, you get these benefits from using Oracle9i's JVM:

- **Better scalability.** Oracle9i's JVM is scalable to support many concurrent users. Other JVM products cannot share resources among concurrent users; therefore, they use ever-greater resources with each additional user.

- **Can be used in place of PL/SQL or in combination with PL/SQL.** This means that you Java fans can skip figuring out PL/SQL and move right to creating triggers, procedures, and functions that work with Oracle database objects.

- **Supports SQLJ.** SQLJ is an extension of JDBC (Java Database Connectivity) and simplifies your programming of database access within Java. JDBC is an industry standard protocol that describes how to access a database within a Java application. SQLJ lets you embed SQL commands within your Java and then creates the corresponding JDBC commands to support the SQL, saving you many lines of code for each SQL command. You use SQLJ in the next section.

- **Better native connectivity to the database.** You can use JDBC on your computer's Java Virtual Machine to reach an Oracle9i database even if the JVM isn't embedded in the database. If you use Oracle9i's JVM, however, your JDBC connects extra fast to your database because Oracle9i uses its internal, proprietary connection to the database (native connectivity). JDBC commands that originate outside the Oracle9i database go through a translation stage where the generic JDBC is translated into Oracle-specific commands. Likewise, the data returned from the database is translated from Oracle-specific formats to generic JDBC formats before returning to the application. All this translating is eliminated when you use Oracle9i's JVM.

The idea is that if you're currently using PL/SQL procedures and functions, you can use them in any Java component that you want to create inside the Oracle9i database. On top of that, you can use Java and SQLJ instead of PL/SQL to create triggers, procedures, and even applications.

Introducing SQLJ

How do you do? I am your new partner, SQLJ. Just call me SJ for short. I can save you a lot of time by writing all your JDBC commands for you. Just give me your SQL statement, and I'll translate it into the proper JDBC commands, keeping your Java program clean and simple. Go ahead, make my day.

Yes, that's right, you're spared the toil of writing all those JDBC commands that open the database, open a cursor, fetch the data row, fetch the next row, close the cursor, close the database . . . you get the idea.

With SQLJ, you simply embed the SQL command in your Java program. And because you run your Java program in Oracle9i's JVM, you have ultrafast access paths into your data. SQLJ may be the most compelling reason to use the Oracle9i JVM — especially if you aren't a coffee-crazed geek wearing a tin-foil hat and sitting in your grandma's basement hacking on your customized turbocharged dual-boot machinery.

Running a Java Applet that Queries the Database

In this section, you create an *applet* (a small Java application) that queries the database. We are going to use SQLJ to save a lot of programming steps. I don't go into all the details of how to program the application — you can dig into the code yourself if you're interested.

You can find the source code for the sample applet in the `Samples\ Chapter13` directory. For this directory and all other sample files, go to the Dummies Web site at `www.dummies.com/extras/Oracle9i.html`.

The applet runs a query that uses dynamic criteria typed into the applet window.

Your environment must include a working copy of the Oracle JDBC driver, SQLJ, and Java 1.1.5 or higher. Your `CLASSPATH` must include the directory that contains the following paths (replace *oraclehome* with the full path name for your main Oracle directory):

- ✔ *oraclehome*`/jdbc/lib/classes111.zip`
- ✔ *oraclehome*`/sqlj/lib/translator.zip`
- ✔ *oraclehome*`/sqlj/lib/runtime12.zip`
- ✔ The current directory (.)

Also, your PATH must include these directories:

- ✔ *oraclehome*/sqlj/bin
- ✔ *oraclehome*/Apache/jdk/bin

If you want to go into detail on how to use SQLJ, you should read and follow the demonstration tutorial provided by Oracle. Find it in the sqlj\demo directory under the Oracle home directory.

Follow these steps to get the applet running on your computer:

1. **Extract the sample directory and all its contents to a directory on your local disk.**

2. **Edit the connect.properties file.**

   Change the connection as needed. Usually, you can use a thin JDBC client connection, so all you have to do is make sure that the Oracle database name is correct. For example, if your database name is ORCL3, the line looks like this:

   ```
   sqlj.url=jdbc:oracle:thin:@localhost:1521:orcl3
   ```

3. **Save the file.**

4. **Open a command-line window in your operating system.**

   In Windows, click Start➪Programs➪Accessories➪Command Prompt.

5. **Go to the directory that you just created.**

   In Windows, UNIX, or Linux, use the cd command.

6. **Run the SQLJ compiler using this command (type the entire command on one line, and then press Enter):**

   ```
   sqlj -profile=false AppletUI.java AppletFrame.java
             AppletBakery.sqlj
   ```

7. **Run the applet with this command:**

   ```
   java AppletBakery
   ```

8. **Type a bread name, such as** Plain White, **and click the Query button to see the results.**

Figure 13-1 shows the applet window you should see.

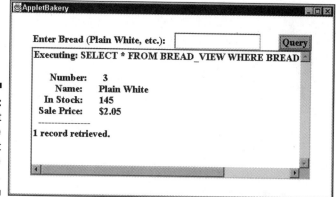

Figure 13-1:
An applet
example
that
queries the
database.

Now you're in the big leagues. Your Java applet connects directly to the database. Be sure to ask your boss for a raise.

Chapter 14

XML and Enterprise Java Beans

● ●

● ●

*H*ere we are onto the hottest new topics to hit Oracle's technologies since Java itself erupted all over the scene! These cool extensions for the Internet and the database can give you a world of choices when it comes to developing applications. They are

- ✔ **XML.** This acronym stands for eXtensible Markup Language. Like HTML (HyperText Markup Language), XML is a way to describe how information is displayed. But unlike HTML, XML has better ways of creating templates and combining them with data, which is better for Web-to-database systems because you can design a template and then reuse that template for lots of different data.

- ✔ **EJB.** This is Enterprise Java Beans. Perhaps you've heard of Java Beans. The concept is to take Java programs and break them into small, self-contained chunks (beans). Stir them up, mix them together, and voila, you have an entire Java program. Do you want whipped cream with that?

I want to give you a taste of this new technology, so I have found the best tools that Oracle has to offer for each of these two styles of working on the Web. Let's start in with XML.

What Is XML?

To use XML, you have to understand just a little bit about how it works. Figure 14-1 shows a diagram listing the process that your Web server goes through to send and receive a Web page based on XML.

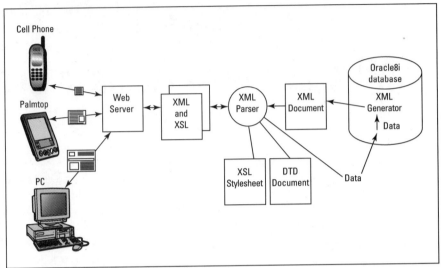

Figure 14-1:
The data
and the
stylesheet
get
combined or
pulled apart
by the XML
parser.

The key difference between XML and HTML is the way that the data and the display features can be combined or pulled apart. In addition, the display features of XML are more flexible and more varied than the display features in HTML.

Following are the main components of XML:

- ✔ **XML document.** This contains data from the database, with markers to identify it as a certain type of data, such as a street address or zip code. The document also specifies what stylesheet and what DTD to use.

- ✔ **XSL stylesheet.** This file (with a suffix of .XSL) has information about each type of data and how to put it on the final Web page. For example, the stylesheet may specify that a street address be displayed in Arial font, bolded, and on a separate line.

- ✔ **DTD document.** A *DTD* (Document Type Declaration) file contains a list of each valid marker used in the XML document and the XSL document and how they fit together. For example, you may have a marker called FISHROW that marks the beginning of a record from the FISH table in your database. Within that, you might have FISHNAME, FISHSIZE, and so on. This is an aid to your XML parser, which combines all these pieces later.

- ✔ **XML parser.** This is the engine that interprets the XML document. If there is a DTD to use, the XML Parser uses the DTD to detect errors in the structure of the document before displaying the document. The other primary job of the parser is to take an existing XML document and separate out the data, so that the data can be inserted into a database of some kind.

So how does Oracle9i fit into all this? Well, Oracle9i has provided some very cool tools that generate the XML and DTD document based on your data! On top of that, they have provided a tool that can be called from the Web server to generate XML documents on the fly — a dynamic Web page generator that begins with a SQL command and ends with an XML document, or vice versa. You can use Java or an XSQL servlet.

Here is a list of all the tools and tips that Oracle9i has on its Technet Web site (technet.oracle.com) today:

- ✔ XML Developer's Kits for Java, Java Beans, C, C++, and PL/SQL
- ✔ Online demonstrations of a roundtrip XML document (used to retrieve and update data in the database)
- ✔ XML Technical Forum for discussing any Oracle-related XML question with the experts
- ✔ How to use the new XML native type in Oracle9i

The tool I feature here is the XML XSQL servlet because that one got me from point A (the database) to point B (the Web browser) the fastest. The XSQL servlet is part of the Oracle9i XML Developer's Kit, which is part of your standard Oracle9i installation.

A Sample XML XSQL servlet

For this example, I want to create a Web page that displays a list of fish in each aquarium I own. Go to the For Dummies Web site at www.dummies.com/extras/Oracle9i.html and download the sample schema that contains the FISH and the AQUARIUM tables that I use for this example (the AMY schema).

The XML servlet driver is installed automatically along with HTTP Web Server, which comes with Oracle9i. The only change you need to make to run this sample is to add the connection string so the servlet knows to connect to the database as AMY when you run the servlet page included in this book.

In a nutshell, here are the steps:

1. **Set up a connection to the database that the XSQL servlet driver knows about.**

2. **Place a query in an XSQL servlet document.**

3. **Create an XSL stylesheet document.**

4. **Execute the XSQL document in the Web server.**

The source code for each document is found at the For Dummies Web site (`www.dummies.com/extras/Oracle9i.html`) in the sample schema for Chapter 14. Figure 14-2 shows the resulting Web page that is displayed.

Aquarium Name	Fish Name	Comment
Fishtank	Fish Two	Eaten by Wesley
Fishtank	Fish Three	Eaten by Wesley
Fishtank	Fish Four	Died while I was on vacation, probably eaten by Wesley
Fishtank	Wesley	
BigDrink	Jerryskids	
BigDrink	Zoe	
BigDrink	Ginger	

Figure 14-2:
This is run from a SQL query and an XSL stylesheet.

To help you understand how it all works, walk through the steps in the following sections.

Step 1: Set up a database connection

When I install Oracle9i, a configuration file includes all the database connection information I need to customize this to log into my sample database as AMY (the username that owns my sample data). The configuration file looks a lot like the `tnsnames.ora` file.

Here is the part that contains my database connection, which I named "amyconn". The file name is `XSQLConfig.xml` and is located in *oraclehome*/ `xdk/admin` (where *oraclehome* is the path to the top-level directory where Oracle9i is installed on your machine). I included this portion of the file in the `Samples/Chapter14/01_xmlconfig.txt` file:

```
<connection name="amyconn">
<username>amy</username>
<password>amy123</password>
<dburl>jdbc:oracle:thin:@dbintern:1521:dbintern</dburl>
<driver>oracle.jdbc.driver.OracleDriver</driver>
</connection>
```

As you can see, there are tags for the user name and password and the JDBC connection.

Step 2: Place a query in an XSQL servlet document

The next step, placing a query in an XSQL servlet document, is pretty easy — there isn't much text inside a servlet document .The first line tells the Web server that this is ultimately an XML document.

```
<?xml version="1.0"?>
```

The next line tells the Web server what stylesheet to use. In this example, the stylesheet is called fish.xsl.

```
<?xml-stylesheet type="text/xsl" href="fish.xsl"?>
```

This next line describes the connection to use when running the query:

```
<xsql:query connection="amyconn"
```

The next line gives some instructions to the XSQL tool on how to treat null values. The true means that nulls are allowed:

```
null-attribute-indicator="true" xmlns:xsql="urn:oracle-xsql">
```

This line shows the actual query to be executed:

```
SELECT AQUARIUM_NAME, NAME_OF_FISH,COMMENT_TEXT FROM FISH
```

This line is the closing tag for the XSQL query connection:

```
</xsql:query>
```

Here is the complete file (named fish.xsql in the Samples/Chapter14 directory):

```
<?xml version="1.0"?>
<?xml-stylesheet type="text/xsl" href="fish.xsl"?>
<xsql:query connection="amyconn" null-attribute-
          indicator="true" xmlns:xsql="urn:oracle-xsql">
SELECT AQUARIUM_NAME, NAME_OF_FISH,COMMENT_TEXT FROM FISH
</xsql:query>
```

Step 3: Create an XSL stylesheet document

Creating a stylesheet is similar to creating an HTML document, except a few extra tags control the retrieved records. I simplify this example just to give you an idea of how it works. You can add many more features to a stylesheet, such as special handling when no rows are returned.

The entire stylesheet is in Samples/Chapter14/fish.xsl.

The first lines tell the Web server how to use the stylesheet. Because I'm using the Oracle examples as a basis for these, I tell it to use Oracle's standards:

```
<html xmlns:xsl="http://www.w3.org/1999/XSL/Transform"
xsl:version="1.0" >
```

The next lines tell the Web server that I want to use a special file to define color classes and font styles. The file is called fishcolors.css. This file resides in the same directory as the stylesheet itself.

```
<head><link rel="stylesheet" type="text/css"
href="fishcolors.css" />
</head>
```

The next lines start the body of the page and add a table that serves as the header for my data. Look at Figure 14-2 to see the table defined here.

```
<body class="page">
<center>
<table border="3" class="title">
<TR>
<TD WIDTH="20%"><I>Aquarium Name</I></TD>
<TD WIDTH="20%"><I>Fish Name</I></TD>
<TD WIDTH="40%"><I>Comment</I></TD>
</TR>
</table>
```

Now, I define the table that has one row for each row of data found in the database table:

```
<table border="3" class="bl">
```

The next tag marks the beginning of a loop that gets repeated one time for each row of data:

```
<xsl:for-each select="/ROWSET/ROW">
```

Here is the part that puts the data into the Web page. There are three columns, and each one is placed into the Web page using its column name in the xsl:value-of tag:

```
<tr>
<td WIDTH="20%"><xsl:value-of select="AQUARIUM_NAME"/></td>
<td WIDTH="20%"><xsl:value-of select="NAME_OF_FISH"/></td>
<td WIDTH="40%"><xsl:value-of select="COMMENT_TEXT"/></td>
</tr>
```

This line closes the loop for the repeating rows:

```
</xsl:for-each>
```

These last lines wrap up the table, body, and the document itself with the appropriate ending tags:

```
</table>
</center>
</body>
</html>
```

Step 4: Execute the XSQL document in the Web server

HTTP Web Server, which comes standard with Oracle9i, is ready to run your XSQL documents without any special changes. Simply place the files you just created in the previous steps into the document directory of the Web server. The Oracle HTTP Web Server's document directory is

```
Oraclehome/Apache/Apache/htdocs
```

For easier organization, I created a subdirectory called `amyfish` and placed the three files there. Now, type the following URL in the location box:

```
http://localhost/amyfish/fish.xsql
```

This runs the query, retrieves the data, applies the stylesheet, and delivers an XML document to the Web server, which in turn displays it on your browser.

XML allows database designers to focus on their work and gives Web page designers a tool that is robust yet easy to work with in the beginning. As a person's knowledge and understanding of XML grows, he or she will find more interesting and creative ways to use this new concept in Web design.

Anyone for EJB?

Here is another vast topic that you look at briefly. The *Enterprise Java Bean* (EJB) idea was born from a bunch of programmers with way too much java in their systems, if you ask me.

As the name implies, EJB is a standard for creating self-contained application objects (beans) that can be strung together and interact with one another. All these beans are based, of course, on Java code. The idea is to give you a way to compartmentalize your programming and reuse some of the Java code spilling all over your keyboard.

Because Oracle is in full-on Java support mode ("Damn the torpedoes, full speed ahead!"), the Java Virtual Machine included in your Oracle9i database server supports Enterprise Java Beans. Oracle has also developed Jdeveloper, a programming tool for Java that supports EJB.

Here's the basic idea of how a bean (of the EJB type) is built:

1. **Set up a definition of what part of the bean gets loaded onto the client.**

   This tells the server what components are needed to be loaded onto the client if it wants to run this bean.

2. **Set up a definition of the bean that runs in the local (home) server site when the client grabs it.**

   This tells the server to start a connection with the client, sending the remote portion of the bean to the client and making a new instance of the local part of the bean for the client's transactions.

3. **Write the bean itself.**

   This consists of the actual Java code that does something. For example, you may write a bean that has three methods for handling changes to a bread recipe in the database:

   - `AddIngredient`. This method adds an ingredient to the recipe, so it must provide the client with a list of available ingredients and ask the amount that's required in the recipe.

   - `ChangeIngredient`. This method revises the amount of an ingredient used in a recipe.

   - `RemoveIngredient`. This method deletes an ingredient from a recipe.

4. **Create a deployment descriptor for the bean.**

   This is a specially formatted list that tells the server how the client and server portions of the bean are connected. In addition, you can add security, the type of bean, the length of time until the bean expires, and so on.

5. **Compile the components.**

   After you've defined all these pieces, you compile them into Java classes.

6. **Stick the beans in a jar.**

   No, really, that is what it is called! After compiling the bean's components, all the resulting classes are stored in a compact unit called a *jar*.

7. **Deploy the jar.**

   If you are using Oracle9i's Java Virtual Machine to deploy your beans, you can use the `deployjb` built-in command to do the work for you.

To find out more about Enterprise Java Beans, check out the Oracle Technet Web site at this location:

```
http://technet.us.oracle.com/tech/java/ejb_corba
```

Take a look at the next chapter for ways to safeguard your data — including those pesky beans and their jars.

Chapter 15

The Five Ws of Safeguarding Your Data

You've heard this story, I'm sure: A poor soul plans to back up his disk drive on Wednesday, but on Tuesday the system crashes, and recovery takes him a month. Another good one: A rookie drops her table instead of deleting a few rows. She has no way to recover because she has no backup.

No, the five Ws is not a singing group (and if it were, this chapter would not be about its backup band). This chapter covers the five Ws of backups: why, what, when, where, and how. I know, I know — that's only four Ws. (Hold up a mirror to see the secret fifth W — who!) I also included a lot of how-to information. Some of the methods describe shortcuts that you can use to speed up the process.

In this chapter, I concentrate on backup strategies that use Oracle9i tools. More backup options exist, such as replication and hot backups, but they are complex and require much study to use properly. If you're interested in those options, you may want to take a class.

Why Back Up

Back up to save face. Do you want to be caught with your pants down because you didn't back up? Worse yet, do you want to face getting caught backing up with your pants down?

When I refer to *backing up,* I'm referring to different methods that accomplish similar tasks. Backing up your database essentially means making a duplicate copy of all, or a portion of, your database — kind of like wearing a belt and suspenders.

Many good reasons to back up your database exist. The reason that motivates me the most is that backing up saves me a great deal of time in the long run. Losing data because you didn't back it up costs you time: time to figure out what's missing, time to get another copy, time to remember all the things that you did during the past month, time to re-create everything that you can't replace. Time to get real about backing up your data.

If you use a PC, periodically backing up your entire PC hard drive helps you recover quickly from hardware problems. How often is *periodically*? The answer depends on how much you use your computer. If you use your computer daily for games and letters, I recommend backing up at the end of each week. If you have a home business and use it daily, you should back up every day. On the other hand, if you're a casual PC user, sitting down once or twice a week to play, work, or perhaps surf the Internet, I recommend backing up once a month.

If you prefer to back up your database using your operating system's backup tools, be careful. One of the default initialization parameters for running your database is the NOARCHIVE setting. The default, NOARCHIVE, requires that the database be shut down before you begin backing up database files. If the database is running, your backup files are useless. You won't be able to restore the files because some of the log files are in a consistent, recoverable state only when the database is closed. Even if you change the setting to ARCHIVE, you must be very careful when restoring from backup copies. Refer to the backup and recovery chapters in my book, *Oracle8i DBA Bible* (Hungry Minds, Inc.), for complete details.

Backing up an entire database allows you to keep a snapshot of the database structure and data. Backing up portions of the database allows you to shorten the amount of time invested in backups while safeguarding parts of the database.

What to Back Up

Here are my guidelines for a backup plan. Ultimately, you are the judge. I am the executioner. We can hang the jury (or at least both attorneys).

- Back up the entire database on a regular basis. For critical database systems that support a business operation on a daily basis, back up nightly. For normal daily use, back up once a week. For occasional use, back up once a month.

> ✔ During database development, when you create and drop tables frequently, back up the table owner before making major changes.
>
> ✔ Use backups to transfer entire groups of tables from one database to another.

When to Back Up

Generally, you don't wait until you crash to fasten your seatbelt. Planning a backup schedule and sticking to it pays off in the long run. No system is immune to losing data. I've seen systems with full backup capabilities get zapped by lightning, which burned up crucial disk drives.

Exactly when to back up depends on what kind of system you're running. If you use common sense and lean a bit to the conservative side, you'll have a good strategy for timing backups.

This chapter covers the following two backup choices:

✔ **Data Manager.** Helps you export and import tables using a wizard. This utility is part of Enterprise Manager. Data Manager can also load the data into the database using a flat file.

✔ **EXP and IMP.** These utilities are like the non-Windows versions of Data Manager, with line commands for exporting (EXP) and importing (IMP) a database, a user, or a specified set of objects. The file that's created is in a highly compressed file structure that can be ported to other platforms. You can restore a backup file created by EXP only by using the IMP command. You can import exports from older versions of Oracle into newer versions of Oracle.

Full database export

A full database export is an alternative way to back up your database. Oracle9i recommends that you use Recovery Manager to handle full database backups and that you perform a full database export every time you do a full system backup (such as a backup of all files to tape). On a practical note, you shouldn't always do this step because it takes extra time.

You use Recovery Manager also to restore from a full database export.

You should do a full database import only when a failure on the disk wipes out your database or when you want to create a new database on another computer. Consult an expert before attempting this task.

Other backup strategies that I don't cover include the list below. All of these are covered in my book, *Oracle8i DBA Bible:*

- ✔ **Backup Manager.** Copies the entire database in a compressed format to disk or tape. You shut down the database to run a full database backup and then restore by using Recovery Manager. If your database runs in `ARCHIVELOG` mode, you have more choices of what to back up. This utility works only if you have more than one database: one to store your repository and one to back up.

- ✔ **Tablespace backups.** Copies selected tablespaces while the database is running in `ARCHIVELOG` mode. This technique is exotic. You generally use the tablespace backup only for large organizations in which the database is online 24 hours a day. Tablespace backups require careful study, and I just can't cover them adequately in a few paragraphs.

- ✔ **Recovery logs.** You can design your recovery logs so that the database recovers activities up to the minute when a failure occurs. You should get expert help before implementing this kind of recovery scheme.

- ✔ **Audit utility.** Not exactly a backup utility, this utility allows you to track all activity in tables. Auditing can be incredibly detailed. You really don't need the Audit utility unless you're wearing a tinfoil hat to ward off evil thought rays and cosmic debris. The audit trail can eat up disk space in a hurry. You can get a fairly good description of this utility in the Oracle9i manual.

Which plan should you use? Again, the answer depends on your situation. Imagine that you're a musician who just produced a CD of your music. You're setting up a cool Web site with promotional materials on your home PC, and you're using Oracle9i to keep track of CD distribution and accounting. You work about an hour a day on the PC, between rehearsals, radio spots, and signing autographs. I recommend that you use Oracle's Backup Manager to back up the database daily. I also recommend that you back up your PC at the end of each week, using software that backs up only changed files to a disk, Zip drive, or tape.

What if your hard disk crashes?

If your hard disk crashes and you're in the process of restoring all your software, first try to start Oracle9i, which has built-in recovery steps that handle many situations. Oracle9i is often capable of restoring your database. If you can't start Oracle9i, use Recovery Manager to restore your database.

Use the Automatic Recovery selection in the Recovery Manager window, and Oracle9i recovers the database to your most recent backup made with Recovery Manager.

On the other hand, what if you work in a federal office and you decide to enhance a set of tables with new features? You plan to add new tables and modify existing ones. I recommend that you use Data Manager or the EXP command to save all the tables before you start making changes.

How to Back Up

The two backup tools that I cover in this book work with Oracle9i platforms. These tools are Data Manager and the EXP tool.

Data Manager can be used with a single database on any platform. However, you must have the Server version of Enterprise Manager (which is not available on Windows 95, 98, or ME). If you are using Personal Oracle9i or are running on Windows 95, 98, or ME, you must use the EXP tool to back up your tables.

Data Manager

Data Manager, which is part of Enterprise Manager, makes saving and retrieving tables from a file easier than it should be. (It should be hard, like the olden days.) Actually, easy is good. I can handle an easy method of backing up and restoring parts of my database.

Use Data Manager when you want to save certain tables or all the tables owned by one or more users but don't want to back up the entire database. This kind of tool can be useful to the systems analyst who has been slaving away on 50 tables and wants to back them up to move them to the production database machine — that sort of thing.

Exporting tables with a wizard

To export several tables to an export file, follow these steps:

1. **Start Console.**

   On Windows platforms, choose Start➪Programs➪Oracle HOME2➪ Enterprise Manager Console. Note that the Oracle HOME2 label may have a different name, such as ORAHOME81, on your computer. The person who installed the software on your machine designates the name.

   On UNIX, Linux, or any other platform, type **oemapp console** at the operating-system command line.

   You see the logo screen for Oracle Enterprise Manager, and then the Oracle Enterprise Manager Console login window appears.

Oracle Agent and Enterprise Management Server must be running before you start Console.

2. **Select the Login to the Oracle Management Server option.**

   The window displays boxes for logging into Management Server.

3. **Type the login information, and then click OK:**

   a. **For the Administrator, type** SYSMAN.

   b. **For the Password, type** OEM_TEMP **or whatever the current password is for SYSMAN on your Management Server.**

   c. **For the Management Server, select the machine name where Enterprise Management Service is started.**

   The first time you log in as SYSMAN with the default password, a pop-up window appears and you are required to change the password. Type a new password and click OK to continue.

   Console's initial screen appears, as shown in Figure 15-1.

4. **Choose Configuration⇨Preferences and then click the Preferred Credentials tab to set the Data Manager login credentials.**

   The Edit Administrator Preferences property window appears. The Preferred Credentials tab lists the login information that is used when administering the database through the Enterprise Manager console.

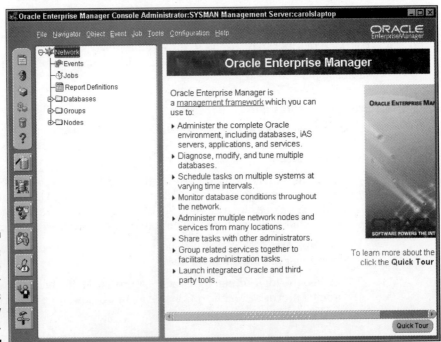

Figure 15-1: Enterprise Manager Console is now ready for use.

5. **Set the login data for the database you want to perform backups on.**

   For example, to back up data from a database named `mydb.world`, edit the login information seen when you select `mydb.world`. You must use a DBA login. The default DBA login for Oracle9i has a user name of SYSTEM and password of MANAGER. Accept the default role of Normal. Figure 15-2 shows the completed window for the database service called mydb.world.

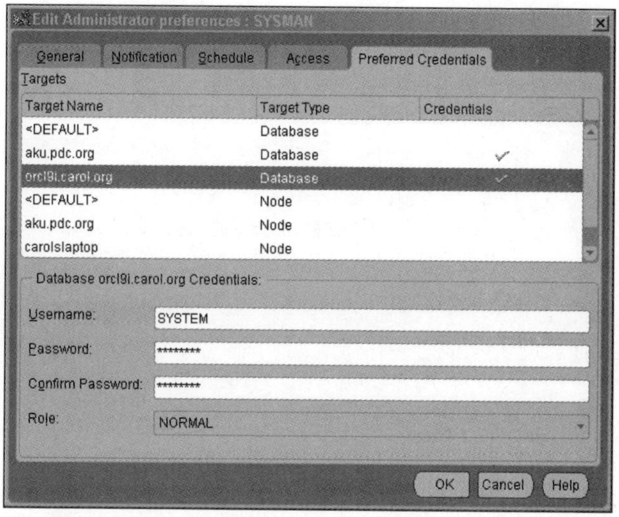

Figure 15-2:
Set the proper database credentials before running Data Manager.

6. **Set the login data for the node where the database resides, and then click OK.**

   The login name for the node must be a user on the node's operating system who has the ability to submit a batch job. On NT, the user must also be an administrator.

   For example, assume the database resides on the localhost node, which is an NT machine, and the user named oracleagent has been set up as the administrator for the NT and has been granted user rights to run a batch job. In this case, the localhost node login information contains oracleagent in the Username box and the oracleagent's password in the Password and Confirm password boxes. Figure 15-3 shows this example.

7. **Double-click the Databases folder.**

   All available databases are listed.

8. **Right-click the database node and choose Data Management⇨Export.**

   The Data Manager Export Wizard window appears, as shown in Figure 15-4.

9. **Click Next.**

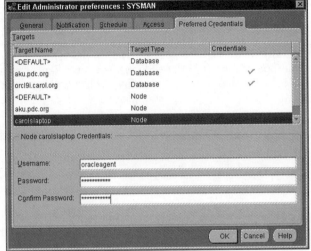

Figure 15-3:
You must
also set
credentials
naming a
valid
operating-
system user.

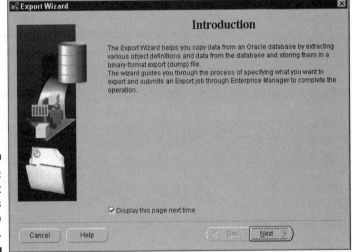

Figure 15-4:
Export
Wizard is
here to help
you.

10. **Name the export file by either accepting the default name or typing your own file name, and then click Next.**

   Be sure that you type the full path and file name if you are choosing your own name.

11. **Choose an export type, and then click Next.**

   You have three choices:

- **Database.** This is the default choice. Use this choice to export the entire database. After you export it, you can restore the entire database from the export file. If you choose this selection, skip Step 12.

- **User.** Here you select one or more users, and the wizard exports all the objects owned by each user. This selection is useful when you are moving an entire schema to another database, such as moving a schema from the test database to the production database.

- **Table.** You can choose individual tables. This option is useful for saving a table just before making structural changes.

For this example, select User.

12. **In the left window, choose users or tables.**

If you chose User in the preceding step, this page allows you to select one or more users. If you chose Table in the preceding step, this page allows you to select one or more tables for export.

Choose a user or table by selecting it in the left window and clicking the arrow pointing to the right. The user or table moves to the right window, indicating that you have chosen the user or table for export.

Continue to choose more users or tables as needed until all the users or tables you need are listed in the right window. Figure 15-5 shows the Export Wizard window with two users, AMY and BAKERY, selected for export. Now you're ready to begin your export.

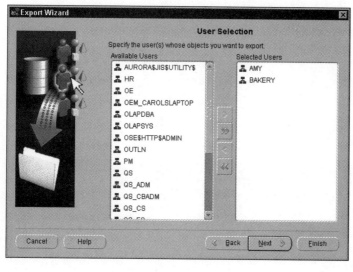

Figure 15-5: Add or remove users to export by selecting and clicking the arrow buttons.

13. Click the Finish button.

You can go through the remaining pages of options if you have advanced knowledge of the database-export process. For now, accept Data Manager's default settings and skip directly to the finish line. Figure 15-6 shows the status window that now appears.

14. Verify the list, and then click the OK button.

Data Manager begins its work, and you see a message stating that the job is submitted.

15. Click the Jobs Icon.

The Active tab in the right window displays jobs currently submitted but not completed.

16. Click the History tab to check the results of your export.

Figure 15-7 shows two export jobs. Double-click the job to view details, including the success or failure of the job.

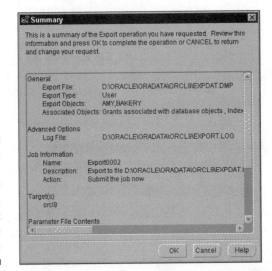

Figure 15-6:
Data Manager Wizard lists what it plans to export.

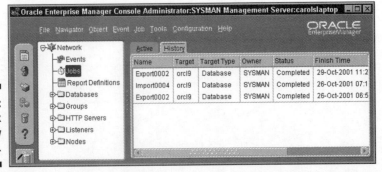

Figure 15-7:
Double-click a job to view its status.

You have completed the steps for exporting tables with Data Manager. You can back up the file you created as you do any other file on your PC. Later, if you want to restore your tables to the state they were in when you created the exported file, you can use the Data Manager's Import Wizard.

Importing with Data Manager's Import Wizard

When is a good time to import? Well, unlike fine wine, which is good any time, you must reserve importing tables for special moments. Most commonly, importing restores tables that have been lost or damaged. The import re-creates the tables and then populates them with the data copied during the export. You can also use the Import Wizard to create a copy of tables on a different Oracle9i database.

To import objects contained in an export file, follow the next set of steps.

1. **From Console, right-click the database node and choose Data Management⇨Import.**

   The Data Manager Import Wizard window appears.

2. **Click Next.**

3. **Name the export file by either choosing a file from the list or typing your own file name, and then click Next.**

   Remember to include the full path and file name if you are typing the file name. The file must be an export file created by Data Manager.

4. **Choose the Read Import File(s) and Select What Objects You Want to Import option, and then click Next.**

   The import file is processed using a batch job that's submitted and run while you watch the status of the job, as shown in Figure 15-8. Don't worry! No data gets imported at this point. The wizard simply reads the file and prepares its next dialog screen for you.

5. **Choose the type of import and what to import, and then click Next.**

   The three possible choices are

   - **Database.** Import an entire database.
   - **User.** Import a user and all its objects.
   - **Table.** Import a table.

   The available choices vary depending on the kind of export. For example, if you chose the User option during the export, the Database selection is not available during the import.

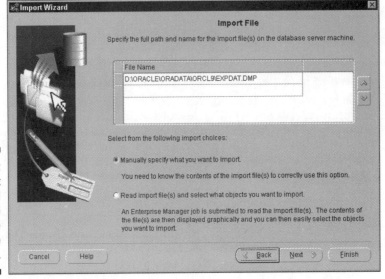

Figure 15-8:
Import
Wizard
reads the
import file
before
continuing.

6. **Select the tables to import, and then click Finish.**

For this example, double-click AMY in the Available Tables area to display all the available tables in the export file. Then select the AQUARIUM table name and click the right arrow button in the middle of the screen to copy the AQUARIUM table to the Selected tables area. The finished window looks like Figure 15-9.

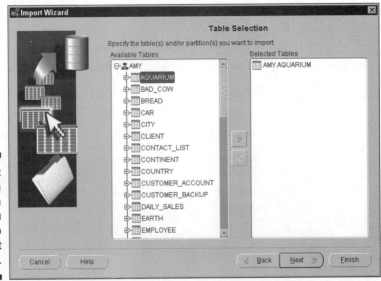

Figure 15-9:
Specify a
user and a
table if you
wish to
import just
one table.

7. **Review the Summary window, and then click OK.**

   Refer to Figure 15-6 for an example of the summary window, which tells you exactly what the wizard plans to do. After you click OK, the wizard submits the job and returns to the main console window.

8. **Click the Jobs icon (near the top of the Navigator tree in Console), and then click the History tab.**

   The jobs you've run are listed, with the most recent one at the top. In Figure 15-10, you can see that the import job was completed. Double-click any job to display its details.

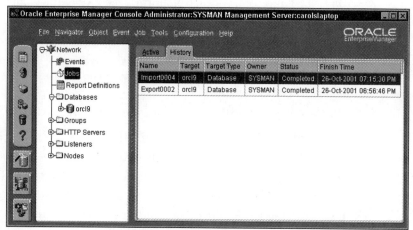

Figure 15-10:
The History tab shows completed jobs.

You made it! You can reuse the same export file as many times as you want, if necessary. Data Manager makes exporting and importing a whiz of a Wiz. Right, Toto?

EXP and IMP commands

The EXP and IMP commands, like my old Maui Cruiser, have been around since the Dark Ages and still run like champs. You can run the EXP and IMP commands from the command line in any operating system, so you don't need Enterprise Manager to use them.

EXP pulls tables or entire schemas (all tables, indexes, and other database objects owned by one Oracle9i user ID) out of the database in a compressed file format that is readable only by Oracle's IMP command.

IMP reads a file created by EXP and restores to the database the tables, indexes, or whatever database objects are in the file. Oracle9i prompts you for choices and can restore all or only specified objects, depending on what you want.

Exporting with the EXP command

Follow these steps to export tables using the EXP command:

1. **Start the EXP utility.**

   On Windows platforms, choose Start⇨Run and then type **EXP**.

   On UNIX, Linux, or any other platform, type **EXP** at the command-line prompt.

2. **Type your user name, and then press Enter.**

   Do not use the INTERNAL or SYS user names with EXP. If you plan to do a full database export, use SYSTEM. Otherwise, use the owner of the tables you want to export.

   Oracle9i responds with a prompt for the password.

3. **Type your password and then press Enter.**

   The default password for SYSTEM is MANAGER.

   Oracle9i checks your user name and password and tells you that you're connected to the database.

4. **If you want to accept the default buffer size (4096), press Enter; otherwise, type a number and then press Enter.**

   The buffer size tells Oracle9i how much data to pull out of the database at a time. The default usually is acceptable unless you're exporting a large table (more than 10,000 rows). In the case of a large table, set the buffer size to the maximum value, which makes the fetching process run faster. (Sometimes I tell my dog, "Fetch, Buffer," but he ignores me.) In cases other than large tables, use the default.

5. **If you want to accept the default export-file location, press Enter; otherwise, type a file name of your own and then press Enter.**

   Remember, Oracle9i creates the file in the current directory unless your file name includes the directory path.

6. **Choose the type of export. You can accept the default by pressing Enter, or you can type in your choice and then press Enter.**

You have three choices:

- **Entire database.** You see this choice only if you are the DBA. Refer to the sidebar titled "Full database export" for details.

- **Users.** This option allows you to export all the database objects (tables, indexes, views, grants, and so on) that belong to one user. If you are the DBA, you can export several users. If you aren't the DBA, you can export only your own user ID.

- **Tables.** This option allows you to export one or more tables that you own. A table export also exports database objects that belong to the table (indexes, grants, primary-key and other constraints, and the data).

The remaining steps assume that you choose 3 (Tables). The prompts for User and Entire Database vary slightly from these prompts.

7. **If you want to export data with your tables, accept the default by pressing Enter. If you don't want to export data, type** no **in lowercase and then press Enter.**

Normally, you want the table data. However, exporting only the structure with no rows can be useful if you intend to use the export file for creating a new table in a separate database.

8. **If you want to compress your table data, accept the default by pressing Enter. If you don't want to compress the data, type** no **and then press Enter.**

You normally want to compress the table data. Compressing extents means that the table takes up less room and you free some wasted space in the table's structure. I can think of only one reason not to compress the extents: when you have deliberately created a table with a great deal of empty space in anticipation of a large number of rows that you may want to insert later. This situation is like calling ahead to a busy restaurant and making reservations.

9. **Type the name of the table or partition that you're exporting, and then press Enter.**

If you're entering a partition name, first type the table name and then type a colon, followed by the partition name. If you're exporting the CUSTOMER_ACCOUNT table, for example, you would type

```
CUSTOMER_ACCOUNT
```

If you log in as SYSTEM and want to export another user's tables, add the OWNER name to the table. For example, to export tables owned by AMY, you would type

```
AMY.CUSTOMER_ACCOUNT
```

Partition export is new for Oracle9i. This feature allows you to export one or more pieces of a table that are in several partitions. For example, if the `CUSTOMER_ACCOUNT` table has a partition named `DENVER`, you would export the partition like this:

```
AMY.CUSTOMER_ACCOUNT:DENVER
```

After you complete this step, Oracle9i responds by exporting a copy of the table and placing it in the export file. The program informs you of the deed and tells you how many rows it exported. Then Oracle9i immediately asks for another table name:

```
Table(T) or Partition(T:P) to be exported: (RETURN to
     quit) >
```

10. **Repeat Step 9 until you've exported all the tables, and then press Enter (without typing a table name) to stop the export.**

    Oracle9i completes the export and sends this message:

    ```
    Export terminated successfully.
    ```

    On Windows platforms, the preceding message flashes on-screen briefly and then the window closes. The message flashes quickly, so reading it is difficult.

After Oracle9i finishes the export, you can use the file to retrieve individual tables or all the tables by running the `IMP` utility.

Importing with the IMP command

The `IMP` command allows you to bring into your database any item (such as a table, an index, or a user) that you saved in an export created by `EXP`. You may import a table if you have made changes in the data that you don't like and want to revert to the older, unchanged data. Another time to import is when you've lost data because of some errors or a database failure. Follow these steps:

1. **Start the IMP utility.**

   On Windows platforms, choose Start⇨Run and then type **IMP**.

   On UNIX, Linux, or any other platform, type **IMP** at the command line.

2. **Log in to the database, entering your user name and password when prompted.**

   For details, see the preceding section.

3. **If the displayed file name is the export file that you want to use, press Enter. Otherwise, type the file name — including the full path if the file isn't in the current directory — and then press Enter.**

4. **If you want to accept the default buffer size (30720), press Enter; otherwise, type your own number and press Enter.**

5. **If you want to import a file, press Enter to accept the default. If you simply want to review an export file, type** yes **and then press Enter.**

   On rare occasions, you may want to review the contents of the export file without doing any importing.

6. **Choose how to handle possible errors caused by tables that already exist.**

   IMP always tries to create the table before importing the rows. If the table already exists, IMP gets an error. Sometimes, you want IMP to add rows to an existing table. To do this, you must tell IMP to continue, even if it gets an error when it tries to create the table.

   If you know that the table exists and you want to add rows to it by using the import feature, type **yes**. If you want the import to stop with an error message if the feature can't create the table, type **no**. Then press Enter.

7. **If you want to import grants, accept the default (yes) by pressing Enter; otherwise, type** no **and then press Enter.**

8. **If you want to import the data from the table, press Enter; otherwise, type** no **and then press Enter to import an empty table.**

   Accepting the default *yes* brings in the data. Answering *no* imports only an empty table.

9. **To import everything in the file, accept the default by pressing Enter; otherwise, to import parts that you specify, type** no **and press Enter.**

   If you type **no**, Oracle9i prompts you for a user name and for table/partition names that you want to import. It then imports them one at a time, prompting along the way. When you've imported all you want, leave the prompt line blank. Then press Enter to complete the import session.

   If you accept the default, Oracle9i completes the import session by informing you of its progress as it imports all the tables and other items (indexes, grants, and so on) from the export file.

   In either case, after Oracle9i completes the import, it displays

   ```
   Import terminated successfully.
   ```

Oracle9i Data Guard can save you from downtime

Data Guard has been improved and enhanced in Oracle9i. One of the best improvements is the use of a standard Enterprise Manager component to allow you to manage Data Guard in a set of easy-to-use windows. You reach Data Guard Manager using the Enterprise Manager console.

Data Guard watches over your database and keeps a backup database ready and waiting. Whenever changes are made to the main database, copies of the log files (which contain the change transactions) are transported to the backup database, where they are immediately applied. Data Guard keeps track of the log files and makes sure they are moved between the main database and the backup database without any corruption.

When Data Guard detects a failure in your main database, it switches all activity to the backup database automatically. For example, suppose that you have a Web-based order system in Dallas for sports equipment. Your main database, which supports the system, is in Chicago. You set up Data Guard so that you have a backup database always ready. The backup is in Cincinnati. If a disaster occurs, such as a blackout, Data Guard immediately reroutes all online activity to your Cincinnati database.

Log Miner: Digging around to find pay dirt

Redo logs, which are created when changes are made to your database, are cryptic and practically unreadable to the average DBA. Log Miner was introduced with Oracle8i to help DBAs analyze database changes, past and present. This first version of Log Miner could read the logs and interpret them into SQL commands, and you could write queries that looked at the logs.

Suppose that you are the DBA for an accounting firm. One day, you discover that everyone in the company has been given the same pay rate as the company janitor. You ask around and discover that Joey, the new junior accountant, was using SQL to update the janitor's pay rate. You must now figure out exactly what time this happened, and then restore your database tables to a state just before that time. You can use Log Miner to find all the changes made to the pay rate table by Joey. Looking at the time of that change gives you what you need to correct this ridiculous error.

Oracle9i's Log Miner has been improved so that you can easily view database changes in Enterprise Manager. The Enterprise Manager component is called the Log Miner Viewer. Before Oracle9i, you had to write SQL queries in SQL*Plus to look at the Log Miner's information.

Another new feature is that you can use Log Miner to look into the future! Well, that is, you can set it up ahead of time to pull out specific information as it happens. For example, you could set up Log Miner to gather all the changes by Joey from now on.

Where to Hide Your Backup Files

Asking you where you hide your backup files is a truly personal question. It's like asking a lady where she keeps that spare $100 bill when she goes on a date.

Zip drives, Jaz drives, and removable hard drives have pretty much over-shadowed tapes as the preferred storage medium for backups. I keep my backup files on a Zip disk in a locked drawer.

Now that CD-ROM writers are becoming more economical, I anticipate that more people will choose to back up on CD-ROM. The new rewriteable CD-ROM technology is catching on.

Regardless of which cool hardware you use to store your backups, be sure that you move your backups to a physical location separate from the computer you're backing up. I know that leaving backup files on the same hard drive as the original data is temptingly convenient. Resist that lazy urge! One of the most common causes of database failure is hardware failure. So move those backup files to some kind of portable unit and then stash it some-where, even if you just move it into the next room or a foot away into your storage cabinet.

Chapter 16

Special Tasks with Enterprise Manager

*B*efore you get into the really fun stuff in Part IV, such as Index Tuning Wizard, take a quick look at the tricks and tips in this chapter. Some of the later chapters require you to log into Console by logging into Enterprise Management Server instead of by starting standalone. I show you how to set up your Enterprise Management Server and even configure it to run on a Web page.

In addition, I have a section each on starting and stopping the database. You might find this handy if you are modifying initialization parameters to tune memory usage, as shown in Chapter 18.

Starting Oracle9i

I know a lot of you are using Oracle9i on a mainframe or a network. If so, Oracle9i should be up and running as part of the initial startup routine for the computer. Even when you set up Oracle9i on your PC, it generally starts when you boot the machine. If not, you can use Enterprise Manager to start it. An alternative is to use the SQL*Plus command-line tool, as I describe later in this chapter in the "Starting the database using SQL*Plus" section.

Starting the database with Instance Manager

To get your Oracle9i database on its feet, follow these steps:

1. **Start Console.**

   On Windows platforms, choose Start⇨Programs⇨Oracle HOME2⇨ Enterprise Manager Console. Note that the Oracle HOME2 label may have a different name, such as ORAHOME81, on your computer. The person who installed the software on your machine designates the name.

   On UNIX, Linux, or any other platform, type **oemapp console** at the operating-system command line

   You see the logo screen for Oracle Enterprise Manager, and then the Oracle Enterprise Manager Console login window appears, as shown in Figure 16-1.

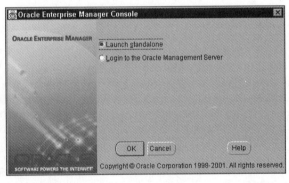

Figure 16-1: Here is where you choose to log in the stand-alone Console.

2. **Make sure the Launch Standalone option is selected, and then click OK.**

   Console's initial screen appears.

3. **Double-click the Databases folder.**

   All available databases are listed.

4. **Double-click the name of the database that you want to work on.**

   If this is the first time you have used Console or you have not saved your login settings, you see a login screen. Otherwise, you see a list of Managers (Instance, Schema, Security, and Storage).

5. **If you do not see a login screen, click Navigator⇨Connect to open the login window.**

6. **At the login screen, log in as the DBA user as follows (your screen should look like Figure 16-2):**

   a. **For the Username, type** SYSTEM.

   b. **For the Password, type** MANAGER **or whatever the current password is for SYSTEM on your database.**

   b. **For the Connect As option, select SYSDBA.**

   d. **Do not select the Save as Local Preferred Credentials check box (the check box should be empty).**

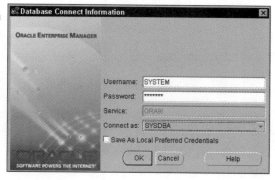

Figure 16-2:
You must log in with the Connect As SYSDBA option before starting the database.

7. **Click OK.**

   After you log in, you see the expanded navigational nodes of the database.

8. **Double-click the Instance icon.**

   Instance Manager's introduction page appears.

9. **Click the Configuration icon and observe the traffic light.**

   The Configuration icon is just under the Instance icon in the left window. The traffic light graphic appears in the right window:

   • A green light means your database is open and running.

   • A red light means your database is closed and needs to be started.

   • A yellow light means that the database is either started or mounted but not open for business. (Oracle automatically handles certain recovery steps when the database is mounted but not open. See Chapter 15 for more information on backup and recovery.)

   Figure 16-3 shows the Instance Manager window with a closed database.

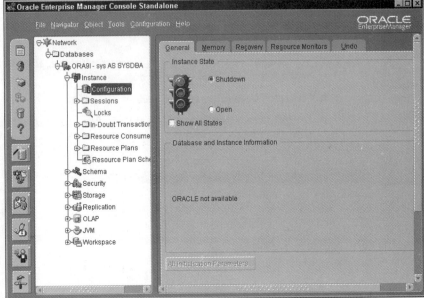

Figure 16-3:
When a database is shut down, the traffic light is red and the Shutdown option is selected.

10. **Start the database, if needed.**

   If the traffic light is red, start the database as follows:

   a. **In the right window, click the Open option.**

   b. **Click Apply.**

   The Apply button is in the bottom-right corner of the window; you may need to scroll down to see it.

   c. **When the database asks what initialization parameters to use, click OK to use the default parameters.**

   You get a status message saying that Oracle9i is performing tasks.

   d. **When the task window displays the "Processing completed" message, click the Close button.**

   The traffic light is now green.

11. **In the left window, click the minus sign next to the Instance icon to exit Instance Manager.**

Starting the database using SQL*Plus

Do not start Oracle9i without permission from your DBA every time. On mainframes, processes that require the database to be shut down (such as a file backup) may be running.

Note: When starting the database with SQL*PLus, you must be sure that TNS Listener is running. Otherwise, SQL*Plus will be unable to communicate with the already shut down database. To start TNS Listener on any platform, issue this command at your system's command prompt:

```
lsnrctl start
```

The most common startup method, even for mainframe databases, is using Enterprise Manager's Instance Manager, as described in the preceding section. Another alternative is to use SQL*Plus. This startup method is probably more common with mainframes but works on all platforms.

Here are the steps to start the database with SQL*Plus:

1. **Start SQL*Plus.**

   On Windows platforms, choose Start⇨Programs⇨Oracle HOME⇨ Application Development⇨SQL*Plus.

   On UNIX, Linux, or any other platform, type **sqlplus** at the operating-system prompt to start the command-line version of SQL*Plus.

2. **Log in as the SYSTEM user.**

   If you see a login window, follow these steps:

   a. **In the User Name box, type** SYSTEM AS SYSDBA.

      Adding the words *AS SYSDBA* to the SYSTEM username is required only when you plan to start the database; otherwise, just the user-name is required.

   b. **In the Password box, type the password for SYSTEM.**

      The default password is MANAGER.

   c. **In the Host String box, type the Oracle Net name of the Oracle9i instance on your local computer or on your network.**

      For a local database, you can usually leave this blank. For a database on a network, ask your administrator to provide you with a valid host string.

   d. **Click OK.**

      The SQL*Plus window appears and displays the `Connected to an idle instance` message.

   If instead of a login window you see a prompt for a user name, follow these steps:

   a. **At the** `Enter User Name` **prompt, type** SYSTEM@*XXXX* AS SYSDBA, **replacing** *XXXX* **with the Oracle Net name of the Oracle9i instance on your local computer or on your network.**

For example, if you want to log into the ORCL database as SYSTEM, you would type SYSTEM@ORCL AS SYSDBA.

b. Press Enter.

c. When you are prompted for a password, type the current password for SYSTEM.

The default password is MANAGER.

d. Press Enter.

The SQL prompt line appears with the `Connected to an idle instance` message. Your session may or may not have the Windows-like screen, but all the commands work the same.

3. **Type** startup **to start the database, and then press Enter.**

SQL*Plus starts the database and replies as follows (note that you might see different statistics):

```
ORACLE instance started.
Total System Global Area 12071016 bytes
Fixed Size 46136 bytes
Variable Size 11090992 bytes
Database Buffers 409600 bytes
Redo Buffers 524288 bytes
Database mounted.
Database opened.
```

4. **Type** EXIT **and then press Enter to close SQL*Plus.**

Whether you use Instance Manager or SQL*Plus, you get the thing running! After the database is started, you can take a look around and see what the database looks like on the inside.

Shutting Down Oracle9i

The following sections show you how to shut down the database.

Be careful about shutting down your database, especially if you share it on a network. Others may be using the database without your knowledge. Shut down Oracle9i only with permission from your DBA every time. If you're sure that everyone is finished with the database, go ahead and shut it down.

Ordinarily, your database gets shut down automatically when the computer is shut down. The main reason to shut down the database manually (as shown in this section) is to reset initialization parameters.

Shutting down Oracle9i on a desktop

Oracle9i gives you a simple solution to shutting down the database. Instance Manager can handle it for you.

Assuming that Console is already started, you can follow these steps to shut down Oracle9i by using Instance Manager:

1. **Double-click the name of the database that you want to shut down.**

   The list of Managers (Instance, Schema, Security, and Storage) appears.

2. **If you do not see a login screen, click Navigator⇨Connect to display it.**

3. **At the login screen, log in as the DBA user as follows:**

   a. For the Username, type **SYSTEM**.

   b. For the Password, type **MANAGER** or whatever the current password is for SYSTEM on your database.

   b. For the Connect As option, select SYSDBA.

   d. Do not select the Save as Local Preferred Credentials check box (the check box should be empty).

4. **Click OK.**

5. **Double-click the Instance icon.**

   Instance Manager's introduction page appears.

6. **Click the Configuration icon and observe the traffic light.**

   If the light is green, your database is open and running. If the light is red, your database is already closed.

7. **Select the Shutdown option, and then click Apply.**

   Oracle9i displays you a pop-up window of choices, as you see in Figure 16-4. These are the different methods of shutting down the database.

8. **Select Immediate (the default) and click OK.**

   The choices for shutdown are:

   - **Normal.** This choice takes longer, but it waits for all users to complete their work before shutting down the database. Use this when you have given your users warning to log off and you want the database to wait for them to complete their work.

   - **Immediate.** This choice stops all users and logs them off no matter what they are doing. Use this when you must shut down right away with no delays.

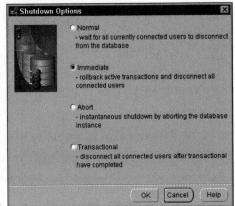

Figure 16-4:
Most of the
time, you
choose
Immediate
for the mode
of shutting
down the
database.

- **Abort.** This choice is for times when your database refuses to shut down using Normal or Immediate. Use this when a previous shutdown was interrupted before completing or if the database does not respond to commands.

- **Transactional.** This choice allows you to specify a time limit in which connected users may complete their transactions before being logged out of the database by the shutdown process. Use this if you want to delay shutdown but not have to wait for all users to log off.

9. **When Oracle9i displays a message informing you that the process has completed, click Close.**

   Oracle9i returns you to Instance Manager, and the traffic light is red.

10. **Close Console.**

    To do so, click the X box in the upper-right corner of the window.

Now your database is put to bed.

Shutting down Oracle9i on a mainframe or a network

Do not shut down Oracle9i without permission from your DBA every time. Mainframes might be running processes that require the database — processes that you may not know about. (Some processes are scheduled to run after business hours so that they don't affect normal operations.)

Check with your DBA, if you have one. If you don't have a DBA, you may have to check the manuals that come with Oracle9i to find out the specific command to shut down Oracle9i. The most common shutdown method is performed by going into Enterprise Manager's Instance Manager, as described in the preceding section.

You can shut down also using SQL*Plus. To do so, follow these steps, assuming that you're already logged into SQL*Plus:

1. **To connect to SYSDBA privileges, type the following command, replacing *XXXX* with the Oracle Net name of the Oracle9i instance:**

   ```
   CONNECT SYSTEM@XXXX AS SYSDBA
   ```

   SQL*Plus prompts for the password.

2. **Type the password for SYSTEM and then press Enter.**

   The default password for SYSTEM is MANAGER. SQL*Plus replies

   ```
   Connected.
   ```

3. **Type** shutdown immediate **and then press Enter.**

   SQL*Plus shuts down the database and replies

   ```
   Database closed.
   Database dismounted.
   ORACLE instance shut down.
   ```

4. **Type** EXIT **and then press Enter to close SQL*Plus.**

Now that you have figured out how to start and stop the database, it's time to dive into Enterprise Management Server, which you need if you want to use some of the advanced tuning tools.

Initializing Enterprise Manager Console

You can do almost everything I describe in this book using Enterprise Manager's Console in stand-alone mode. You can access Console in this stand-alone mode or by logging into Enterprise Management Server. Generally speaking, bypassing Management Server is faster. However, if you get Console hooked into Management Server, you may want to use some of its cool features, such as the job scheduler or the notifier (which can e-mail you if a remote database runs out of space, for instance).

Anyway, for those of you who like to tinker, I include instructions on how to get Enterprise Management Server started. You have to perform a few tasks to get it all set up, but you need to do these steps only once. After that, you can log in straight into Enterprise Management Server. The tasks are

1. **Create a repository.**
2. **Start Intelligent Agent.**
3. **Start Enterprise Management Server.**

You can use a variety of configurations to set up Enterprise Management Server, Intelligent Agent, the Oracle9i database with the repository, and Enterprise Manager Console. In the simplest configuration, all four of these reside on the same computer. You can't do this with Windows 98, however, because you need an Oracle9i Enterprise Edition database to handle the repository.

The following sections show how to do each of these tasks on Windows 2000. The instructions are similar in Windows NT, UNIX, and Linux. Check your *Getting Started* documentation from Oracle for details.

Creating a repository for Enterprise Manager

You may find that the task of creating a repository has already been completed during the installation of Enterprise Manager. If you don't have a clue, check with the person who installed Oracle9i. Pray that he or she does. Otherwise, better buy the person a copy of this book. Really!

If a repository already exists, skip to the next section. Otherwise, follow along with the bouncing ball. . . .

1. **Start Enterprise Manager Configuration Assistant.**

   On Windows platforms, choose Start⇨Programs⇨Oracle HOME2⇨Configuration and Migration Tools⇨Enterprise Manager Configuration Assistant. Note that the Oracle HOME2 label may have a different name, such as ORAHOME81, on your computer. The person who installed the software on your machine designates the name

   On UNIX, Linux, or any other platform, type **emca** at the operating-system command line.

   The first window of the Configuration Assistant appears.

2. **Click Next.**

   The screen shown in Figure 16-5 appears.

3. **Select the first option (to configure a local Oracle Management Server), and then click Next.**

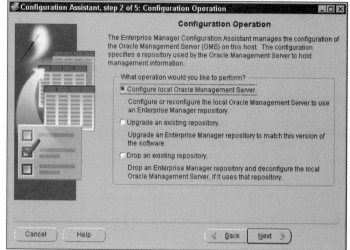

Figure 16-5:
Begin
creating a
repository
with
Configura-
tion
Assistant.

4. **Select the first option (to create a new repository), and then click Next.**

5. **Select the Custom option, and then click Next.**

6. **Select the second option, In Another Existing Database, and then click Next.**

   Your new repository will be loaded into your existing Oracle9i database.

7. **Log in as the DBA user (see Figure 16-6), and then click Next.**

   a. **For the Username, type** SYSTEM.

   b. **For the Password, type** MANAGER **or whatever the current password is for SYSTEM on your database.**

   c. **For the Service box, type the Oracle Net name of the remote database or the local name or the database.**

   You must type a name. If you are using a local database or your Oracle Net is not configured for the repository database, type the name as instructed in the tip shown at the bottom of the screen.

   d. **For the Connect As option, select SYSDBA.**

8. **Specify the repository owner and password (see Figure 16-7), and then click Next.**

   Define a brand-new user name and password. This user ID becomes the owner of all the repository tables. You may use the standard name displayed by the assistant, or you may type a different name.

   Do not use the name of an existing user!

9. **Choose a tablespace for the repository tables, and then click Next.**

   You can simply accept the defaults for this page, as shown in Figure 16-8, or you can choose different tablespaces by using the pull-down selection lists.

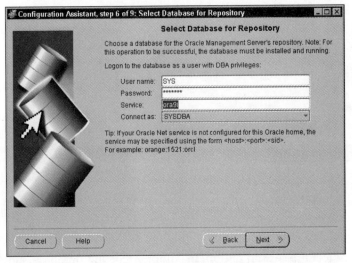

Figure 16-6:
The repository lives in one database — name it here in the Service box.

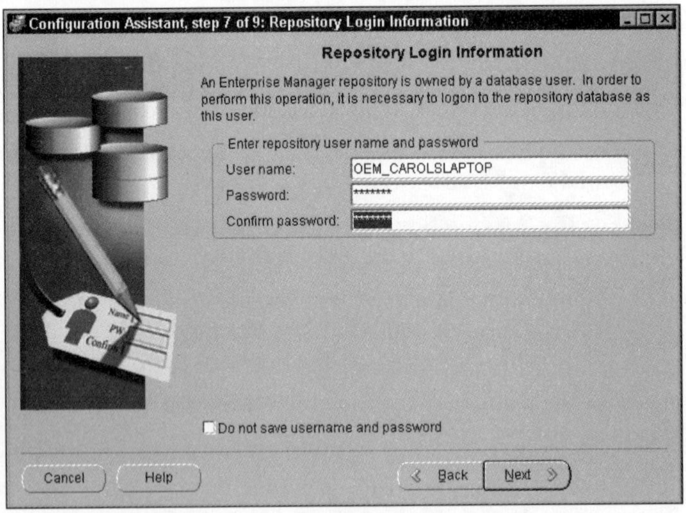

Figure 16-7:
The repository needs a brand-new user as its owner.

10. **Verify the data you entered, and then click Finish.**

    Configuration Assistant goes about creating the repository for you. You can watch the progress in the status window.

11. When Configuration Assistant is finished, click Close.

Now you are ready to start Intelligent Agent.

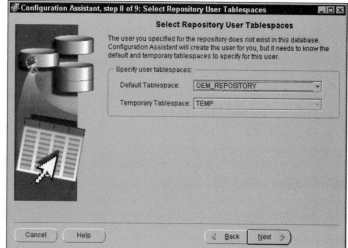

Starting Intelligent Agent

Intelligent Agent exists only on a computer that has an Oracle database installed. Intelligent Agent's job is to monitor the status of the local database and communicate with Enterprise Management Server on the local machine and Intelligent Agents on other machines.

Typically, Intelligent Agent is already set up and running when you start your computer.

On UNIX or Linux, you can start the Intelligent Agent service by typing the following command:

```
lsnrctl dbsnmp_start
```

On Windows platforms, follow these steps:

1. Open Control Panel or Services Panel.

In Windows 2000 or NT, open Services Panel. For all other Windows platforms, choose Start⇨Settings⇨Control Panel. A window of icons opens.

2. Double-click the Services icon.

You see a list of services.

3. **Right-click the service called OracleHOME1Agent and choose Start.**

   Note that the OracleHOME1 part of the name depends on your installation. It may be OracleHome90, for example.

   A status window appears, and after a few seconds, you return to the Services window. The service shows a status of Started.

The final step of initializing Enterprise Manager is to start the Enterprise Management service.

Starting the Enterprise Management service

On UNIX or Linux, type the following command to start the Enterprise Manager Server service:

```
oemctrl start oms
```

On Windows platforms, follow these steps:

1. **Open Control Panel or Services Panel.**

   See Step 1 in the preceding section.

2. **Double-click the Services icon.**

   You see a list of services.

3. **Start the service called OracleOraHome2ManagementServer.**

   Note that the OracleOraHome2 part of the name depends on your installation. It may be OracleHome90 or some other Home. To start the service, select it and click the Start button. A status window appears, and after a few seconds, you return to the Services window. The service shows a status of Started, as shown in Figure 16-9.

Now you can start Console in its full-fledged Enterprise Management Server mode! But first, let me show you how to make the Console available through a Web browser.

Setting a Web-based Console

After you have your Console up and running locally, you can set up a Web server to deliver the same thing over the Internet.

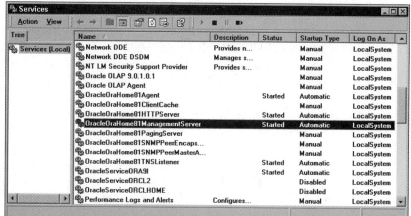

Figure 16-9:
The Enterprise Management service has been started.

Note: Oracle9i supports the Web-based Console only on Windows 98, NT, and 2000.

Serving Console on a Web server does not automatically open it up to the entire Internet. That depends on your computer's Internet connections. At the very least, you must have an assigned ISP (Internet Service Provider) number. More typically, you must have your own domain name (such as www.solarflarehats.com) on the Internet. To find out how to get these, you need another book or a friendly Web genie in the back office.

You can use the Web-based Console within your own office's network system or on the Internet — you get to decide what to do.

Here is an overview of the steps for getting things served up to the Web. You need a computer with a Web server and with access to the Oracle9i database running Enterprise Management service. Oracle9i comes with the Oracle HTTP Web Server automatically installed and configured to work with Enterprise Manager.

To access the browser-based Console, follow these steps:

1. **Start the preconfigured Oracle HTTP Web Server.**

   On Windows, choose Start⇨Programs⇨Oracle HOME2⇨Oracle HTTP Server⇨Start HTTP Server powered by Apache. The HOME2 portion of the name may vary on your installation.

2. **Access the Enterprise Manager Web site at this address:**

   ```
   http://hostname:3339/
   ```

   Replace *hostname* with the Web server computer host name, such as `aloha.oi.net`. If you're running on your local PC, type **localhost** or **127.01.01** as the host name. Figure 16-10 shows the initial Enterprise Manager Web page.

3. **Click the <u>Download Plug-in</u> link and follow the instructions to download and install the Jinitiator plug-in.**

   The plug-in is located in the `oem_webstage` directory and is called Oracle Jinitiator. After installing it once, it is available each time you go to the Web site. The installation requires you to close your browser after downloading the plug-in and before starting the installation.

4. **Open the browser again, as in Step 2.**

5. **Type the Management Server host name, and then click the Launch Console button.**

   The Management Server name is the name of the machine where you installed Oracle Management Server. For example, if you're running it on a PC called MYOWNPC, you would type MYOWNPC in the box.

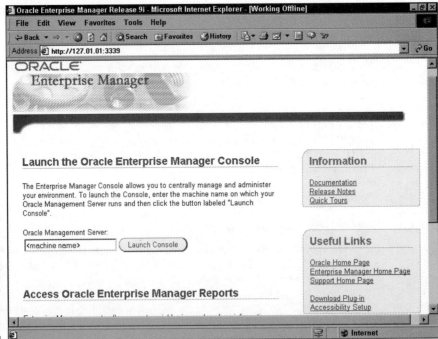

Figure 16-10: The Web-based Enterprise Manager starts with this page.

The first time you access the Web-based Console, a set of program components are downloaded, which takes a few minutes. Then the Console login window appears.

6. **Type the Management Server Administrator name and password, and then click OK.**

   The default administrator name is SYSMAN, and the default password is OEM_TEMP. Console now appears, ready for use, as shown in Figure 16-11.

7. **Close Console by simply closing the browser.**

Each browser must have the Oracle Jinitiator installed. For example, if you use the Web site from home and at the office, you have to install the Oracle Jinitiator plug-in at home and at the office. The plug-in is large (more than 3MB) for downloading across the Internet, so I recommend that you make a copy on a CD or on a Zip drive and install it from there.

The next section takes you on a tour of the features of Console when you log into Enterprise Management Server, as you must when using the Web-based version of Console.

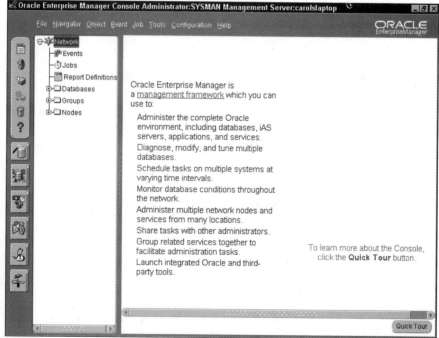

Figure 16-11: The Web-based Console looks just like the regular console.

Taking a quick tour of Enterprise Manager Console

To start Console and look around a bit, follow these steps:

1. **Start Console.**

   On Windows platforms, choose Start⇨Programs⇨Oracle HOME2⇨ Enterprise Manager Console. Note that the Oracle HOME2 label may have a different name, such as ORAHOME81, on your computer. The person who installed the software on your machine designates the name.

   On UNIX, Linux, or any other platform, type **oemapp console** at the operating-system command line

   You see the logo screen for Oracle Enterprise Manager, and then the Oracle Enterprise Manager Console login window appears.

   Oracle Agent and Enterprise Management Server must be running before you start Console.

2. **Click the Login to the Oracle Management Server option.**

   The window displays boxes for logging into Management Server.

3. **Type the login information, and then click OK.**

   a. **For the Administrator, type** SYSMAN.

   b. **For the Password, type** OEM_TEMP **or whatever the current password is for SYSMAN on your Management Server.**

   c. **For the Management Server, select the machine name where Enterprise Management service is started.**

   The first time you log in as SYSMAN with the default password, a pop-up window appears and you are required to change the password. Type a new password and then click OK to continue.

   Console's initial screen appears, as shown in Figure 16-12. I suggest that you take the Quick Tour for lots of great tips on how to use Console.

4. **Click the Quick Tour button in the lower-right corner of the window.**

   Console has four parts, plus extras:

   • **Databases.** Here you can see your databases and drill down into their components.

   • **Groups.** Here you can collect groups of related tasks, jobs, or databases for convenience. Cute, and perhaps even useful if you run a worldwide network of databases.

   • **Jobs.** If you want to schedule a nightly backup, here is where you do so.

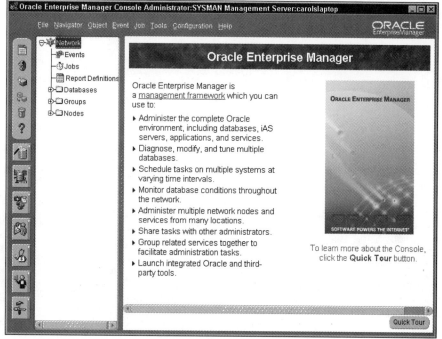

Figure 16-12:
Enterprise
Manager
Console has
all kinds of
bells and
whistles.

- **Events.** Here you can monitor your database's activities, including when it was shut down and rebooted. You can tell Console to e-mail you or even call you on the phone (if you have the right combination of software, hardware, and technical support) when some disaster occurs to your database. For example, you probably want to know whether the database fails to function on Thanksgiving night, right? Sure you do!

- **Management Packs.** A *Management Pack* is a set of tools that are related to a particular subject and available as a package from Oracle. Some Management Packs, such as the DBA Management Pack, are included with the Oracle9i database. Others, such as the Performance Pack, are available for sale. Each Management Pack has an icon along the left side of Console. These icons expand into a long bar of icons for individual tools in the Pack. Click the little icon to see any of the tools included in each DBA Management Pack tool (such as Performance Manager). In addition, if you spend money and buy other Management Packs, you can access them the same way.

5. **After you've finished the tour, close Console by clicking the X box in the top-right corner of the window.**

Now you're really flying! To tune up, flip to the next chapter. Don't delay — tune up today.

Part IV
Tuning Up and Turbocharging

The 5th Wave — By Rich Tennant

"Your database is beyond repair, but before I tell you our backup recommendation, let me ask you a question. How many index cards do you think will fit on the walls of your computer room?"

In this part . . .

You're running like a Cadillac — cruising with your Oracle9i schema with all its related queries, scripts, and online screens in perfect harmony. Then, out of the blue, the engine starts to sputter. Now your cruising machine gets sluggish and sometimes won't even get out of first gear. What went wrong?

This section covers things that go wrong in Oracle9i and how to correct them. Oracle9i has a handful of little bugaboos that haunt every database after awhile. A little tuning up here and there can get your database engine back into racing form.

And be sure to check out Chapter 18, where I show you around a new tool called Memory Manager that helps you tune your database memory usage to perfection.

Chapter 17

What's Slowing Down Your Query?

In This Chapter

▶ Looking into tune-ups, timing, and performance

▶ Analyzing your table for Optimizer

▶ Taking little bites versus wolfing down your data

*P*erhaps you write SQL code in your spare time. If so, you probably have no spare time; I suggest that you get a life. On the other hand, you may use some additional software programs that generate all your queries for you. Everything goes well until one day you create a query that runs so slowly you consider taking it out and shooting it. The database administrator (DBA) starts yelling in your face. You take three ginko tablets and grab your manuals.

This chapter is all about performance tuning, or speeding up your query. I cover the bases with useful information for tuning up your SQL code. This chapter and the others in Part IV will have your code flying as never before.

The Oracle Tuning Pack

The Oracle Tuning Pack is an additional set of tools you can add to your Enterprise Manager toolbox. You get a trial version of the Tuning Pack when you receive your CD set for Oracle9i. Use the Universal Installer to install the pack, as you do any other Oracle product, and try out the features described in this section. Then, if you find them useful, don't forget to purchase the license.

Note: The book doesn't have enough room to go through all the steps to install and run the Oracle Tuning Pack tools described in this section. Instead, I illustrate examples of how the tools can be used.

A database needs tuning in two primary areas:

✔ **Indexes.** Adding an index that speeds up a frequently used query can help speed up overall performance in your database. In addition, removing unneeded indexes can reduce the overhead of inserting and updating data. Index Tuning Wizard reviews your system for places where new indexes are needed or old indexes should be removed.

✔ **SQL query code.** The flexibility of the SQL language means that you can often write the same query in more than one way. Sometimes, you might find yourself using code you are familiar with when there is a more efficient technique. SQL Analyzer assesses your SQL code and suggests improvements.

Watch Index Tuning Wizard work its magic

To use Index Tuning Wizard, you simply start Oracle Expert. Follow these steps:

1. **Start Oracle Expert.**

   On Windows platforms, choose Start⇨Programs⇨Oracle HOME2⇨ Enterprise Management Packs⇨Tuning⇨Expert. Note that the Oracle HOME2 label may have a different name, such as ORAHOME81, on your computer. The person who installed the software on your machine designates the exact name.

   On UNIX, Linux, or any other platform, type **xpui** at the operating-system prompt.

   You see the logo screen for Oracle Enterprise Manager, and then the Expert Login window appears. This is just like logging into Enterprise Manager Console. Review Chapters 1 and 16 if you are not familiar with Console.

2. **Log in as the Management Server Administrator user as follows:**

   a. **In the Administrator box, type** SYSMAN.

   b. **For the password, type** OEM_TEMP **or whatever the current password is for SYSMAN on your database.**

   c. **In the Management Server box, type the name of the node on which the Management Service is running, such as** LOCALHOST.

   d. **Click OK.**

   The Oracle Expert main window appears, as shown in Figure 17-1.

3. **Double-click the Databases folder.**

4. **Double-click the database you want to work on.**

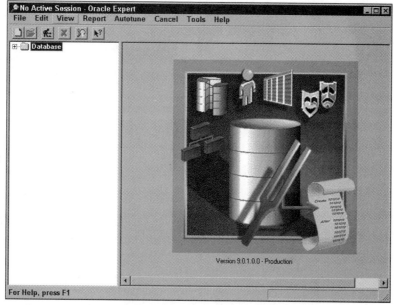

Figure 17-1:
Oracle
Expert
requires you
to log into
Enterprise
Manage-
ment Server.

5. **Choose Tools⇨Index Tuning Wizard.**

   An introduction window appears.

6. **Click Next to continue.**

   Figure 17-2 shows the Index Tuning Wizard page that appears.

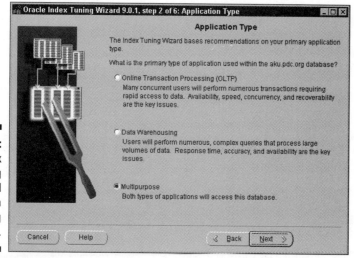

Figure 17-2:
Index
Tuning
Wizard will
begin
gathering
statistics.

7. **Click the appropriate option for your database, and then click Next.**

   Read the descriptions to help you decide which choice is correct.

8. **Accept the defaults settings by clicking Next.**

   The schema selection screen allows you to narrow down Index Tuning Wizard's scope to a few schemas rather than all schemas.

9. **Click Generate to begin the data-gathering process.**

   This process takes several minutes. The result is a list of recommendations, as shown in Figure 17-3.

10. **Click Next.**

11. **View the report and the SQL script.**

    Review the report and the script. You can print and save the report and script as you want, using the buttons on the screen.

12. **Click Next.**

13. **Select an action you want to take.**

    On the final screen of Index Tuning Wizard, you can implement the changes now or save them for later. You can also save the data gathered by the wizard as a Tuning Session that you can use later with other parts of Oracle Expert. For now, accept the default setting, which saves the recommendations as a script that you can use later.

14. **Click Finish to close the wizard.**

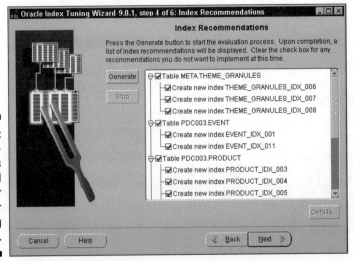

Figure 17-3: Recommendations are listed here for adding or removing indexes.

Index Tuning Wizard is the easiest tool in Oracle Expert to use because it gathers its own data independently from a working database. Use it to discover needed indexes that may help improve your system's performance.

The next section tells you how to review specific SQL commands and tune them for better performance.

Let SQL Analyze help tune queries

You can use SQL Analyze to review the worst SQL commands currently in your database or to review any SQL statement you have created. This section shows you how to display the ten worst SQL statements and how to get SQL Analyze expert to review one of those statements.

Note: This tool requires a working Enterprise Management Server, which I show how to set up in Chapter 16. Please review this if you have not already started your Management Server.

If you don't own the Oracle Tuning Pack, you can still get tuning information using EXPLAIN PLAN in SQL*Plus. See the last section in this chapter to find out how.

To run SQL Analyze, follow these steps:

1. **Start SQL Analyze.**

   On Windows platforms, choose Start⇨Programs⇨Oracle HOME2⇨ Enterprise Management Packs⇨Tuning⇨SQL Analyze. Note that the Oracle HOME2 label may have a different name, such as ORAHOME81, on your computer. The person who installed the software on your machine designates the exact name.

   On UNIX, Linux, or any other platform, type **vmq** at the operating-system command line.

   You see the logo screen for Oracle Enterprise Manager, and then the SQL Analyze Login window appears. This is just like logging into Enterprise Manager Console. Review Chapters 1 and 16 if you are not familiar with Console.

2. **Log in as the Management Server Administrator user.**

   See Step 2 in the preceding section for details. After you log in, the Getting Started with Oracle SQL Analyze screen appears.

3. **Click OK.**

   The main SQL Analyze window appears, as shown in Figure 17-4.

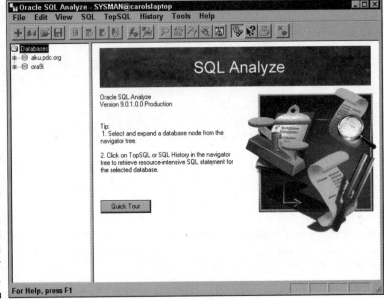

Figure 17-4:
The SQL
Analyze
main menu
displays
databases
available for
analysis.

4. **Double-click a database to connect to that database.**

   The node opens up and displays TopSQL and SQL History as nodes below the database.

5. **Click TopSQL.**

   An options window appears for setting the parameters that determine which SQL commands you want to see. For now, accept the default settings.

6. **Click OK.**

   The system whirs and thinks for a while, and then the screen displays some SQL commands and statistics, as shown in Figure 17-5.

7. **Double-click the first SQL command.**

   This creates an entry below the database name with a name such as SQL003. In addition, the right window displays the full text of the command and the Optimizer's execution plan in the Explain area below the SQL statement.

   Figure 17-6 shows a query that I double-clicked.

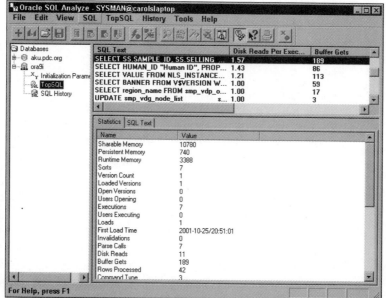

Figure 17-5:
The SQL commands shown rate highest in resource consumption.

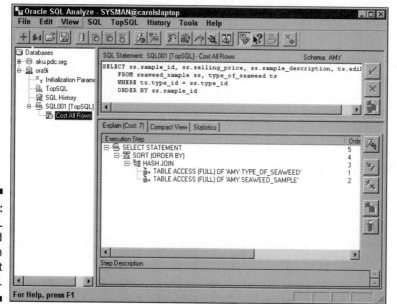

Figure 17-6:
One SQL command has been singled out for scrutiny.

8. **Click Get Index Recommendations (one of the icons along the top of the screen).**

To view the name of an icon, point your mouse at the icon and wait. In about one second, the title of the icon appears in a small box near the mouse.

When you click the icon, a process reviews the SQL command and the tables involved and suggests how to create a new index if that will improve performance. The recommendation shows up in the lower right window. If no indexes are needed, it says so in the same lower right window.

9. **Click SQL Tuning Wizard (another icon along the top of the screen).**

This starts a wizard that reviews inefficient coding in your SQL command. If any recommendations are shown, you can implement them in your SQL command.

10. **Close SQL Analyze.**

Click the X in the top-right corner.

SQL Analyze has a lot of potential for sniffing out problem areas when you have a lot of applications running. It has option settings for focusing on different aspects of tuning, such as memory or buffers. But that is more than I can cover in this chapter. Just remember that if your system starts to slow down, SQL Analyze or Oracle Expert may be able to pinpoint the best area to start your hunt for bad SQL code.

Another important part of your bag of tricks as a DBA or SQL code creator is a good understanding of how Oracle's internal tuner, called Optimizer, works to process your SQL commands. The next section discusses Optimizer. Stay tuned!

Helping Optimizer Do Its Job

Oracle9i has a brain called *Optimizer* that has the unenviable job of figuring out the best way to execute your SQL code, no matter how garbled. If you help Optimizer, it rewards you with good performance (meaning low overhead costs and fast response times) on your SQL code. The best way to aid this overworked bit of software is to give it the information it needs to do its job.

Because SQL is a fourth-generation language, it leaves many things open to interpretation. Basically, SQL outlines the ingredients and how they fit together as well as what the results should contain. SQL does not, however, clearly define the exact instructions for getting from point A to point B — that is where Optimizer comes into play. Optimizer looks over your SQL code and figures out a half-dozen angles of attack to get the data you want out of the database. Each of these angles is called a *plan*.

Optimizer looks at the tables or objects involved in your query (or INSERT, UPDATE, and so on). It compares the size of the tables, the size of their rows, the available indexes, and other statistics it has on hand, and then makes its calculations. It figures out the amount of I/O (disk reading and writing) and the amount of CPU (computer brainpower) needed for all the various plans. The plan with the lowest overall cost wins.

Optimizer makes decisions based on information it has in the data-dictionary views. The information it needs is updated only when you (or the DBA) update it using the ANALYZE command. Each table that you don't analyze suffers because Optimizer doesn't have important decision-making information for that table.

Keep your data-dictionary views current by running the ANALYZE command regularly on all your tables.

If you still have a query or other SQL code that seems to be running slowly, read on. I have some great hints for adjusting your code to speed up your query.

Moods and modes of Optimizer

Which is the root word for Optimizer: *optimist* or *miser?*

Your Oracle9i database comes equipped with the most up-to-date Optimizer. However, it won't use any of its new features unless you give it statistics on at least some of your tables and objects.

Your Oracle9i Optimizer functions in two modes:

- ✔ **Cost-based.** This is the default mode, and it chooses the plan that delivers your data at the lowest cost in terms of system resources. System resources include central processing unit (CPU) time, input and output (I/O) traffic, and volume of data.

- ✔ **Rule-based.** This was the only mode available in Oracle6. It remains in Oracle9i primarily to allow backward compatibility. If you have legacy SQL that was explicitly tuned for rule-based optimization, you can instruct Optimizer to continue to use this mode. Be forewarned, however, that rule-based optimization is being phased out in future releases.

If you have a new database and have never gathered statistics for any of its tables or objects, Oracle9i Optimizer always uses its older, less-efficient mode: rule-based optimization. So get with it! Analyze those tables!

If you're working with an older database (one that has been upgraded from earlier releases), verify that the database has the OPTIMIZER_MODE initialization parameter set to its default value of CHOOSE. This setting allows Optimizer to use cost-based optimization whenever it can.

Follow the steps in the next section to gain access to the best Oracle9i optimization: cost-based optimization.

One command to analyze your entire schema

The GATHER_SCHEMA_STATS command is a great feature that helps you be lazy and efficient all at once (which is actually the definition of *smart*). Either the schema owner or the DBA can run this command in SQL*Plus. The general syntax is

```
-- 01_gatherstatistics
EXECUTE DBMS_STATS.GATHER_SCHEMA_STATS('schema_name');
```

Replace *schema_name* with the Oracle user name that owns the tables and objects.

To gather statistics for a schema, follow these steps:

1. **Start SQL*Plus.**

   On Windows platforms, choose Start⇨Programs⇨Oracle HOME⇨Application Development⇨SQL*Plus.

   On UNIX, Linux, or any other platform, type **sqlplus** at the operating-system prompt to start the command-line version of SQL*Plus.

2. **Log in as the Oracle user.**

   If you see a login window, follow these steps:

   a. **Type the user name and password. If you installed the sample schema, type AMY for the name and AMY123 for the password.**

   b. **In the Host String box, type the Oracle Net name of the Oracle9i instance on your local computer or on your network.**

   For a local database, you can usually leave this blank. For a database on a network, ask your administrator to provide you with a valid host string.

   c. **Click OK.**

   The SQL*Plus window appears.

   If you see a prompt instead of a login window, follow these steps:

     a. **In the Username box, type** AMY@*XXXX*, **replacing** *XXXX* **with the Oracle Net name of the Oracle9i instance on your local computer or on your network.**

      For example, if you want to log into the ORCL database as AMY, you would type **AMY@ORCL.**

     b. **Press Enter.**

     c. **Type the password.**

      If you log in as AMY, type **AMY123** for the password.

     d. **Press Enter.**

      The SQL prompt line appears. Your session may or may not have the Windows-like screen, but all the commands work the same.

3. **Type the following command, replacing** schema_name **with the Oracle user name that owns the tables and objects:**

```
EXECUTE DBMS_STATS.GATHER_SCHEMA_STATS('schema_name');
```

For the example, replace schema_name with AMY. This command gathers statistics on all the tables, columns, and indexes owned by AMY. The command looks like this:

```
-- 01 gatherstatistics
EXECUTE DBMS_STATS.GATHER_SCHEMA_STATS('AMY');
```

4. **Press Enter to execute the command.**

After working for a while (this takes longer when you have more tables and more data), SQL*Plus displays

```
PL/SQL procedure completed successfully.
```

Completing the GATHER_SCHEMA_STATS command makes sure that you have statistics on your tables, columns, objects, and indexes, which in turn ensures that you can use cost-based optimization. The next section shows you how to gather statistics for one table.

Personal attention: Analyzing one table at a time

Suppose that you have a new table or a table that has a new index. You want to refresh the statistics for the table so that Optimizer knows about your changes. In the old days, you had to run the ANALYZE command for the table, the columns, and the index. Now you can take care of all three at once with the GATHER_TABLE_STATS command. Here is the general syntax for this trick:

```
-- 02 --gathertablestats
EXECUTE DBMS_STATS.GATHER_TABLE_STATS('sname','tname');
```

Replace *sname* with the Oracle user name that owns the table and *tname* with the table's actual name. For example, the syntax for gathering statistics on the `AMY.CAR` table is

```
EXECUTE DBMS_STATS.GATHER_TABLE_STATS('AMY', 'CAR');
```

The table owner or the DBA can run this command in SQL*Plus.

Because you're using the `EXECUTE` command, you must list all the parameters on a single line. Otherwise, you get syntax errors when you execute the command.

Another way to gather table statistics is to use the `ANALYZE` command, which is the underlying task that the `GATHER_TABLE_STATS` package handles. The basic syntax is

```
-- 03_analyzetable
ANALYZE TABLE table_name COMPUTE STATISTICS;
```

Replace *table_name* with the actual table name. The owner of the table can run this command in SQL*Plus Worksheet or SQL*Plus.

Whenever you add a new table, use the `GATHER_TABLE_STATS` command to update your data dictionary's statistics. Another time to gather statistics is when columns or indexes are added to or removed from the table.

Sometimes you want to change the cost-based Optimizer's tuning to accomplish a different goal. The next section discusses how to do that.

A hint . . . you're getting warmer

When using the default settings, Oracle9i Optimizer, in its infinite wisdom, knows that you usually want it to choose the most efficient plan. But there are exceptions to every rule, and we mere mortals are graced with the following choices in optimization modes:

- ✔ **ALL_ROWS.** This mode tells Optimizer that you want the most cost-effective plan it can devise using the cost-based Optimizer. Optimizer uses default statistics for tables that are in the SQL statement and do not have statistics available.

- ✔ **FIRST_ROWS.** Fastest response time. This mode is best for interactive applications, such as Web pages, that display data. Because the objective of this kind of optimization is to deliver the first row of the query in as little time as possible, this goal is called `FIRST_ROWS`.

✔ **CHOOSE.** This is the default mode for Oracle9i databases. Optimizer looks at the SQL statement and uses the ALL_ROWS (cost-effective) plan if at least one table in the statement has statistics available. If none of the tables has statistics available, Optimizer uses the RULE plan (backward compatible).

✔ **RULE.** Uses rule-based optimization. Rule-based optimization determines the most cost-effective plan without considering the table statistics, such as distribution of data and volume of data. Even if statistics have been gathered, Optimizer ignores them. This mode is equivalent to Optimizer in older versions of the Oracle database. If you have legacy SQL code that is well tuned for the rule-based Optimizer, you can rest assured that Oracle9i Optimizer will carry on the proud tradition by specifying this Optimizer mode. You can impose any of these modes on the entire database by specifying the mode in the OPTIMIZER_MODE initialization parameter.

If you prefer to impose a mode other than the one set up for the entire database, you can set the mode for a single SQL command by using the hint feature. A *hint* is an instruction to Optimizer that changes which plan it chooses for the SQL statement.

You can use a great many hints, but they require careful study of Optimizer plans. I cover only those hints that change the overall Optimizer mode. The remaining hints are more obscure and seldom used.

The general syntax of the Optimizer mode hint is

```
SELECT ... /* mode_name */
FROM ...
WHERE ...;
```

Replace *mode_name* with the actual Optimizer mode that you want to use.

Suppose that you've created a lovely report for the manager of your bread company to use. The report is executed from her desktop and delivers the data to her Web browser. Naturally, you want to impress her with how incredibly quickly and efficiently your report can run. So you add the FIRST_ROWS hint to the query. The query looks like this:

```
-- 04_querywithhint
SELECT B.BREAD_NAME, /* FIRST_ROWS */
B.SELLING_PRICE,
INGREDIENT_NAME, R.OUNCES*I.PRICE_PER_OUNCE
FROM INGREDIENT I,
BREAD B,
RECIPE R
WHERE R.BREAD_NO = B.BREAD_NO
AND R.INGREDIENT_NO = I.INGREDIENT_NO
ORDER BY BREAD_NAME, INGREDIENT_NAME;
```

The first line contains the hint, FIRST_ROWS, enclosed inside a comment:

```
SELECT B.BREAD_NAME, /* FIRST_ROWS */
```

This type of hint must always appear in the first line of the query.

Getting Ahead While Testing and Tuning

You can extract data from your relational database a hundred different ways. This section covers a few of the simpler techniques that help you create efficient, well-tuned queries and avoid common mistakes.

When you have a query that is running slowly, how can you determine what part of the query is causing the problem? Maybe an index will help. Or perhaps rewriting a subquery is the answer. The SQL*Plus EXPLAIN PLAN command can help. This command loads Optimizer's plan into a table (called, surprise!, the PLAN table), and you can display the results with a simple query. Give it a try!

The steps involved in using the EXPLAIN PLAN go like this:

1. **Create the PLAN table.**

   The table should be owned by the user who runs the EXPLAIN PLAN command. This step needs to be performed only once.

2. **Prepare and run the EXPLAIN PLAN command.**

   This involves taking a sample command, selecting a plan name, adding the query statement, and then running the command.

3. **Run a query to display the plan.**

   This query is long, but after you have it ready, you can reuse it.

For example, suppose you are a saucy mermaid with your seaweed selections all lined up on a shelf. You want to find out the total worth of the edible portions of your seaweed collection and also list the highest price and the lowest price. Here is the query:

```
SELECT SUM(S.SELLING_PRICE), MAX(S.SELLING_PRICE),
MIN(S.SELLING_PRICE)
FROM SEAWEED_SAMPLE S, TYPE_OF_SEAWEED TOS
WHERE S.TYPE_ID = TOS.TYPE_ID
AND TOS.EDIBLE = 'EDIBLE';
```

Now that you have a query, follow the next set of steps to view Optimizer's plan for this query.

You can find all the commands in the `Samples/Chapter17` directory on the For Dummies Web site (`www.dummies.com/extras/Oracle9i.html`).

1. **Start SQL*Plus and log in as the Oracle user.**

   For details, see Steps 1 and 2 in the "One command to analyze your entire schema" section.

2. **Create the `PLAN` table if it does not exist.**

   You need to do this step only once. After that, you can skip to the next step.

   To create the table, type the following command and press Enter. Remember to replace *X* in the command with the full path where you stored the downloaded files for Chapter 17:

   ```
   START X:\Samples\Chapter17\05_plantable.sql;
   ```

   Oracle responds

   ```
   Table created.
   ```

3. **Copy `EXPLAIN PLAN` to your hard drive so you can edit it.**

   Here is a fast way to do it, right in SQL*Plus:

   a. **Load the file into the SQL*Plus buffer by typing the following command and then pressing Enter:**

   ```
   GET X:\Samples\Chapter17\06_explain.sql
   ```

   Again, replace *X* with the full path where you stored the downloaded files.

   b. **Save the file to your hard drive by typing the following command and then pressing Enter:**

   ```
   SAVE explain.sql
   ```

4. **Open the new file for edit by typing the following command and then pressing Enter:**

   ```
   EDIT explain.sql
   ```

5. **Add your query in the file, placing it between these two lines:**

   ```
   -- >>>> begin your query below this line <<<<
   -- >>>> end your query above this line (no semicolon!)
          <<<<
   ```

For example, after adding your seaweed collection query, the lines look like this:

```
-- >>>> begin your query below this line <<<<
SELECT SUM(S.SELLING_PRICE), MAX(S.SELLING_PRICE),
MIN(S.SELLING_PRICE)
FROM SEAWEED_SAMPLE S, TYPE_OF_SEAWEED TOS
WHERE S.TYPE_ID = TOS.TYPE_ID
AND TOS.EDIBLE = 'EDIBLE'
-- >>>> end your query above this line (no semicolon!)
          <<<<
```

Notice that you have correctly removed the semicolon from the end of the query.

6. **Save the file with your changes and exit.**

   If you are in Notepad, choose File⇨Save and then choose File⇨Exit. Otherwise, issue the appropriate command to save the file and exit the editor you are using. You return immediately to SQL*Plus.

7. **Run the file by typing this command and then pressing Enter:**

```
START explain
```

   SQL*Plus prompts:

```
Enter the value for Plan_name:
```

8. **Type a plan name and then press Enter.**

   The plan name is used as the primary key when the EXPLAIN PLAN process adds records to the PLAN table and used also to extract those records in a query.

   SQL*Plus first deletes records with this plan name (if any). It displays:

```
        5 rows deleted.
```

   The actual number of rows varies from zero to a dozen or so. Next, the EXPLAIN PLAN command runs. SQL*Plus says

```
Explained.
```

   Finally, the query runs and SQL*Plus displays the plan. Here is the plan for the example:

```
OPERATION OPTIONS OBJECT_NAME POSITION
--------------- ------------- ---------------- --------
        SELECT STATEMENT SORT AGGREGATE 1
NESTED LOOPS 1
TABLE ACCESS FULL SEAWEED_SAMPLE 1
TABLE ACCESS BY INDEX ROWID TYPE_OF_SEAWEED 2
INDEX UNIQUE SCAN TYPE_OF_SEAWEED_PK 1
```

The plan is also saved in a file for you. The file name is the plan name with a .txt suffix. For example, if you typed MINE as the plan name, the file name would be MINE.txt.

9. Type EXIT and then press Enter to end SQL*Plus.

Look at the plan. If you find any lines that say TABLE ACCESS FULL, the database will look at every record in the table — slowly! Add an index to this table (refer to the next chapter) and rerun EXPLAIN PLAN to see whether it eliminates this type of scan.

Want to find out more about indexes and other tuning secrets? Just go on to Chapter 18 and become the tuning guru you always dreamed of being.

Chapter 18

Improving Performance with Indexes and Memory Buffers

· ·

· ·

Speeding up a slow query is a dilemma faced by almost anyone who works with Oracle9i. Oracle9i has a brain called an Optimizer that has the job of deciding how to go after the data that's requested in your query. In most cases, you can transform a slow tortoise query into a speedy rabbit query by adding an index to an important column in the query. In this chapter, you find out how to create the keys and the indexes.

Another common bottleneck that causes performance anxiety is memory. The proper care and feeding of the Oracle9i memory space will ease your distress. Lucky for you, a new tool called Memory Manager comes to the rescue.

Why Create an Index?

Speed, speed, and speed are the main reasons to create an index. When you run a query, you tell Oracle9i which parts of which tables you want to see. Oracle9i looks at its own resources and decides the most efficient way to get the data to you. An index helps Oracle9i get the data faster.

What are a row ID, a UID, and an OID?

A *row ID* contains the physical location of the row in a table and is the fastest retrieval method that Oracle9i uses. If Oracle9i knows a row ID, it knows the location of that row and can go directly to it without any delay. The row ID consists of several hexadecimal numbers that identify the storage space used for a single row from a single table. Every row has a row ID. You can query a row ID as you can any column, but you can't modify the ID. When a table is reorganized, such as during export and import of the entire table or database, the row ID changes.

A *UID*, or universal identifier, is used in place of a row ID for certain types of tables and can contain a variety of formats. For example, the UID contains the value of the row's primary key if the table is an index-organized table. The UID contains some other key value if a table is pointing to an entity in a different kind of database, such as SQL Server.

Every row in an object table contains an object ID, or OID. An *OID,* like a row ID, is a unique identifier that describes the location of the row's data to the Oracle9i database engine. Unlike the row ID, however, the OID is needed to relate two objects. It works as a foreign key. The structure of the OID is similar to the row ID, but unlike a row ID, you can't directly query an OID. The only time that you can retrieve an OID is when you put it into the REF datatype (often within a PL/SQL procedure).

Oracle9i doesn't sift or sort the storage of your table's rows based on any index (unless you're working with complex, parallel, or indexed table structures). As you add rows to a table, Oracle9i always adds them to the end of the current rows. Sometimes, Oracle9i moves a row from its original position to the end of the current rows. This happens if a row gets updated with a great deal of data at one time — data that doesn't fit into its current space in the table. Therefore, table rows become jumbled up in sequence, even if you originally entered them in order.

The problem with a disorderly bunch of table rows is not in the retrieval itself but in the time it takes to retrieve and then sort the rows back into order. When you add an ORDER BY clause to your query, your results are listed in proper sequence. Behind the scenes, Oracle9i has grabbed all your data, thrown it into a temporary table, created an index on the temporary table, and then sorted and retrieved the data to deliver it to you in order. This takes precious time. Indexing a table gives Oracle9i an easier and faster method of retrieving sorted data.

Oracle9i keeps indexes as independent objects in the database. An index looks much like a table when you look at its internal structure, and it consists of rows of data. The columns in the index include a copy of the indexed column(s) and the row ID of the corresponding row in the table that you indexed.

Unlike tables, indexes are kept in perfect sorted order by the index columns. Every new row added to a table creates a row in the index. Oracle9i automatically adds the row to the index in its sorted order, which allows Oracle9i to use fast search algorithms on the index. After Oracle9i finds the row in the index, it uses the row ID (or primary key, depending on the type of index and the type of table) to retrieve the table row.

If you create a primary-key constraint on your table, Oracle9i automatically creates an index on the primary-key column or columns. A primary-key constraint is a feature of Oracle9i that defines the table's primary key as a rule (constraint) enforced by the database.

Oracle9i doesn't require indexes or primary keys on any table. If you have neither, Oracle9i uses its only option, a full table scan, when you query the table. A *full table scan* is similar to starting at the 100s on the library shelf and reading every book label until you find the book you want. Likewise, using an index is like going to the card catalog, looking up your book's Dewey decimal number, and then walking right to the appropriate aisle and finding the exact location of the book.

What can you use an index for? Lots of stuff:

✔ **Faster queries.** You can make an index on columns that you use for searches. If you have an online screen that allows searches by last name, for example, add an index on the LAST_NAME column of the table. This kind of index doesn't require unique values.

✔ **Unique values.** A primary key always requires unique values, meaning that the value of the primary-key column (or columns) in one row of the table is unique when compared to the values of the primary-key column (or columns) in all the other rows in the table. Oracle9i automatically generates an index to enforce unique values in the primary key of a table. You can also use this feature for any other column (or set of columns) that requires unique values in your table.

✔ **Foreign keys.** Foreign keys are used frequently in queries. You can speed up the performance of queries using foreign keys by adding an index on them.

In the next section, you find out how to create primary and foreign keys and their indexes.

Creating Your Own Indexes

Oracle9i has few restrictions on what you can do when you create indexes. The main rules are these:

✔ You can't make two indexes on one table that include all the same columns.

✔ You can't index columns that have the LONG, BCLOB, NCLOB, or BFILE datatypes. These kinds of columns can contain huge amounts of data, and indexing them makes no sense anyway. The folks at Oracle made a logical choice on this one.

Make a rule of creating an index on a foreign key. This practice speeds up your queries because Oracle9i efficiently stores and maintains indexes for fast matching and lookups. Queries that join two tables always use the foreign key and the primary key in the WHERE clause. Having an index on the foreign key allows Oracle9i to quickly match the two indexes — the foreign-key index and the primary-key index — before going after the data.

Indexes can also speed up response time in a popular online screen. If you create a screen in which users search for phone numbers based on a person's last name, for example, you can create an index for the LAST_NAME column.

Avoid adding an index on a column that includes many of the same values in many rows. A column called SEX, for example, has three possible values: MALE, FEMALE, and NULL. In a table with 10,000 rows, an index that narrows down the number of rows to 3,333 may not speed up the performance much.

When you want to create an index, you can use Schema Manager to help you. You can easily remove and modify an index as well.

An index can be unique or nonunique. A *unique* index validates every new or changed row in a table for a unique value in the column or set of columns in the index. A *nonunique* index allows duplicate values in rows. You add a nonunique index to speed up the query.

The 20 percent rule

The fastest way to retrieve rows from a table is to access the row with the exact row ID. An index is the second-fastest way, but it decreases in performance as the proportion of rows retrieved increases. If you're retrieving approximately 20 percent of the rows in a table, using an index is just as fast. But beyond that magic 20 percent, *not* using an index is faster.

Keep this rule in mind when you create indexes intended to help speed up a query. Queries vary

in the rows that they select from a table. If you have a query that you use often, determine the number of rows that it selects from the table. If this number is more than 20 percent of the total number of rows in the table, an index on the table may not improve the performance of the query. You may just want to try both methods. If the number of rows is less than 20 percent, an index will almost certainly help performance.

Adding an index

Use Enterprise Manager Console to reach Schema Manager and create an index. To do so, follow these steps:

1. **Start Console.**

   On Windows platforms, choose Start⇨Programs⇨Oracle HOME2⇨ Enterprise Manager Console. Note that the Oracle HOME2 label may have a different name, such as ORAHOME81, on your computer. The person who installed the software on your machine designates the name.

   On UNIX, Linux, or any other platform, type **oemapp console** at the operating-system command line.

   You see the logo screen for Oracle Enterprise Manager, and then the Oracle Enterprise Manager Console login window appears.

2. **Make sure the Launch Standalone option is selected, and then click OK.**

   Console's initial screen appears.

3. **Double-click the Databases folder.**

   All available databases are listed.

4. **Double-click the name of the database that you want to work on.**

   If this is the first time you have used Console or if you have not saved your login settings, you see a login screen. Otherwise, you see a list of Managers (including Instance, Schema, Security, and Storage).

5. **If you see a login screen, follow these steps to log in:**

   a. **For the Username, type** SYSTEM.

   b. **For the Password, type** MANAGER **or whatever the current password is for SYSTEM on your database.**

   c. **For the Connect As option, select Normal.**

   d. **Click to add a check mark to the Save As Local Preferred Credentials option.**

   e. **Click OK.**

   Console asks whether it's okay to save your credentials in a local encrypted file.

   f. **Click OK to continue.**

   The list of Managers (including Instance, Schema, Security, and Storage) appears.

6. **In the left half of the window, double-click the Schema icon.**

   This action opens Schema Manager within Console. A list of schema objects appears below the Schema icon.

7. **In the left half of the window, double-click the Table folder.**

   A list of tables appears in the right half of the window. A list of schemas (table owners) appears under the Tables folder in the left half of the window.

8. **Double-click the schema that owns the table that you want to index.**

   Both the right and left windows show you a list of tables owned by that schema. If you want to follow along with the example, select the AMY schema and the RECIPE table.

9. **Right-click the table that needs an index and choose Create Index On, as shown in Figure 18-1.**

   A window appears for completing the definition of the index.

10. **In the Name box, type the index name.**

    Follow the usual naming standards for Oracle objects, as you do for tables and columns. For the example, type **RECIPE_INGREDIENT_X.**

11. **Select the indexed columns by clicking them in order.**

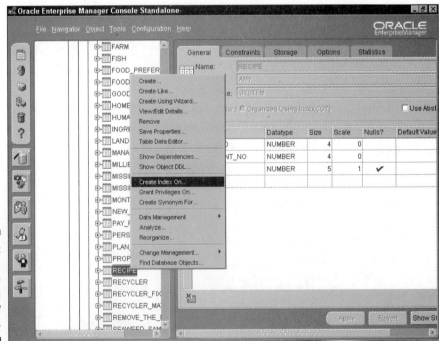

Figure 18-1:
Right-click a table to pop up a menu of new options.

Select the first column in the index first, the second one next, and so on until you've numbered all the columns in the index. Figure 18-2 shows you what the sample index looks like. In the example, only one column, the `INGREDIENT_NO` column, has been selected.

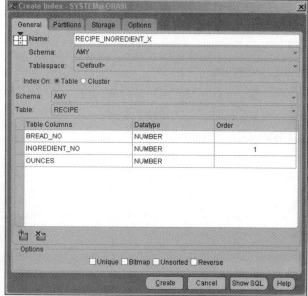

Figure 18-2: Choose columns to be indexed by clicking the Order box for each column — the sequence numbers are added automatically.

12. **Click the Create button to finish.**

    Oracle9i executes the SQL it generated and returns to the main window.

The index creator in Schema Manager can create as many indexes as you need in a flash.

Removing an index

Removing an index using Schema Manager is easier than creating one. Follow these quick and easy steps:

1. **Start Console as shown in the preceding section.**

2. **Double-click the Schema icon.**

   Schema Manager's introduction page appears.

3. **In the left window, double-click the Table icon.**

   A list of schemas appears below the icon in the left window, and a list of all the indexes appears in the right window.

4. **Double-click the schema that owns the table and index that you want to remove.**

   Both the right and left windows display a list of tables owned by that schema. To remove the index you created in the preceding section, double-click AMY.

5. **Click the plus sign next to the table with the index that you want to remove.**

   A list of folders, including the Index folder, appears below the table name in the right window. To follow along with the example, click the plus sign next to RECIPE.

6. **Click the plus sign next to the Indexes folder.**

   The folder expands to show a list of indexes.

7. **Right-click the index that you want to remove and then choose Remove, as shown in Figure 18-3.**

   Schema Manager asks you whether you're sure that you want to remove the index.

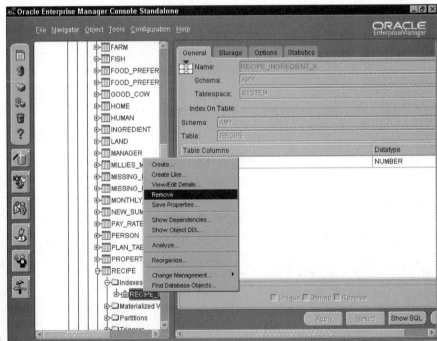

Figure 18-3: Indexes are listed under each table's name in the navigator window of Schema Manager.

Index versus primary-key constraints

You probably know that you can create your own unique index for a table's primary key if you do not define a primary-key constraint.

If you're working with a legacy system, you may face a situation in which many of these indexes are attached to older tables. Why go through all the trouble of removing those indexes and adding the primary-key constraints? Do you get royalties every time the primary key is used?

The best reason for replacing unique indexes with primary-key constraints is that you can't create any foreign-key constraints that refer to

a table that has no primary key. You may start with the older tables and then build on new tables that fit in and enhance these older ones. Foreign keys define all the connections between the old and new tables. If you don't create a primary-key constraint, you are handicapped. Ultimately, you can't create the foreign-key constraints that make your schema (set of database tables) have integrity with good values in all the foreign keys. You don't have to be a Boy Scout to know that good values and integrity are desirable traits.

   8. **Click Yes.**

      Schema Manager removes the index and returns to the main window. You see that Oracle9i has removed the index from the list of indexes.

   The index is gone, just like that.

Using Indexes with Object Tables and Nested Tables

Like relational tables, object tables and nested tables store data. You can experience better performance when retrieving data from object tables and nested tables by adding an index.

The next sections cover the how-tos of index creation with object tables and nested tables. If you don't like objects, I object! Skip these sections. Otherwise, read on.

Creating an index on an object table

As you find out in Chapter 2, there are two kinds of object tables: tables of objects and tables with columns of objects.

You can create an index on various objects in the following cases:

- ✔ **You can create an index on the relational columns within a table, just as you do on a relational table.** This applies to tables that use a combination of relational columns and object columns. In this case, follow the instructions in the "Adding an index" section, earlier in this chapter.

- ✔ **You can create an index on a nested table.** This requires using SQL, which I describe in the next section, "Creating an index on a nested table."

- ✔ **In special circumstances, you can create an index on a column that has the** REF **datatype.** I don't discuss this aspect of indexing objects because it is too complex.

Creating an index on a nested table

To create an index on a nested table, you need a nested table. Refer to Chapter 10 for plenty of information on the exciting job of nesting tables.

For now, I assume that you already have a nested table somewhere and you want to add an index. The general syntax of the command to use is

```
CREATE INDEX indexname ON
nestedtablename (columnname, columnname...);
```

Replace *indexname* with the name of your new index. Replace *nestedtablename* with the name of the nested table's physical storage table. Replace *columnname* with one or more columns to be indexed.

Use the following variation on the syntax when you want to create a unique index on a nested table (this enforces uniqueness, similar to a primary key):

```
CREATE INDEX indexname ON
nestedtablename (NESTED_TABLE_ID, columnname,columnname...);
```

This format includes the pseudocolumn called NESTED_TABLE_ID. NESTED_TABLE_ID is the unique ID that Oracle9i assigns to each row of a nested table. Including the unique ID in the indexed columns assures that the unique values of other columns are included in the index.

Suppose that you have a table called BREAD_OBJ that contains a nested table of ingredients for your bread. The nested table is stored in the RECIPE_NT_STORAGE table. The SQL to create the index is

```
-- 01_nestedtable
CREATE INDEX RECIPE_NEST_INGRED_IX ON
RECIPE_NT_STORAGE (AMOUNT_IN_OUNCES);
```

Use SQL*Plus to execute the command.

Removing an index on an object table or a nested table

If you have a table that contains column objects, you may have created an index on one of the relational columns. In this case, remove the index by following the instructions in the "Removing an index" section earlier in this chapter.

If you've created an index on a nested table, use SQL to remove it. The syntax is

```
DROP INDEX indexname;
```

Execute the command in SQL*Plus.

For example, to drop the RECIPE_NEST_INGRED_IX index, you use the following command:

```
-- 02_dropindex
DROP INDEX RECIPE_NEST_INGRED_IX;
```

Now that you know how to create indexes, you're ready to look at some extra tools that Oracle provides for tuning.

Enterprise Manager's Memory Manager

"Add more RAM!" is the battle cry of all PC users. For Oracle9i, RAM is useful, and more is probably better. Oracle9i uses memory to avoid reading data from a hard drive disk. When a database user or application runs a query, the data is retrieved from disk and stored in memory as well as delivered to the user. Oracle9i saves the retrieved data, clinging to it in the hope that some other user or application will want that same data. When that happens, Oracle9i grabs the data straight out of its memory, avoiding a trip to the disk. Disk retrieval is hundreds of times slower than memory retrieval, so any time Oracle9i can reuse data stored in memory rather than go out to the disk, your response times will improve.

How Oracle9i uses memory

Oracle9i divides its memory allocation into several areas, called *caches*. The entire set of caches is called the *SGA,* or *System Global Area.*

Your SGA should not exceed the total RAM on your machine; otherwise, Oracle9i will have problems trying to use disk space to make up for missing RAM. This is called *paging* and should be avoided.

You can view the size of the SGA in SQL*Plus by typing this command:

```
SHOW SGA
```

The output looks like this:

```
Total System Global Area    118255568 bytes
Fixed Size                     282576 bytes
Variable Size                83886080 bytes
Database Buffers             33554432 bytes
Redo Buffers                   532490 bytes
```

The SGA size is changed by adjusting SGA-related parameters in the initialization parameters of your Oracle9i database instance. These can be viewed and modified within Instance Manager inside Console.

Enterprise Manager can help you determine what adjustments you should make to the SGA to improve performance speed.

Getting advice from Enterprise Manager

A lot of tools can help you tune memory for Oracle9i. Some, such as STATSPACK, are complex tools that require megabrains to use. Others, such as the Performance Overview Charts, help even a beginner get a clue.

Oracle9i also provides plenty of documentation on performance tuning. The best place to begin in the documentation is the *Oracle9i Database Performance Guide and Reference*.

The Performance Overview Charts have been improved and made easier to use in Oracle9i. Let's take a look at some of the features.

One area of memory that was difficult to tune before Oracle9i was the Program Global Area, or PGA. New settings allow you, as the DBA, to tell Oracle9i to automatically and dynamically adjust the PGA size for best performance. For databases with lots of online users, you should set the new initialization parameter, PGA_AGGREGATE_TARGET, at about 16% of total system memory.

What if you need advice about memory settings? Let's look at Enterprise Manager Console to see how you can seek advice from the Performance Overview Charts and the expert help screens inside the tool.

To check out the Performance Overview Charts, follow these steps:

1. **Start Console.**

    See Step 1 in the "Adding an index" section for details.

    Oracle Agent and Enterprise Management Server must be running before you start Console.

2. **Click the button to select the Login to the Oracle Management Server option.**

    The window displays boxes for logging into the Management Server.

3. **Type the login information, and then click OK.**

    a. **For the Administrator, type** SYSMAN.

    b. **For the Password, type** OEM_TEMP **or whatever the current password is for SYSMAN on your Management Server.**

    c. **For the Management Server, select the machine name where Enterprise Management Service is started.**

    The first time you log in as SYSMAN with the default password, a pop-up window appears and you are required to change the password. Type a new password, and then click OK to continue.

    Console's initial screen appears.

4. **Double-click the Databases folder.**

5. **Double-click the database you want to tune.**

    If this is the first time you have used Console or if you have not saved your login settings, you see a login screen. Otherwise, you see a list of Managers (including Instance, Schema, Security, and Storage).

6. **If you see a login screen, follow these steps to log in:**

    a. **For the Username, type** SYSTEM.

    b. **For the Password, type** MANAGER **or whatever the current password is for SYSTEM on your database.**

    c. **For the Connect As option, select Normal.**

    d. **Click to add a check mark to the Save As Local Preferred Credentials option.**

    e. **Click OK.**

    Console asks whether it's okay to save your credentials in a local encrypted file.

    f. **Click OK to continue.**

    The list of Managers (including Instance, Schema, Security, and Storage) appears.

7. **Choose Tools➪Diagnostics Pack➪Performance Overview.**

   This starts up the Performance Overview Charts, as shown in Figure 18-4.

8. **Click the green flag button next to the Database Memory label on the chart.**

   The flag is circled in Figure 18-4. A pop-up menu of subjects related to Database Memory appears near your mouse.

9. **Choose % Shared Pool Free, and then choose Advice.**

   A window appears with advice about the statistic on your chart, as shown in Figure 18-5. Reading this advice shows you how to monitor, adjust, or detect problems related to your Shared Pool. Bring your earplugs and your sunscreen.

10. **Close the advice window, the Performance Overview Charts, and finally Console by clicking the X box in the top-right corner of each window.**

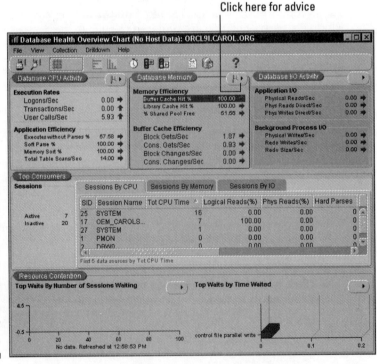

Figure 18-4: The Performance Overview Charts are dynamic and refresh every few minutes.

Figure 18-5:
Oracle9i has
built a
wealth of
expert
advice into
its tools.

As you can see, you could spend plenty of time perusing the information in
the Performance Overview Charts.

Suppose that just when you get your entire database system humming along,
you discover that one of your tables needs a new column! Curses, foiled
again. Read the next chapter to discover all the tricks for making corrections
to tables.

Chapter 19

Correcting Flaws

· ·

· ·

*O*ften, you create tables as you develop your plans — this is called the prototype (or "wing it!") method. You may want to read this chapter when you notice an error — such as a column that has the wrong datatype — just after you finish creating a table. Another time that you may scurry to these pages is when you have a table or *schema* (set of tables) that you want to update with more tables and additions. As the old swami sez: "Whatever the reason, now is the time to change things!"

Categories of Changes

You can *attempt* to make two kinds of changes in a table: the kind that you can make and the kind that you can't make. Oracle9i has rules about what parts of a table you can change. So if you need to change part of a table and Oracle9i says, "Not!," you can get around the rule only by dropping the table and then re-creating it. But don't worry: Later in this chapter, I show you how to do this without losing your data — or your mind.

Table 19-1 shows the breakdown of table changes by category. Each of these categories has its own section in the chapter, so look here for the change that you want to make and then head to the appropriate section for details on how to do it.

Table 19-1	Changes to Tables and Columns		
Description	Best Tool	Save Data first?	Drop/ Create Table?
Easiest to perform			
Lengthen column size	Schema Manager	No	No
Add new column (at end of table)	Schema Manager	No	No
Drop old column	Schema Manager	No	No
Change NOT NULL to NULL	Schema Manager	No	No
Disable constraint	Schema Manager	No	No
Drop constraint	Schema Manager	No	No
Drop index	Schema Manager	No	No
Drop table	Schema Manager	No	No
Change table storage	Schema Manager	No	No
Easy to perform			
Move table	SQL*Plus	No	No
Rename table	SQL*Plus	No	No
Change NULL to NOT NULL	SQL*Plus	No	No
Difficult to perform			
Shorten column size	SQL*Plus	Yes	No
Rename column	SQL*Plus	Yes	No
Most difficult to perform			
Reorder columns	Schema Manager and SQL*Plus	Yes	Yes
Add new column (to beginning or end of table)	Schema Manager and SQL*Plus	Yes	Yes

Changes that can be performed inside Schema Manager (which is in Enterprise Manager Console) are easiest because you don't have to write any SQL commands. Instead you just use your mouse. These changes list Schema Manager as the best tool (the second column in Table 19-1).

Changes best performed in SQL*Plus require you to write the SQL command yourself and execute it in SQL*Plus. I give examples of these in this chapter.

Changes that require saving data ("Yes" in the third column in Table 19-1) are harder to do. You must preserve the data, remove the data from the original table, make the change, and then restore the data.

Finally, changes that require dropping and recreating the table ("Yes" in the fourth column in Table 19-1) are the most difficult. When you drop and re-create a table, you must not only restore the original data, but also restore all the constraints, indexes, and storage parameters of the table and restore foreign keys that reference the table. Tricky, but doable.

This chapter covers all these kinds of changes. Enjoy! On top of that, at the end of the chapter, you find out how to change object tables. As they always say, "Nothing is constant in this world except change." Anyone who can accurately prove to me just who "they" are gets a free copy of my next book, *Godlike Alterations of the Time/Space Continuum For Dummies.*

Changing Columns

Changing column features is like taking care of your garden. Sometimes it's easy, like picking tomatoes. Other times it's hard, like weeding the green bean patch. This section covers both varieties of changes, starting with the super-easy stuff.

Baby Bear: Easy as porridge

This section shows you how to make the types of changes to columns that are a no-brainer. You can make these changes any time, regardless of what data is in the column that you plan to change. You can freely make these kinds of changes:

- Lengthen a column
- Add a new column
- Drop an old column

You can also make the following changes in certain circumstances without any additional steps:

✔ Shorten a column but only if the column is null in every table row. The next section describes how to handle a column with existing data.

✔ Change from NOT NULL to NULL but only when the column is not part of a primary key. Primary keys cannot be null.

✔ Change from NULL to NOT NULL but only when every row has data in the column. Otherwise, you have to fill in a value first using an UPDATE command.

✔ Change the datatype of a column but only when the column is null in every table row. Otherwise, it's better to add a new column with the desired datatype and drop the old column. See the next section.

In these cases, you must review the data in your table. The number of rows of data you have doesn't matter, nor does the contents of all the other columns of data. Focus on the column that you want to change. Look at the data in that column in every row of your table. If every single row has nulls in that column, you can go ahead and shorten the size or change the datatype of the column. If even one row contains data, you can't make the change without first doing something to that row of data. Refer to the "Mama Bear: A few medium steps" section for information on how to correct the data so that you can make the change.

Everything that you change in the table structure is changed in the table property page. To get to the table property page and start making changes using Schema Manager, follow these steps:

1. **Start Console.**

   On Windows platforms, choose Start➪Programs➪Oracle HOME2➪ Enterprise Manager Console. Note that the Oracle HOME2 label may have a different name, such as ORAHOME81, on your computer. The person who installed the software on your machine designates the name.

   On UNIX, Linux, or any other platform, type **oemapp console** at the operating-system command line.

   You see the logo screen for Oracle Enterprise Manager, and then the Oracle Enterprise Manager Console login window appears.

2. **Make sure the Launch Standalone option is selected, and then click OK.**

   Console's initial screen appears.

3. **Double-click the Databases folder.**

   All available databases are listed.

4. **Double-click the name of the database that you want to work on.**

5. **If you see a login screen, follow these steps to log in:**

   a. **For the Username, type** SYSTEM.

   b. **For the Password, type** MANAGER **or whatever the current password is for SYSTEM on your database.**

   c. For the Connect As option, select Normal.

   d. Click to add a check mark to the Save As Local Preferred Credentials option.

   e. Click OK.

   Console asks whether it's okay to save your credentials in a local encrypted file.

   f. Click OK to continue.

   The list of Managers (including Instance, Schema, Security, and Storage) appears.

6. **In the left half of the window, double-click the Schema icon.**

   Schema Manager appears, along with a list of schema objects below the Schema icon.

7. **In the left half of the window, double-click the Table folder.**

8. **Double-click the schema that owns the table that you want to change.**

   To follow along with my example, select the AMY schema.

9. **Select the table that needs correcting.**

   A properties page for the table appears in the right window. For the example, select the TICKET table.

10. **Type any changes that you want to make to the table.**

    As shown in Figure 19-1, you can make the following changes:

    - **Lengthen column.**

      To change a column length, type the length that you want in the Size box, or the Scale box, or both for that column. For the example, change the FULL_NAME column from 31 characters to 50 characters by typing **50** in the Size box in the FULL_NAME row.

    - **Add column at end of table.**

      Schema Manager always has a blank row at the end of the list of columns ready for you to add a new column. Just type the column name and so on to add the column.

    - **Remove a column.**

      Click the Drop Column icon in the lower-left corner of the Table Properties window. A new box appears. Select all the columns you want to drop, choose Drop Selected Columns as your operation, and then click the OK button.

    - **Shorten column (column has nulls in all rows).**

To shorten a column, all the rows must contain a null value in the column. If this is so, just type the change in the Size box, or the Scale box, or both, for that column. If not, go to the next section and follow those instructions.

- **Change from** NOT NULL **to** NULL **(column can't be in primary key).**

  Toggle the value in the Null? column for each row by clicking the box. A check mark means that nulls are allowed (NULL constraint). A red X means that nulls are not allowed (NOT NULL constraint).

  Note: If the column is part of the primary key for the table, you can't remove the NOT NULL constraint.

- **Change from** NULL **to** NOT NULL **(column has data in all rows).**

  Again, use the Null? box for the column and click to toggle the value. Remember that your table data must have a value in this column in every row to successfully change the column from NULL to NOT NULL. If you get an error like the following you must go to the next section and follow the instructions:

  ```
  ORA-02296: Cannot enable (...) - null values found.
  ```

- **Change datatype of column (column has nulls in all rows).**

  In the Datatype box for the column, select a new datatype. You can also change the datatype to object types if you select the schema that owns the object type in the Schema box (just left of the Datatype box) and then select the desired object type in the Datatype box.

11. **Click the Apply button when you're finished.**

    Schema Manager makes the change. If you don't see an error message, you can be sure that the change took place. (No news is good news in this case.)

    If you get an error message after you click the Apply button, you probably tried to change a column in a way that has other restrictions, as noted in Table 19-1. For example, you may have tried to change the size of a column from 20 characters to 10 characters. If the table has data in the column that you tried to change, you get an error message. Read the error message carefully to determine what's wrong. You may have to resort to the Mama Bear approach, discussed in the following section.

By the way, the SQL command for making these kinds of changes is

```
ALTER TABLE tablename MODIFY | DROP (columnname [changed]);
```

Replace *tablename* and *columnname* with the table and column, respectively, that you're working on. Replace *changed* with the changed datatype and length, or the changed NULL/NOT NULL constraint.

Change datatype here   Change to NULL or NOT NULL here

Change
length here

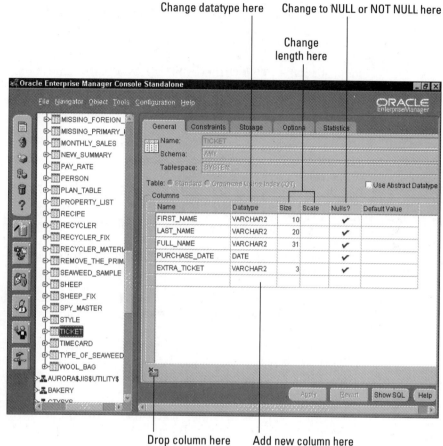

Figure 19-1:
Make
changes to
the column
attributes of
a table here.

Drop column here   Add new column here

For example, to change the length of the FULL_NAME column as I do in the
example, the SQL command is

```
-- 01_modifycolumn
ALTER TABLE AMY.TIMECARD
MODIFY (FULL_NAME VARCHAR2(50));
```

To remove a column, such as the CHANGE_DATE column, type

```
-- 02_dropcolumn
ALTER TABLE AMY.TIMECARD DROP (CHANGE_DATE);
```

Mama Bear: A few medium steps

Don't ask me why. Oh, go ahead and ask. *Reply hazy; ask again later.* Whatever the reason, Oracle9i has nitpicky rules about making changes in column attributes. My own theory is that these rules came about because of the space-saving conventions that Oracle9i uses when it stores table definitions and data. Shuffling the order of columns is more difficult when they're arranged in compact, abbreviated form. Just a theory, really.

You get an error message from Oracle if you try to make the following kinds of changes when you have data in a column you're trying to correct. These changes are

✔ Shorten a column (the column has data in some rows)

✔ Change the datatype of a column (the column has data in some rows)

One type of change is just the opposite. Every row *must have data* in the column for changing to NOT NULL.

The following two sections show you how to handle cases in which your data just doesn't fit into the restrictions. All these changes are performed in SQL*Plus. Follow these steps:

1. **Start SQL*Plus.**

   On Windows platforms, choose Start➪Programs➪Oracle HOME➪ Application Development➪SQL*Plus.

   On UNIX, Linux, or any other platform, type **sqlplus** at the operating-system prompt to start the command-line version of SQL*Plus.

2. **Log in as the table owner.**

   If you see a login window, follow these steps:

   a. **Type the user name and password. If you installed the sample schema, type** AMY **for the name and** AMY123 **for the password.**

   b. **In the Host String box, type the Oracle Net name of the Oracle9i instance on your local computer or on your network.**

      For a local database, you can usually leave this blank. For a database on a network, ask your administrator to provide you with a valid host string.

   c. **Click OK.**

      The SQL*Plus window appears.

If instead of a login window you see a prompt for a user name, follow these steps:

a. In the Username box, type AMY@*XXXX*, **replacing *XXXX* with the Oracle Net name of the Oracle9i instance on your local computer or on your network.**

For example, if you want to log into the ORCL database as AMY, you would type **AMY@ORCL**.

b. Press Enter.

c. Type the password.

If you log in as AMY, type **AMY123** for the password.

d. Press Enter.

The SQL prompt line appears. Your session may or may not have the Windows-like screen, but all the commands work the same.

If the column must be null . . .

Changes that require every row in the table to have a null value are

- ✔ Making a column shorter
- ✔ Changing the datatype

Because you can add and drop columns more easily than shortening or changing the datatypes of existing columns, I suggest you consider an alternative to modifying the existing column: Add a new column that is the correct length or datatype. Then use an UPDATE command to copy data from the old column to the new column, and drop the old column.

But if you must change that pesky existing column, here is how to do it. If any row of your table has data in the column that you're about to change, you can't make the change right away. You must first eliminate the data in this column for all the rows in your table. If you use Schema Manager to try to make the change without fixing the data, you get an error message, stating the problem. This error message may be similar to these messages:

```
ORA-01439: column to be modified must be empty
to change datatype
ORA-01441: column to be modified must be empty
to decrease column length
```

Your two choices for fixing the data are

- ✔ **Get rid of it.** Think about it. Do you really need that data? Maybe the data is just test data anyway and isn't worth the hassle of saving. Maybe just retyping it later is faster.

✔ **Preserve it.** Often, your data is valuable, and you should preserve it. In the "Saving the data" section later in this chapter, I show you how to preserve your data and still make the change that you want to make.

Throwing out the data

Congratulations — you've decided that you don't need the data in your column after all. In this case, you can run the SQL command that removes the data quickly. Log into SQL*Plus to run your SQL commands.

Before running the following SQL command, make sure that you don't need the data in the column you're updating.

The general format for removing all data from a column is

```
UPDATE tablename SET columnname = NULL;
```

Replace *tablename* and *columnname* with the actual table and column that you're working on.

For example, this SQL command changes all the data in the EXTRA_TICKET column of the TICKET table:

```
-- 03_set_null
UPDATE TICKET SET EXTRA_TICKET = NULL;
```

By the way, if you change your mind after running this command, issue a ROLLBACK command:

```
ROLLBACK;
```

The ROLLBACK command restores the data but it works only during your current SQL session and only if you haven't issued any DDL commands. A DDL (Data Definition Language) command is any command that creates, modifies, or removes a database object such as a table or index. For example, the ALTER TABLE command is a DDL command.

After updating the data, issue a COMMIT command to save your work to the database:

```
COMMIT;
```

Saving the data

Many times, you may want to keep your data. In these cases, you can use SQL*Plus to save your data in a table that you create just for that purpose. Then you make your change and put the data back in the table. Start SQL*Plus and follow along with this example.

Suppose that you use a table called DAILY_SALES to track your total sales each day. You decide to shorten the maximum size of the SALES_AMOUNT column from ten digits to eight digits. Because you have good data in the table, you definitely want to save the data. Before you adjust the column size, you use SQL*Plus to create a holding column for the data. The holding column is added to the end of your DAILY_SALES table and will be dropped when you are finished.

You create the holding column by using this SQL code:

```
-- 04_addcolumn
ALTER TABLE DAILY_SALES
ADD (HOLD_SALES_AMOUNT NUMBER(10,2));
```

Oracle9i responds

```
Table altered.
```

Next, you copy the data from the original column to the new column as follows:

```
-- 05_copydata
UPDATE DAILY_SALES
SET HOLD_SALES_AMOUNT = SALES_AMOUNT;
```

Oracle9i complies and says

```
17 rows updated.
```

Next, null out the data in the original column:

```
-- 06_set_null
UPDATE DAILY_SALES
SET SALES_AMOUNT = NULL;
```

Oracle9i complies and says

```
17 rows updated.
```

Now you can modify the column size. Here is the SQL code for making the change:

```
-- 07_altercolumnsize
ALTER TABLE DAILY_SALES
  MODIFY (SALE_AMOUNT NUMBER(8,2));
```

Oracle9i complies and says

```
Table altered.
```

Finally, you copy the data back into the newly modified column, as follows:

```
-- 08_copydata
UPDATE DAILY_SALES
SET SALES_AMOUNT = HOLD_SALES_AMOUNT;
```

Oracle9i answers

```
17 rows updated.
```

The final step removes the holding column you created:

```
-- 09_dropholdingcolumn
ALTER TABLE DAILY_SALES
 DROP (HOLD_SALE_AMOUNT);
```

Oracle9i complies and says

```
Table altered.
```

You've completed the task. Congratulations! Well done.

Before you go to all this trouble, make sure that the data is worth saving. This project is like cleaning out your closet. As you remove all the stuff from your closet, you notice how much of it you don't want or can't squeeze into anyway. Don't waste time saving data that is old or incomplete or that you haven't been able to fit into since high school; send it off to the Salvation Army thrift store for someone else to enjoy.

Set column from NULL to NOT NULL

The second kind of restricted column change requires that every row have some data in the column that you want to change. Only one change falls into this category: changing a column constraint from null values allowed to null values not allowed. Every row in the table must comply with this new constraint. In other words, all the rows need data in the column that you want to change. If any of the column's rows include nulls, you get an error message like the one shown here, which informs you that you can't change the column:

```
ORA-02296: cannot enable ... null values found.
```

What do you do if you have null values in this column? Decide what to put in each row that contains nulls and then update the rows with the value. Use SQL*Plus to run the SQL statement that plugs in a default value for every null value.

The steps for starting SQL*Plus are shown earlier in the chapter.

A simple option that may work for you is plugging a standard default value into every row that has null in the column. Here is an example:

```
-- 10_fillinnullcolumn
UPDATE CONTACT_LIST
SET REASONS = 'UNKNOWN'
WHERE REASONS IS NULL;
```

Oracle9i answers

```
1 row updated.
```

You can update your column any way that you want. You can use any valid update command, including those update commands with subqueries and correlated subqueries. Use your head.

After you fill in the default data, you can go back to the "Baby Bear: Easy as porridge" section and make your table changes. Easy as porridge.

Rename a column

To rename a column, you must create a new column with the new name, copy the data into the new column, and then drop the old column. This effectively moves the column to the end of the table.

To rename a column without changing its order in the table, skip to the "Papa Bear: A lotta steps" section because you have to drop and re-create the whole table.

Here's a true example of why you might need to rename a column: Your sales force has gone ballistic at the name of a column in the database. For some reason, the fact that they must type the name of a city into a column called TOWN is totally unacceptable to them. You, being a peace-loving manager, announce that indeed, you shall rename the column to CITY! Applause rings out and flowers litter the stage before your podium.

Down to business! To rename a column, first log into SQL*Plus, as shown earlier in the chapter.

Next, add the column with its new name to the end of the table.

```
-- 11_addnewcolumn
ALTER TABLE HUMAN
ADD (CITY VARCHAR2(20));
```

Oracle9i replies

```
Table altered.
```

Copy the data from the old column to the new column (skip this step if the old column contains no data):

```
-- 12_copyold_to_new
UPDATE HUMAN
SET CITY = TOWN;
```

Oracle9i replies

```
5 rows updated.
```

Finally, drop the old column:

```
-- 13_dropoldcolumn
ALTER TABLE HUMAN
DROP (TOWN);
```

Oracle9i replies

```
Table altered.
```

That wasn't so bad after all!

Papa Bear: A lotta steps

Changes that involve restructuring your table are the hardest. These kinds of changes include the following:

- Reordering columns
- Adding a column to the beginning or middle of the table
- Renaming a column (while keeping its order intact)

Oracle9i's great storage efficiency and retrieval speed come at a cost: Changing certain parts of a table structure can be laborious. Here's what you do when you need to make these kinds of changes:

1. **Copy the table, including the data, to a new table. Skip this step if the table contains no data or if you can throw out the data permanently.**

2. **Document all dependent foreign-key constraints, plus all dependencies such as indexes, constraints on the table, and table privileges.**

3. **Remove the old table.**

4. **Rebuild the new table, incorporating the changes.**

5. **Copy the data from the old table that you created in Step 1 to the new table. Skip this step if you skipped Step 1.**

6. **Re-create all the dependent foreign keys documented in Step 2.**

7. **Re-create all dependencies documented in Step 2.**

How do you perform these tasks? Glad you asked. Watch closely as I perform magical feats with a dazzling combination of Schema Manager and SQL*Plus.

Now you're ready to embark on a multistep journey to restructure the entire known intergalactic time-space continuum. Well, you restructure a table for starters.

Because this kind of change is so difficult, think of ways to avoid it. For example, instead of renaming a column, how about doing this instead: Add a new column with the good name, copy the data from the old column to the new column using the UPDATE command, and then drop the old column. Taking these steps saves a lot of work. Also, consider the reasons behind changing the order of columns — these reasons are usually for aesthetics and have no real bearing on performance. If this is the case, why not leave the columns as they are?

Danger, Will Robinson! One of the numbered steps later in this section removes a table from the database. When you remove a table, you also remove three other important database elements:

- ✔ Any indexes that you created for the table; they must be re-created.
- ✔ Any active foreign keys in other tables that refer to this table's primary key; they should be disabled beforehand and then enabled after the table is re-created.
- ✔ Any privileges that you gave for the table; they must be granted again.

The Change Manager tool in Enterprise Manager Console may be a great way to save you time and trouble because it remembers constraints for you.

Being a diligent DBA, you have discovered that the CONTACT_LIST table owned by AMY is sadly lacking. Who designed this table in the first place? Well, at any rate, you decide that adding two new columns for storing information about the reviewer of each contact should take care of the problem. The two columns are

- ✔ REVIEWED_BY. This stores the name of the person who checks up on the contact for the first time.
- ✔ REVIEWED_DATE. This, of course, stores the date of the review.

These columns need to be added next to the existing column, REVIEWED_CASE, rather than at the end because you have a generator that creates all your table update screens and uses the order of the columns as the order of the data entry fields. So, you are faced with the task of inserting two columns into the middle of the table.

Now, follow these steps to accomplish your task.

1. **Start SQL*Plus and log in.**

   For details, see the steps at the beginning of the "Mama Bear: A few medium steps" section.

2. **Create a new table that contains a copy of the old table's data.**

   ```
   -- 14_createholdingtable
   CREATE TABLE CONTACT_LIST_HOLD AS
   SELECT * FROM CONTACT_LIST;
   ```

3. **Start Console.**

   For details, see the steps at the beginning of the "Baby Bear: Easy as porridge" section.

4. **Right-click the CONTACT_LIST table and choose Save Properties.**

   A window appears for choosing a location, file name, and format for a report.

   The Save Properties Report is a new feature in Oracle9i's Enterprise Manager Console. The report describes the table and generates a `CREATE TABLE` SQL command for `CONTACT_LIST` that you can use later. Make a note of the file location and name.

5. **Click OK to accept the default values and generate the report.**

   A status window appears briefly. When this disappears, the report has been generated.

6. **Right-click the CONTACT_LIST table and choose Show Dependencies.**

   A window appears, listing dependencies (items that the table needs for its own existence, such as tables referenced in foreign keys).

7. **Click the Dependents tab.**

   All tables with foreign keys that reference this table appear. These must be disabled before you can safely remove the table. Figure 19-2 shows that the `CONTACT_HISTORY` table is dependent on the `CONTACT_LIST` table.

8. **Document all foreign keys.**

   Use Schema Manager to view foreign keys in other tables. For the example, click the CONTACT_HISTORY table. Then click the Constraints tab and note that the CONTACT_FK constraint references the CONTACT_LIST table.

9. **Remove the old table.**

   Right-click the table (CONTACT_LIST) and choose Remove. When Oracle9i pops up a confirmation window, click Yes.

Figure 19-2:
Oracle9i's
new report
describes
all the
attributes of
a table and
even
generates
the SQL
command to
create the
table.

10. **View the Properties report in your browser.**

    The report is in HTML format, so it can be viewed with a Web browser. Open your browser, and then open the file that was generated. In Internet Explorer, you can open a file by choosing File⇨Open and then clicking Browse to find and select the file.

11. **Scroll down and then select and copy the entire SQL command that creates the table (object definition).**

    You will be pasting this into a file in the next step. In Windows Explorer, click and hold the mouse to highlight the text. Release the mouse and click Ctrl+C to copy the highlighted text. Figure 19-3 shows a portion of the report.

12. **In SQL*Plus, open a new file named** CREATETABLE **by typing this command and pressing Enter:**

    ```
    EDIT CREATETABLE
    ```

13. **Paste the copied text into the** CREATETABLE **file.**

    In Windows, simply click Ctrl+V.

14. **Edit the file, making adjustments to the command as needed.**

    For the CONTACT_LIST table, add two new columns right after the REVIEWED_CASE column. The SQL for these two columns looks like this:

    ```
    REVIEWED_BY      VARCHAR2(20).
    REVIEWED_DATE    DATE,
    ```

15. **Save and close the file.**

    This returns you to the SQL*Plus session.

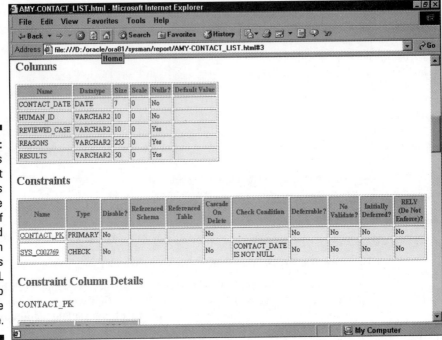

Figure 19-3:
Oracle9i's new report describes all the attributes of a table and even generates the SQL command to create the table.

16. **Create the table by executing the file you edited using this command:**

    ```
    START CREATETABLE
    ```

    Oracle9i replies

    ```
    Table created.
    ```

17. **Copy the data from the holding table into the new table by typing this command in SQL*Plus and pressing Enter:**

    ```
    -- 14_copyrows
    INSERT INTO CONTACT_LIST
    SELECT CONTACT_DATE, HUMAN_ID, REVIEWED_CASE,.
    NULL. NULL. REASONS. RESULTS
    FROM CONTACT_LIST_HOLD;
    ```

18. **Commit the changes by typing this command in SQL*Plus and pressing Enter:**

    ```
    COMMIT;
    ```

19. **Exit SQL*Plus by typing** EXIT **and pressing Enter.**

20. **Return to Console, where you should still have Schema Manager open.**

21. **Re-create any foreign key constraints that were disabled.**

    Refer to Chapter 9 to refresh your memory.

22. **Re-create any additional dependents.**

    Refer to the dependencies report and use it to re-create indexes or other dependencies that were on your original table.

23. **Remove the holding table.**

    Right-click the table and choose Remove. For this example, remove the CONTACT_LIST_HOLD table. Schema Manager displays a window to verify your choice.

24. **Verify the table name and click Yes.**

    You've completed the final steps of restructuring your table.

Finished! You've restructured your table just as you wanted it. This kind of change is difficult to do and requires careful attention to detail. Good job!

Now, for a real treat, read on to take a look at how to change tables.

Changing Tables

In Table 19-1, five changes involve the table, rather than the columns inside the table. These are

- Dropping the index
- Dropping the table
- Changing the table storage
- Moving the table
- Renaming the table

The first three changes can be made in Schema Manager. For the last two, you must use SQL*Plus. So, let's go ahead and take a quick tour of where to make all these changes.

Schema Manager table changes

Begin the process of dropping an index, a table, or changing table storage by logging into Console and displaying the Table Properties window of the table you want to change. This is described in the "Baby Bear: Easy as porridge" section.

Drop an index or table

Dropping a table is simple: Just right-click the table in Schema Manager and choose Remove from the pop-up menu.

To drop an index, you must first find the index in Schema Manager.

Take a look at the CONTACT_HISTORY table owned by AMY. Imagine that you have run the Oracle Expert tool and it has recommended that you remove the CONTACT_HISTORY_X index in this table.

To drop the index, follow these steps:

1. **Double-click the table icon for** CONTACT_HISTORY.

2. **Double-click on the Indexes folder.**

3. **Click the index that you want to drop.**

   Figure 19-4 shows the window that appears when you select an index in Schema Manager.

4. **Right-click the index and choose Remove.**

   Oracle9i asks if you want to drop the index.

5. **Click Yes to complete the task.**

That was so easy, let's look at the next one, which is just as easy.

Change table storage

Another suggestion frequently made by Oracle Expert is to change the storage parameters of a table. The more uniform you make your table storage parameters, the easier it is for Oracle9i to allocate storage and use all the corners of your datafile efficiently.

To modify table storage, follow these simple steps:

1. **Click the Storage tab of the Table Properties window in Schema Manager.**

   Figure 19-5 shows the Storage tab. Values that appear dimmed can't be changed.

2. **Type the changes.**

3. **Click Apply.**

   Oracle9i makes the change. The Apply button appears dimmed, indicating that Oracle9i is finished.

It's good that these things are easy because it saves you a lot of time and effort as a DBA.

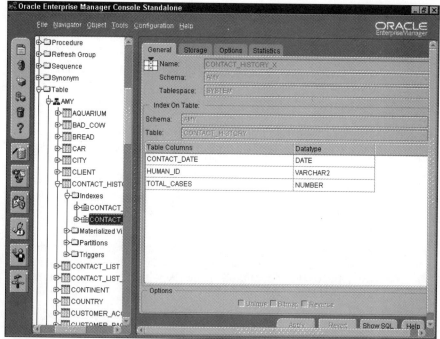

Figure 19-4:
An index
has a
property
window
similar to a
table.

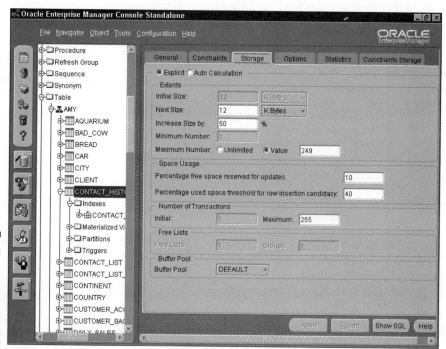

Figure 19-5:
Change
storage
settings by
typing in the
boxes.

SQL*Plus table changes: Move or rename a table

To move or rename a table, you have to write some SQL code. You should log into SQL*Plus, as described earlier in this chapter in the "Mama Bear: A few medium steps" section.

Moving a table to a different tablespace can make your system more efficient by spreading the reading and writing of data to disks across several disks.

To move a table, use the following SQL syntax:

```
ALTER TABLE tablename MOVE tablespace
```

For example, suppose that the CLIENT table owned by AMY was accidentally created in the SYSTEM tablespace. Because Oracle9i recommends that only system-related tables reside in the SYSTEM tablespace, you decide to move the table to the USERS tablespace. Type the following command in SQL*Plus and press Enter:

```
-- 16_movetable
ALTER TABLE CLIENT MOVE USERS;
```

Oracle9i replies

```
Table altered.
```

Renaming a table has its own unique syntax:

```
RENAME oldname TO newname
```

Suppose that the CLIENT table has grown to hold clients all over the world. To reflect this, you rename it to WORLDWIDE_CLIENT. Type the following command in SQL*Plus and press Enter:

```
-- 17_renametable
RENAME CLIENT TO WORLDWIDE_CLIENT;
```

Oracle9i replies

```
Table altered.
```

And now for something completely different: object tables.

Modifying Object Tables and Object Types

Here you have an interesting problem. When you make an object table, you identify what object type is to be used for each row in the object table. The attributes that you see when you look at the table in Schema Manager are actually the attributes of the object type.

You can modify a few characteristics of the object table, as shown in the following section. Adding or removing attributes in an object table, however, must be performed by modifying the underlying object type, which is discussed in the second section.

Modifying object tables

The only changes to the attributes that you can make to the object table are

- ✔ Changing NULL to NOT NULL
- ✔ Adding a default value
- ✔ Adding constraints, such as primary-key or check constraints

You handle these changes the same way that you do with relational tables, so you can follow the directions in the previous sections of this chapter. Refer to Chapter 9 for details on how to create a primary key.

Modifying object types

When you modify an object type, the changes are inherited by all the object tables and all the object types that use the changed object type.

If you're not sure which object type was used to create an object table, you can get some help from the table properties window in Schema Manager. To view this window, follow these steps:

1. **Start Console, as described earlier in the chapter.**

2. **Click the object table that you're interested in.**

   A properties window for the table appears in the right window. For my example, I selected the BREAD_OBJ table in the BAKERY schema. Figure 19-6 shows the properties window. Notice that if you peer intently at the window, you can just make out the object type that defines the object table rows.

Object type

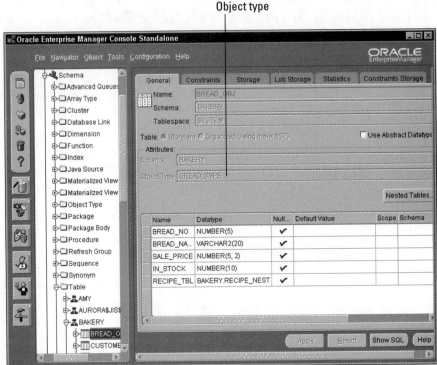

Figure 19-6:
Make all the
adjustments
you need to
your column
definitions.

To modify an object type, use SQL*Plus. You can add, change, or remove an attribute in an object type. Following is the syntax for adding an attribute to an object type:

```
ALTER TYPE typename
ADD ATTRIBUTE (attributename datatype)
CASCADE;
```

Replace *typename*, *attributename*, and *datatype* with the names and datatype. The CASCADE parameter tells Oracle9i to make the change to all dependent objects and object types.

For example, to add a new attribute called MANUFACTURER to the INGREDIENT_ TYPE object type owned by BAKERY, use this SQL command:

```
-- 18_addattribute
ALTER INGREDIENT_TYPE
ADD ATTRIBUTE (MANUFACTURER VARCHAR2(40))
CASCADE;
```

Modifying an attribute uses the same syntax as adding, except you replace ADD with MODIFY.

For example, to modify the MANUFACTURER attribute to be 60 characters long, use this command:

```
-- 19_changeattribute
ALTER INGREDIENT_TYPE
MODIFY ATTRIBUTE (MANUFACTURER VARCHAR2(60))
CASCADE;
```

When removing an attribute, use the following syntax:

```
ALTER TYPE typename
ADD ATTRIBUTE (attributename)
CASCADE;
```

Replace *typename* and *attributename* with the actual names. The CASCADE parameter tells Oracle9i to make the change to all dependent objects and object types. For example, to remove the MANUFACTURER attribute from the INGREDIENT_TYPE object type owned by BAKERY, use this SQL command:

```
-- 20_dropattribute
ALTER INGREDIENT_TYPE
DROP ATTRIBUTE (MANUFACTURER)
CASCADE;
```

The Oracle Change Management Pack — Something New to Try!

The Change Management Pack is an extra addition to Oracle's Enterprise Manager that you can install from a free download from Oracle's Technet Web site (technet.oracle.com). I found it an interesting tool, but you may find that it takes a bit of time to begin using its more advanced features.

For starters, I find that the DB Quick Change feature is useful when you have a database schema change that requires you to drop and re-create a table. In a previous section of this chapter ("Papa Bear: A Lotta Steps"), I show you how to go through about two dozen steps to add a column in the middle of a table. DB Quick Change can handle this task with fewer steps, especially when it comes to restoring indexes and foreign keys that are lost when you drop the table.

The installation of the Change Management Pack also installs the Oracle Tuning Pack and Performance Monitor. All of these are fun tools to explore! Remember, Chapter 18 covers the Performance Overview Charts, and Chapter 17 explores the Tuning Pack.

To get going on a quick database change, follow along with these steps. Make sure that Enterprise Management Server is running before you begin:

1. **Click the Change Management Pack icon.**

   This icon is along the left side of the Console panel. If you hold your mouse cursor over the icon, a pop-up text box displays "Change Management Pack." Click this icon. Another icon scrolls out of the first icon. (Oracle calls these icons that slide out of another icon *drawers*.)

2. **Click the Change Manager icon.**

   Change Manager appears, as shown in Figure 19-7.

3. **In the right window, click DB Quick Change.**

   This opens the DB Quick Change tool, which is a wizard of sorts.

4. **Follow along with the wizard pages and select a table to change.**

   For this example, select the FISH table in the AMY schema. Figure 19-8 shows the DB Quick Change page at this point. This should look familiar because it is almost identical to the table properties page in Schema Manager.

5. **Make changes here, as you would in Schema Manager, and then click Next.**

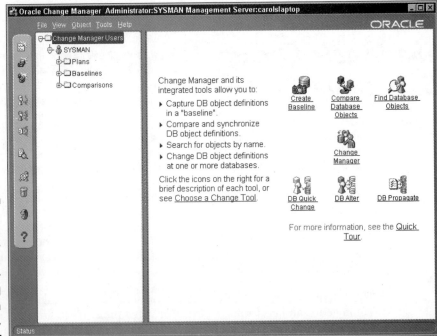

Figure 19-7: Change Manager has a navigator and a tool selection list.

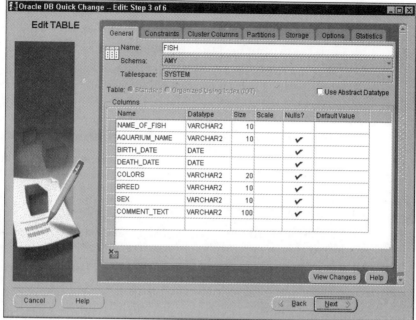

Figure 19-8:
DB Quick
Change
appears to
have stolen
its format
from
Schema
Manager.

For the example, add a new column called FAVORITE_COLOR after the column BIRTH_DATE. Be sure to click the Nulls? box to allow nulls in the new column. Change the length of the COMMENT_TEXT column to 250 characters. Move the COLORS column up one by right-clicking and choosing Move Up. Recall that in Schema Manager, you were not allowed to insert columns in the middle of an existing table or move existing columns! Here, you are able to do so. The View Changes button gives you a quick list of all the changes you have made on the screen.

6. Type a plan name, and then click Next.

The plan name stores documentation about the change. Change Manager uses plans in its other tools, so creating a plan is standard when using Change Manager.

7. Click Generate to create a script for the changes.

After you click Generate, you see two things: the Impact report, which lists all the things that your change will affect, and the Script summary, which lists what the DB Quick Change script plans to do to the database. If you want, you can pause at this point to get a good understanding of the mind behind the DB Quick Change wizard.

8. Click the Next button.

The Execution Log appears.

9. **Click the Execute button to run the script.**

   The wizard gives you one last chance to change your mind.

10. **Click Yes to continue barreling along.**

    The script is executed. In this example, the script renames the original table, creates a new table, copies rows from the old table to the new table, and then drops the old table. Figure 19-9 shows you the results window you see.

11. **Click the Keep button to finalize these changes to the database.**

    If you click the Undo button at this point, the wizard will try to undo all the changes it did to the database. Depending on what it did, it may or may not succeed. The wizard sends a warning if it can't undo changes.

12. **Click Finish to end the process.**

    This ends the DB Quick Change feature and returns you to Change Manager.

13. **Click the X in the top-right corner to leave Change Manager and return to Console.**

Consider using this new tool as an alternative when you are faced with changes to many tables or changes to multiple databases.

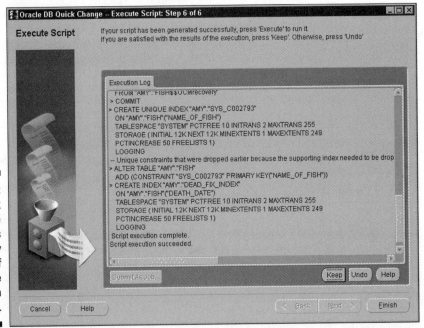

Figure 19-9:
DB Quick Change makes child's play out of database schema changes.

Part V

The Part of Tens

The 5th Wave — By Rich Tennant

"I STARTED DESIGNING DATABASE SOFTWARE SYSTEMS AFTER SEEING HOW EASY IT WAS TO DESIGN OFFICE FURNITURE."

In this part . . .

This is my favorite part. Here are a couple of short and sweet chapters, each containing ten gold-encrusted jewels for your treasure chest of Oracle9i know-how. You leave this section with a trick up your sleeve for every occasion. Plus, you find out about all the Internet tools that Oracle9i has to offer — there's something for everyone in here.

Have fun! I did!

Chapter 20

Ten Tips for Good Design

In this chapter, I share some useful ideas that may lighten your load when you sit down to create an Oracle9i database schema of your own. Then again, I guess that sitting down already sort of lightens your load, huh? These ideas save you time and make it easier to convince your boss that you know what you're doing.

Name Tables and Columns Creatively and Clearly

Scott and his cat, Tiger, who prowl the bowels of every Oracle9i database from here to Mars, probably had something to do with the rules about naming Oracle9i tables, columns, and so on. Refer to Chapter 2 to see the naming rules spelled out in detail. When you know the rules, you can create names as you see fit.

The best way to annoy your own brain is to name tables and columns inconsistently. Imagine that you own a real estate business. Figure 20-1 shows two of the tables that you use. One of the tables, called HOME, has a column called HOME_DESC in which you enter a short description of the house. Another table, called LAND, has a column called LAND_DESCR in which you enter a description of the land. You have abbreviated *description* two different ways: DESC and DESCR.

Abbreviations should be spelled the same in all columns

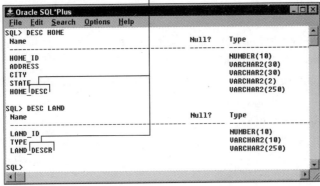

Figure 20-1:
The pitfall of naming columns inconsistently is that you must memorize the differences.

A month later, you write a query using the LAND table and type LAND_DESC by mistake. Because you weren't consistent in the way you abbreviated *description,* you need to look up the exact column name.

You multiply this problem each time you add another table designer to your company's team of designers. Each person has his or her own style for naming columns, tables, indexes, and so on. Soon, you have to keep a list by your side that contains the name of every table and every column, just to keep all the names straight.

Make sure that you establish a naming standard to share with the group. Establish clear and concise naming standards for tables, columns, indexes, primary keys, foreign keys, synonyms, views, and roles so that others can quickly understand your table design. Decide ahead of time what abbreviations and acronyms you plan to use; then be consistent. Don't hesitate to use force, threats, bribes, or name-calling to make your team members see things your way.

Get creative in your names so that they truly describe their real-life counterparts. Suppose that your LAND table has a column called TYPE, as shown in Figure 20-2. What does that name mean? Type of what? Land? Soil? Vegetation? Perhaps it means the type of selling contract or type of parcel.

Column name should be more meaningful

Figure 20-2:
Is this type
of type the
type you
think it is?
Not my type,
for sure.

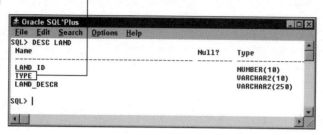

A table and its columns are much like a filing drawer. Have you ever tried valiantly to find a letter that you know you filed but can't recall which folder you filed it in? Perhaps you asked your spouse to get a paper from your desk drawer or file drawer at home, but you had a hard time describing exactly where you wanted your spouse to look, even though you could clearly visualize the place. The more intuitively you name your tables and columns, the better.

Here's another example of how not to name columns. This problem crops up even in commercial databases. It appears when a table evolves to handle a more diverse amount of data than you originally designed it to hold. Often, one column becomes obsolete, and you need a new column. Rather than create a new column, you recycle the old column, using it for new data. What you get is a single column containing a mixture of data. A column named MANUFACTURER, for example, initially stored only manufacturers' names, but now it also stores distributors' names. You have no way of telling whether you're looking at the name of a manufacturer or a distributor.

Look Before You Leap (Design Before You Build)

I find that a little planning goes a long way. Grasping the big picture of your database project may seem overwhelming. Even so, no matter how big the project appears to be, when you have a vision for it and can see that vision as a whole in your mind, you're better equipped to create the product. I don't mean that you have to know how you'll build the database; you can figure out the details as you go along. I mean that you need to picture the final product. What will it look like on the computer screen? If you don't know what it will look like, pretend you do at first. Who will use it and how? Who on your team is helping you? Would you like fries with that?

Envisioning the final product this way may seem silly, but years of designing and leading database projects has convinced me that doing so really works. Fixing a vision of the result in some tangible way (how it feels, looks, and sounds) can smooth out the process tremendously. Vision is critical. Conveying your vision to others is also critical.

Go Ahead, Leap! (Build a Prototype)

Building a prototype has become standard operating procedure these days for projects large and small. A *prototype* is a small working model of the product. The prototype may work on a small scale, or it may be a simulation. With an Oracle9i database, you can easily build the tables that you plan to use. By adding only 10 or 20 rows to your tables, you can experiment with queries, relationships, reports, or online screens built with Oracle Forms or other software.

If you're on your own using Oracle9i, not much stands in the way of experimenting. In a larger organization, you may have to follow some ground rules. When planning your prototype, include these critical portions of your project:

- ✔ **Bottlenecks.** Bottlenecks are the parts that can slow you down, such as converting data from an old database.

- ✔ **Popular features.** Include the features that you know people are excited about. One feature that many projects include is a table that stores multimedia files.

- ✔ **A little of everything.** Add a small portion from each major part of your entire plan. Incorporating small parts of your plan helps you refine the prototype so that when you're ready to create the real thing, you have valuable experience under your belt.

Don't be afraid to throw out the entire prototype. The beauty of a prototype is its disposability. In the beginning, put a small amount of time and effort into a prototype so that if you go down the wrong road, you don't lose too much time and energy. You can create another prototype. You can create two more prototypes. Ideally, you're paid by the hour. Later, if your prototype seems to be working, continue developing it as a springboard to the final product.

Share — Don't Reinvent the Wheel

Share information, share ideas, share your fears, and share your new red bike. Tell others that you'll even share your *Oracle9i For Dummies* book with them, and then go buy several copies of the book to share. Remember that others have gone down the same path that you're traveling, unless you're really on the cutting edge.

People are usually proud to share what they know. Don't be afraid to ask for help. Meeting with your coworkers can bring you a fresh perspective that helps speed up your design and development time.

A great resource is the International Oracle Users Group. The International Oracle Users Group–Americas (IOUG-A) is an independent, not-for-profit organization of users of Oracle products and services. The group's goal is to help you, the Oracle9i user, create great databases with Oracle9i. The IOUG-A publishes a newsletter and holds meetings across the country. The group also has a European branch.

Another great resource is the Oracle Technet Web site at `technet.oracle.com`. This site gives you access to discussion forums on the hottest Oracle topics, such as XML, Java, and Oracle9i. Register for free — after you register, you can download advanced copies of Oracle's products, read White Papers (technical how-to guides from the experts), and get sample code.

Remember That Primary Keys Are Your Friends

Primary keys form a core for your tables. Foreign keys contain primary keys from other tables. Primary keys are among the few pieces of data that you must carry in multiple tables. You can retrieve all the other data in a row from a table when you know the primary key.

The size and intelligence of primary keys help you streamline tables. The primary key should be small and stupid (not intelligent), which sounds strange, especially to my single friends. "Small and stupid?" they ask. "That was my last date!" Allow me to explain why primary keys should be small and stupid.

Small keys take up less room

Any column that holds a 4-digit number takes up less space than a column that holds 20 characters. This obvious fact is magnified when the column is a primary key. People almost always copy primary keys to other tables as foreign keys. The more rows that you have in the second table (the one with the foreign key), the more space that you use. Saving 16 characters in several thousand rows may seem insignificant at first, but it does make a difference.

Nonintelligent keys are easy to maintain

An *intelligent key* (as opposed to a nonintelligent key) is a column or set of columns that you use as the primary key for a table and at the same time use to store meaningful data. (My musician husband suggests B-flat minor.)

A nonintelligent key is a column, or set of columns, whose sole purpose is to be the primary key for the table. (Definitely C major.) The advantage of using a nonintelligent key as the primary key in your table lies in its stability. No matter what happens to the data in that row, the data in the primary key remains the same. This advantage is magnified as soon as you duplicate the primary key in the foreign key of another table.

The primary disadvantage in using intelligent keys is that this type of key can and does change over time. You must always change any foreign key that uses this primary key to match. This can change a simple single row update into a cascading update involving several rows in many tables. Even though it is possible to specify cascading updates automatically when you define a foreign key, the overhead of this operation may slow down your response time.

What is an intelligent key, anyway? An *intelligent key* is a primary key that has meaning for the row of data.

Suppose that you, as self-proclaimed ruler of the universe, have a table called HUMAN that tracks this tiny corner of your domain. This table helps you locate your subjects and call them on your cellular phone. The primary key, HUMAN_ID, is a unique identifier that you create for your subjects. This key is an intelligent key because it contains information about the person rather than a simple sequential number. HUMAN_ID has two parts: a code number that identifies the town that a person lives in and a sequential number assigned when you hand out the person's ID card. The sequential number is not unique by itself, but it is unique within the town.

Figure 20-3 shows the table with example rows. The figure also shows how two other tables, CONTACT_LIST and PROPERTY_LIST, connect with the HUMAN table. These tables have foreign keys that reference the HUMAN table's primary key. Now you have an intelligent key replicated as a foreign key in two tables. This setup seems fine until something happens that causes you to reconsider your choice of the intelligent key. Read on — the suspense thickens.

One day, a subject moves to another town. You forgot to impose a law preventing this sort of nonconformist act. Now the primary key (the intelligent key) contains the wrong town code, so you need to change the key to keep the data in your table accurate. You assign the person a brand-new HUMAN_ID with the correct town code and a new sequential number. You print a new ID card for your loyal but mobile subject and then go about modifying your data.

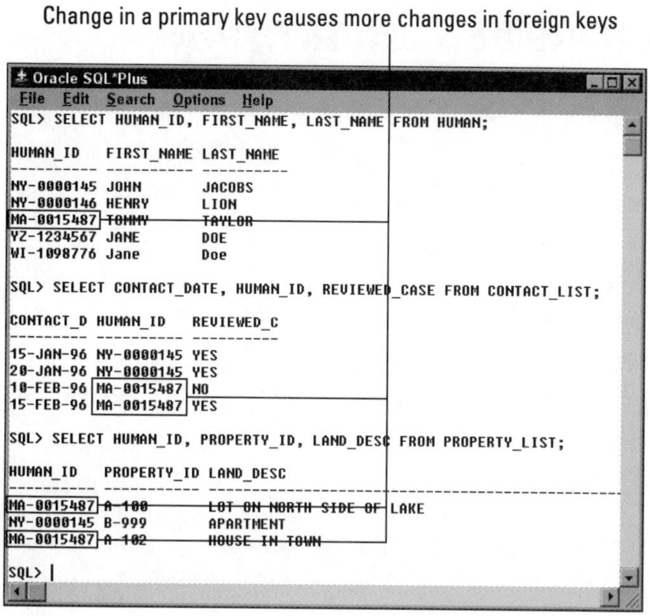

Change in a primary key causes more changes in foreign keys

Figure 20-3:
When a primary key changes, all related records in other tables must change also.

```
Oracle SQL*Plus                                          _ □ ×
File  Edit  Search  Options  Help
SQL> SELECT HUMAN_ID, FIRST_NAME, LAST_NAME FROM HUMAN;

HUMAN_ID     FIRST_NAME  LAST_NAME
----------   ----------  ---------
NY-0000145   JOHN        JACOBS
NY-0000146   HENRY       LION
MA-0015487   TOMMY       TAYLOR
YZ-1234567   JANE        DOE
WI-1098776   Jane        Doe

SQL> SELECT CONTACT_DATE, HUMAN_ID, REVIEWED_CASE FROM CONTACT_LIST;

CONTACT_D    HUMAN_ID    REVIEWED_C
---------    ---------   ----------
15-JAN-96    NY-0000145  YES
20-JAN-96    NY-0000145  YES
10-FEB-96    MA-0015487  NO
15-FEB-96    MA-0015487  YES

SQL> SELECT HUMAN_ID, PROPERTY_ID, LAND_DESC FROM PROPERTY_LIST;

HUMAN_ID     PROPERTY_ID LAND_DESC
---------    ----------- ---------------------------------
MA-0015487   A-100       LOT ON NORTH SIDE OF LAKE
NY-0000145   B-999       APARTMENT
MA-0015487   A-102       HOUSE IN TOWN

SQL> |
```

First, you update the HUMAN table with the change in the primary-key column for this person. Next, you change all the rows of data in the CONTACT_LIST and PROPERTY_LIST tables that are connected to this person so that they reflect the new correction in the primary key. Finally, just to be sure that you remember what you did, you create a new table called ID_HISTORY, which tracks the changes in HUMAN_ID as people move from town to town. What a lot of work!

The problem with intelligent keys crops up when all or part of the information in a key changes. Updating a primary key causes a ripple effect that requires more work, time, and effort to maintain. There must be a better way! There is: nonintelligent keys. Nonintelligent keys are much easier to manage.

Imagine the same scenario, but this time you generate unique sequential numbers for subjects as you sign them up. The number that you assign to a person has no significance to that subject. If he or she moves to a new town, the primary key (nonintelligent key) stays the same. If the subject gets married and changes his or her name, the key stays the same. If the subject gets a promotion for all that incredible work designing databases, the key stays the same. This means that you don't need to change any of the related tables, such as CONTACT_LIST and PROPERTY_LIST.

Presto and voilà — small and nonintelligent make a great combination for primary keys.

Use Caution When Modifying Table Definitions

Remember last Christmas Eve when you were determined to peek at your presents under the tree? You sneaked down the stairs and cleverly pried open the corner of the wrapping paper on your biggest present. Having seen the big secret, you went off to bed feeling smug. The next morning, however, the excitement of the day seemed to be spoiled. The climax of opening that big box had lost its thrill. You can never undo the knowledge after you have it.

Similarly, you can't easily undo changes that you make in a table's structure. Changing a column name requires a series of tedious and time-consuming steps.

When you make table structure changes that require you to remove and re-create the table, you need to remove and re-create all the foreign keys in every table that relates to the table that you change. You may need to run a report first to be sure that you catch all the foreign keys.

One useful new command is SET UNUSED. This command lets you tell the database that the column will be dropped later but the old data will remain in the table's existing rows. For example, suppose that the FOOD_AGE column in AMY's FOOD_PREFERENCE table will be dropped during the next fiscal quarter's database review. Meanwhile, by running this command, the column is marked as unused to document the fact that it will be dropped:

```
-- 01_setunused
ALTER TABLE AMY.FOOD_PREFERENCES SET UNUSED (FOOD_AGE);
```

When it's time to actually drop the column, the DBA issues this command:

```
-- 02_dropunused
ALTER TABLE AMY.FOOD_PREFERENCE DROP UNUSED COLUMNS;
```

Handle Derived Data Efficiently

Derived data is any data that exists as an extrapolation from other data. A column contains derived data, just as it contains any other data. The difference is simply that the source of the data in the column is some kind of manipulation of the data in other columns. If you add the subtotal and the tax, for example, you derive the total sale. The easiest way for me to explain derived data is to show you an example.

Suppose that you track daily sales totals in your DAILY_SALES table. You create a new table called MONTHLY_SALES so that you can compare monthly totals quickly. I show the two tables in Figure 20-4.

Derived data is usually calculated from other data

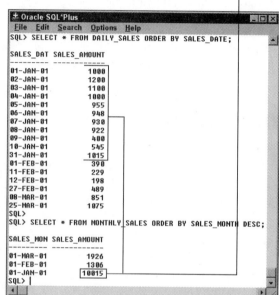

Figure 20-4:
The
MONTHLY_
SALES table
is a table of
derived
data.

The SALES_AMOUNT column in the MONTHLY_SALES table is derived data. Oracle9i arrives at the figure in the MONTHLY_SALES table by using the data in the SALES_AMOUNT column of the DAILY_SALES table. Here's the SQL code that calculates SALES_AMOUNT for the month of February 2001 and places the amount in the MONTHLY_SALES table:

```
-- 03_derived
UPDATE MONTHLY_SALES SET SALES_AMOUNT =
(SELECT SUM(SALES_AMOUNT)
FROM DAILY_SALES
WHERE SALES_DATE BETWEEN '01-FEB-01' AND '28-FEB-01')
WHERE SALES_MONTH = '01-FEB-01';
```

This example illustrates data that you derive by summarizing data in many rows of a table. Derived data can also be calculated within a row; one example is a person's age, which you calculate from a birth date. Another form of derived data results from comparing data in two columns. An example is a column that indicates when a bank account is below its established minimum balance. In all these cases, you can always re-create the value that you store in a column of derived data by redoing the calculation or comparison.

Derived data has a tendency to become outdated quickly. In the preceding example, the monthly total for the current month changes daily. Should you recalculate the monthly total every day? Once a week? Only at the end of the month? You decide and then delegate the task, because it's a pain in the you-know-where.

If you decide to store derived data, I recommend that you do so with a materialized view. This way, the database keeps the derived data up-to-date as often as you decide is necessary. Using materialized views saves you the time and effort of creating code and running job schedules to update your derived data. See Chapter 12 to review materialized views.

Approach Internet Security in Practical Ways

A million opinions exist on how to handle security for databases. I hope that this section helps you sort out a good strategy to use for your unique situation.

Security concerns vary greatly. Some of the factors to consider are

- ✔ **The number of people who use your database.** The more people who use the database, the more likely that someone will try accessing data that he or she isn't authorized to access.

- ✔ **The kind of access you allow over the Internet.** You may be able to completely separate your Internet Web site from your internal data, making accessible data less sensitive. On the other hand, you may have on-the-road salespeople entering their sales reports into your central database across the Internet. In this kind of example, your Internet system may need more security features.

- ✔ **The kind of data in your database.** Data that you must keep private needs tight security. Bank and government information, for example, may need this kind of high security.

The Oracle security strategies that use Oracle Net are called, as a group, Oracle Advanced Security. You can choose from a wide range of possible combinations when setting up a Web-enabled database system. I describe three of the choices in the next three sections.

Low security — application proxy

Imagine that you have a Web site where your visitors can browse an online catalog of goods. You provide text-based search capabilities. When visitors are ready to order a product, they must call your toll-free phone number to place the order. In this kind of setup, Oracle's Application Proxy is an appropriate choice. The database contains only one or two users, which are connected to the one or two database applications you use on the Internet. You specify inside the database the source of the connection (your own application server) and the user with which to connect to the database. This way, other requests that come across the Internet won't be allowed to log in to the database. In addition, you can limit the access allowed to the user inside the database by granting roles and privileges, as I describe in Chapter 11.

Medium security — application context

The medium-security approach uses application context and works well for the average internal corporate database, and it works even if the public has limited access to the database.

Application context is the storing of each user's security attributes in a protected data cache for quick and secure access. Application context restricts and filters database records. The basic idea is that your users log into an application with a unique user name and password.

The application context procedure gathers all users' attributes in a secure memory area that is used to run applications. Each user's security information is set at login and held in a secure area for the duration of the user's session. The application uses the context by calling a built-in function. Whenever called, the context function links with a procedure and gathers the necessary data out of the database, filtering the data access based on the context attributes. The process is fast and seamless.

With application context, casual and Web users don't need database accounts. The nightmare of maintaining hundreds or even thousands of users in a database can be eliminated. Application context also helps performance.

To implement application context, you do the following:

- **Build the context area.** You must create a package that sets which user attributes will be held for the application context. You can set as many context attributes as you need in that package.

Inside the package, you need a procedure that sets context attributes. The only way to set values in a context area is to use the DBMS_SESSION. SET_CONTEXT command. For example, if you're saving the user's name in the context area, the procedure would have a command something like this:

```
-- 04_context1
DBMS_SESSION.SET_CONTEXT('access user'.
'username',v_username);
```

After creating a package, you also execute a command that establishes the application context area. For example, if your package is named DO_THE_CONTEXT and your context area will be named MY_NEW_CONTEXT, the command is

```
-- 05_context2
CREATE OR REPLACE CONTEXT MY_NEW_CONTEXT
USING AMY.DO_THE_CONTEXT;
```

✔ **Modify your views, procedures, and triggers to call the context area.** Reference any value in the context area with the SYS_CONTEXT built-in function. For example, to retrieve the user's name from the context area just described, use this command:

```
-- 06_context3
SELECT SYS_CONTEXT('access user'.'username')
FROM DUAL;
```

The SYS_CONTEXT function can be added to the WHERE clause of views in place of the PSEUDOCOLUMN USER so that your view filters data based on the value of the context area rather than the value of the Oracle user who is logged in.

✔ **Modify your application to set the user's attribute.** Your application might be written in Java, Oracle Forms, or any number of other packages. Any one of these can be modified to call a procedure that sets the context area. The SQL command to set context must use the package you defined. Continuing with the example, you might use this command to set the user's login name to the user's context area:

```
-- 07 context4
EXECUTE AMY.DO_THE_CONTEXT.SET_USERNAME('GEORGE');
```

High security — SSL

Oracle9i allows you to apply SSL (Secure Sockets Layer), the most popular security protocol on the Web, to your database connections. SSL encrypts data that is sent across the Internet from your browser to the Web server. Oracle9i has been enhanced to extend encrypted data all the way into the

database server. In addition, Oracle9i supports SSL encryption for thin JDBC (Java Database Connectivity) connections — a popular type of connection between Web applications and the database.

Be Smart about Test Data

Test data is a set of fake rows of data. The purpose of test data is to verify the schema that you designed and any queries, screens, or other fancy finagling that you intend to use with your data. Most people fail to use test data because it is boring and seems like a waste of time. First, you have to create all the test data yourself, and then you have to use it for a while. The final step is getting rid of the test data so that it doesn't get confused with real data.

Why would anyone ever want to use test data? Several good reasons exist for taking the time and care to create and use test data. Test data allows you to create a controlled environment for experimenting and exercising your queries and SQL commands. The benefits of using test data are as follows:

✔ You control the data and, therefore, can predict and verify the results of queries and other SQL commands.

✔ You work with a smaller set of data compared with real-life data. I limit test data to a small number of rows (10 or 20 usually are enough) in each table.

✔ You don't have to worry about destroying actual data when trying new SQL commands, screens, or other changes.

If you choose to create and use test data, remember these pointers about Oracle9i:

✔ Oracle9i's ROLLBACK command in SQL*Plus Worksheet can speed testing because the command gives you a fast way to restore data to its original state. The ROLLBACK command undoes inserts, updates, and deletions to all tables as far back as the last time you used the COMMIT command or logged on.

✔ Another fast way to return to your starting point with test data is to use EXP and IMP. After you create the test data, use EXP to make a copy of all the tables. After you run SQL commands or use online screens to experiment with changes in the data, you may want to restore everything to its original state. Use IMP to bring back all your original data. Refer to Chapter 15 for a description of the EXP and IMP commands.

Talk to Non-Techie-Type Humans

Ricky Ricardo, talking about a neighbor's dog, says, "Oh, she doesn't mind sleeping in the yard. She's used to it."

Lucy, talking about the neighbor's wife, says, "Well, if that's the way he treats her, I don't blame her for going home to mother!"

A misunderstanding like this one can sometimes creep into an otherwise solid design. I once worked on a project in which everyone misinterpreted the word *grantee* for months. I was halfway through the project, after hundreds of hours of work, before an outsider made an offhand comment about *grantee*. Upon hearing the comment, I realized that I had designed part of the system incorrectly.

Make sure that you take your design for a walk to meet the people in your neighborhood. Sometimes, getting feedback from other people helps you improve your design and saves you a great deal of time and trouble down the road. At other times, you wind up scooping up a lot of you-know-what.

Chapter 21

Ten Handy Oracle9i Internet Features

This chapter is food for thought. Take it with you in the tub, relax, and dream of all the possibilities! Oracle9i was designed with the Internet in mind, and each section here shows you a handy feature ready and waiting for you.

interMedia

The really cool thing about interMedia is that it has all kinds of handy built-in capabilities for audio, video, and graphic files. For instance, Figure 21-1 shows the interMedia Clipboard utility, which you can download from Oracle's Technet Web site (`technet.oracle.com`). You can develop an image on your desktop, and then copy it into the desktop clipboard and paste it into the database. Or you can save it to a file and load the file into the database.

interMedia has a predefined object type for images called `ORDIMAGE` that enables you to define image-related information, such as the type of file format you saved the image with (GIF, JPG, and so on). You can search this information, which is stored along with the image itself when you load it into the `ORDIMAGE` column of the table.

In addition to all its predefined object types, you can add your own object types to interMedia and customize it to your needs. For example, you may want a special interMedia object type for your interstellar transporter schematic drawings.

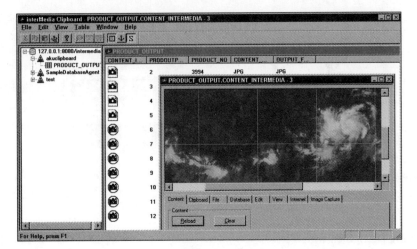

Figure 21-1:
interMedia's
Clipboard
for
Windows
is the
easiest way
to load
images into
Oracle9i.

iSQL*Plus

Get on the Web wave now! A new tool, called iSQL*Plus, is installed with your basic Oracle9i software package. This tool lets you run a SQL*Plus session on a Web page. You need the Oracle9i database, a Web browser (such as Internet Explorer or Netscape) and a Web server (such as Apache or the standard Oracle HTTP Server). Everything is set up for you when you install the Enterprise Edition of the database, so you can dive right in.

Figure 21-2 shows an example of a query that was run using iSQL*Plus and one of the sample tables used in this book, SEAWEED_SAMPLE.

PL/SQL on the Web

You can deliver Web documents straight from the database when you use the HTML extensions that are now built into Oracle's programming language, PL/SQL. This procedural language has been in Oracle's core database engine since its infancy but had to be upgraded for the World Wide Web.

Here are your choices:

- ✔ **PL/SQL Web Toolkit.** This tool helps you create PL/SQL server pages. These are PL/SQL packages stored in the database that generate HTML code by combining database data and HTML tags. The HTP and OWA_* packages that come with all Oracle9i databases are used to accomplish this feat.

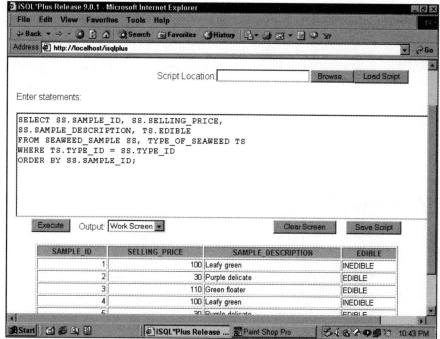

Figure 21-2: iSQL*Plus, the new Web-based tool, lets you run any SQL command you want in a browser window.

✔ **PL/SQL Server Pages (PSP).** This alternative allows you to create HTML documents and embed PL/SQL calls directly into the document. This kind of document then gets executed and delivered to the Web using a PL/SQL connection, such as WebDB's PL/SQL gateway.

Either way, you have to learn both HTML and PL/SQL to do this, so put on your tinfoil hat immediately.

Internet File System

Internet File System, or iFS, is a Java-based, Oracle9i-delivered, file management system. "What does that mean, oh goddess of Oracle?" you say. Let me tell you.

Suppose that you're browsing through documents and images and other files in Windows Explorer. You've found the document that explains all the timesheet rules. Now you need to create a form letter that contains this information and is addressed at the top with every employee's name and address. But wait! Your employee information is stuck inside the Oracle9i monster. How can you ever get it into your letter?

What if the employee information looks like another document file and is formatted so that you can grab names and addresses and throw them into your form letter? This is where iFS comes to the rescue. You can design a directory and file structure for your Oracle9i tables that look like all the other directories and files found when you browse around in Windows Explorer. You can specify the format of the files (tab-delimited, HTML, preformatted documents, and so on) using the iFS toolset.

With this tool, your users can read and write Oracle data as if it were in a text file. What will they think of next?

JDeveloper

The JDeveloper toolset contains all kinds of utilities and aids for you savvy Java programmers. This toolset has caught on recently and is rivaling other toolsets in the race to have the best and most versatile tools on the market for Java development. Figure 21-3 shows the main window of the JDeveloper programming tool.

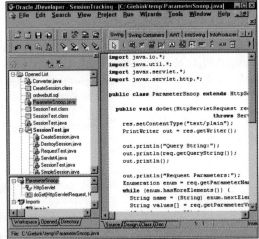

Figure 21-3: Get with it and start doing that Java thing!

Following are some of the cool tasks that the JDeveloper design tool can do:

✔ Create validation code in Java using a simple point-and-click navigator window

✔ Debug your code from a remote site as it runs in server-side or client-side components

> ✔ Generate XML automatically from a schema design
>
> ✔ Write code for Enterprise Java Beans (EJB), PL/SQL (Oracle's extended SQL programming language), Java servlets, and Java Server Pages (JSP)

Web Single Sign-On

New to Oracle9i, the Web Single Sign-On tool comes with the application server components of Oracle9i. The dream of a single entry point for users of your in-house network, your Web site, your file system, and your database has been around for years, but the reality was usually that users had to sign in at least twice.

When you set up Oracle9i's Internet Directory service, your systems administrator has the tool for creating a single sign-on that works both inside and outside the database. Once inside the initial login screen, a user can navigate among Web pages, database tools such as SQL*Plus, and even normal data files in network directories without having to log in to any new areas. This useful tool will be welcomed by a lot of systems designers as a dream come true.

Java Stored Procedures

Here's a way to use Java programming inside the database. *Java stored procedures* are Java methods stored in the database for everyone to use. In addition to residing in the database, these procedures use special call specifications (communication instructions) that automatically convert Java methods and parameters to SQL components. This means your Java and your SQL are totally compatible without any reprogramming.

You can use JSP to create Java methods that can be used within the database in procedures, triggers, and functions. For example, you can write a Java method that updates the date and time that a row is changed, and then use this Java method in a table's trigger. To use it in the trigger, follow these steps:

1. **Create the Java method and store it in the database.**

2. **Create a procedure (`CREATE PROCEDURE` command) that calls the Java method and passes the appropriate parameters.**

3. **Create a trigger that executes the procedure.**

One advantage of using stored procedures is that calls to the database are executed in groups instead of individually, making the procedure more efficient than a set of individually executed commands.

Web Assistant

Web Assistant is a simple tool that lets you get your data out to the Web in record time. Web Assistant is limited to read-only, simple HTML pages. What's cool about this tool is that you can set it up to refresh pages periodically. For example, suppose you have a surf report that is entered into the database twice a day. Set up a Web Publishing Assistant report that queries the data, creates a Web page from it, and posts it to your Web site at 10:00 and 2:00 every day.

Figure 21-4 shows a Web page that I generated in about one and a half minutes! I used two tables, FISH and AQUARIUM, in the AMY sample data. I didn't have to tell the tool anything about how to join the two tables or how to display the results of the query, and the page looks great! Web Assistant is an intuitive and simple tool for fast, easy work. The tool is automatically installed when you install the Enterprise Edition of Oracle9i.

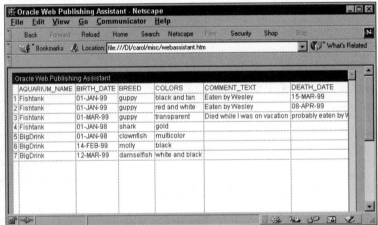

Figure 21-4: Using Web Publishing Assistant, you don't even need to know how to write SQL queries.

Ultra Search

Ultra Search, as the name implies, is the ultimate Web-based search tool for your database-driven Web site. Ultra Search can go crawling through all your Web pages, like a normal search engine. But here's the cool part: Ultra Search can also crawl through your database in the same search.

Suppose you have a database that contains catalog entries for your online store that include updated prices, new features, sales, and so on. You also have static pages that describe the catalog items in detail. When folks run a search on your site, it's desirable to give them all the pages, whether they are database-generated or static. That's where Ultra Search comes to the rescue.

Faster than a speeding bullet, it grabs your customer's search request, shuffles through all your static Web pages, and then plows into the database data, retrieving everything pertinent in a single bound. Very ultra cool.

Oracle9i Application Server Wireless

Oracle9i Application Server Wireless is an interesting addition to Oracle's toolset that can be downloaded from Oracle's Technet Web site (`technet. oracle.com`). The idea is to provide an interactive connection for all those portable devices out there, such as palmtop computers, cell phones with e-mail capability, and laptops that can plug into a network.

Oracle9i Application Server Wireless is based on the XML concept, which is used to deliver and format data according to what kind of device you use. On the data side, your application needs only to be developed one time to extract and deliver the required data. On the display side, the XML format allows you to design many different looks for that data, depending on what kind of device is viewing the data. For example, you may have a full-color, image-laden Web page for display on a laptop and a simple, text-only layout for the same data on a cell phone.

Glossary

alias: A nickname or alternative name for a table or column used in SQL.

attribute: A feature or characteristic. For example, the datatype and size of a column are two of the column's attributes.

authentication, external: This form of authentication allows users to pass into the database using their identities from the operating system. To log into SQL*Plus or some application, you simply type a slash where you normally enter your Oracle9i user ID and password.

authentication, global: This form of authentication was new in Version 8 of Oracle. Intended for use across distributed database systems, this method requires authentication to be performed outside the database using the Oracle Security Service (OSS). It lets you use a common user ID and password to reach any database in your distributed network of databases.

authentication, password: This is the traditional method of authentication in which the user must type a password to enter a database transaction.

block: A unit of storage for data and other information in the database.

column: A component of a database table. A column contains the definition of what kinds of data are to be collected and stored in the rows of the table.

comma-delimited file: A format for extracting data out of a database and placing it into a plain text file. Each line in the file contains one row, and each column is separated from the following column by a comma.

commit: To permanently save all changes since the last commit was performed to the database.

constraint: A rule applied to a table or a column that restricts the data that is allowed in any row in the table. For example, a primary-key constraint defines the primary key for a table. All rows must have unique values in the columns included in the primary-key constraint.

correlated subquery: A subquery that has references to the outer query.

database engine: The set of programs that runs the database, keeping track of information, monitoring usage, checking security, checking for errors, and so on.

datafile: The operating system file used by Oracle9i to store table data and other information. Each datafile is assigned to one tablespace. Datafiles can expand incrementally if needed.

datatype: Defines the type of information that can be stored, such as dates, numbers, or characters.

DBA: The database administrator.

derived data: Data that can be calculated, summarized, or otherwise extracted entirely from other data in the database.

dictionary managed tablespace: A type of tablespace that uses the database data dictionary to keep track of space usage. *See also* locally managed tablespace.

DTD: Document Type Declaration. A part of XML. The DTD file contains valid datatypes so that your XML parser can evaluate all the commands in an XML document as either valid or invalid.

EJB: Enterprise Java Beans. A programming guide for Java in which small stand-alone programs (beans) are combined into larger components so that the beans interact with one another and accomplish program tasks.

entity: A table or group of tables. Used interchangeably with *table* in this book.

Entity Relationship Diagram: A style of drawing a relational database model that uses boxes, text, lines, and a few simple symbols to represent the entities and relationships in the model.

explicit data conversion: The user controls conversion of a column or expression from one datatype into another. The data conversion thus happens in a predictable manner. *See also* implicit data conversion.

export: Oracle9i utility to pull data out of the database into a file. The file is in a special format for use only with the Oracle9i import utility. Also used to refer to the act of using the export utility.

expression: A column, a literal, or a column with some function applied to it, such as addition. In SQL queries, expressions can be used almost anywhere a column can be used.

field: *See* column.

foreign key: The primary key of a reference table that is stored inside another table. The foreign key connects the two tables. It allows access to all the information stored in both tables without repeating data from either table, other than the key column.

fragmented table: A table that contains wasted space in the form of empty blocks and chained blocks.

full table scan: One of several choices of table access that the Oracle9i optimizer uses. This type of access requires the optimizer to read each row in the entire table. A full table scan is similar to starting at the 100s on the library shelf and reading every book label until you find the book you want.

GB: Gigabyte. Approximately one billion bytes.

GRANT: SQL command for adding security privileges on a table, view, or synonym.

hierarchy: A relationship of tables in which a parent table has a child table, that child table has its own child table, and so on.

HTML: HyperText Markup Language. The primary language used to create Web pages. HTML consists of normal text and special codes, called *tags,* which tell a Web browser how to display the text. Tags determine the size of the font, the color of the background, and other formatting details.

implicit data conversion: Oracle9i converts a column or expression from one datatype to another using its own internal logic. This function is unpredictable and subject to change with new releases. *See also* explicit data conversion.

import: Oracle9i utility to bring data into the database from a file. The file must be in a special format created by using the export utility. Also used to refer to the act of using the import utility.

incremental space: In a table definition, the amount of space reserved if the table runs out of room and needs more space. The same amount of space is reserved again if the table needs more space until the table hits the maximum space limitation.

index-organized table: A table stored in index order. As rows are inserted, all rows are arranged into physical order in the tablespace.

initial space: In a table definition, this parameter sets the starting size of the table.

INSERT: A command to add a new row to a table.

instance: A single complete Oracle database. Each instance has its own name, number, and initialization parameters. Multiple instances can run on one computer.

intelligent key: A primary key that has meaning for the row of data.

interactive: Any process in which the computer asks for information from the user and then acts on it.

Internet: A global, public network of computers linked together with telephone lines and network software. *See also* World Wide Web.

intranet: A network of computers (connected by phone or cable lines) that is inside one organization for internal use only.

Java: A programming language designed to be independent of operating systems so that Java programs are fully portable between computers.

join: A type of query in which two or more tables are connected, or *joined,* together.

JVM: Java Virtual Machine. A translator for Java programs that translates some Java commands into commands that the local operating system acts upon, such as a read or write command.

key: A column or set of columns in a table that identifies a unique row of data. *See also* primary key and foreign key.

legacy system: A set of tables (schema) that has been brought into your Oracle9i system from an older source, such as Oracle8, or another database system.

literal: A word or phrase, number, or letter that is used at its face value (exactly as it is written) in a query or in a SQL*Plus command. A literal is always surrounded by single quotes.

local database: A database that resides on the computer the user is logged into.

locally managed tablespace: A type of tablespace that maintains a header within the tablespace to store information about its storage use. *See also* dictionary managed tablespace.

logical operator: A connection between two columns or expressions in a WHERE clause. Examples are = (equal), <> (not equal), like, between, < (less than), and > (greater than).

Management Pack: A set of tools related to a particular subject and available as a package from Oracle. Some Management Packs, such as the DBA Management Pack, are included with the Oracle9i database. Others, such as the Performance Pack, are available for sale.

Markup tag: In HTML or XML documents, a markup tag is a code enclosed in brackets that defines how a document is formatted. For example, an HTML markup tag for displaying text in bold looks like this: <B>.

method: A self-contained bit of programming code that travels with an object, delivering parts or modifying data according to the method code.

nonintelligent key: A key that is unique and does not change, even when information in the row changes. A sequential ID number is an example of a nonintelligent key.

nonunique index: Allows duplicate values in rows in the table. Nonunique indexes are used to speed retrieval of data.

null: Unknown or missing. A row can be created in a table without all the columns filled in. Columns where no data has been entered are defined as containing a null value.

object column: A column in a table with an object type as its datatype.

object table: A table whose rows or at least one of its columns are defined by an object type rather than by explicit columns. The elements within the object type define what data is stored in the object table.

object type: Enables you to extend the definition of datatypes (classes of data) into customized user-defined datatypes. Oracle calls these special datatypes object types.

object view: Maps relational tables into an object table. Like relational views, the object view doesn't have data of its own; it's merely a way of looking at underlying tables. The object view allows you to use existing relational tables in an object-oriented way.

object-relational database: A database that combines features of a relational database with features of an object-oriented database. Oracle9i is an object-relational database.

objects: Things in a database or groups of things that stand on their own. For example, a table is an object, but a row is not an object.

optimizer: An internal part of the Oracle9i database engine that determines the fastest access path for any given SQL command.

overhead: Information about tables, columns, rows, indexes, and other structures in the database.

owner: The user who creates a table.

package: A database program consisting of one or more procedures. A package executes when called using SQL or a programming language interface.

partitioned table: A table that spans more than one tablespace. Each table-space contains one partition of the table.

primary key: A column or set of columns in one table that uniquely identifies each row in the table. Every row in a table has a value in the primary key that is different than that of every other row in that table.

private synonym: A synonym that can be used only by the synonym creator, unless the creator grants privileges to others.

procedure: A database program that contains PL/SQL commands. A procedure can be contained in a package or can stand alone. A procedure executes when called, using SQL or a programming language interface.

pseudocolumn: A column defined by Oracle9i that you can use in a query. For example, USER is a pseudocolumn that always contains the Oracle9i user ID of the current user.

public synonym: A synonym created by a database administrator (DBA) that can be used by anyone.

query: A question posed in SQL to look at data in the database.

record: *See* row.

relational database: A collection of tables connected in a series of relation-ships so that they model some small part of the real world.

remote database: A database that does not reside on the computer that the user is logged into.

reorganize: To rebuild the internal physical structure of a table by dropping it and re-creating it. One way to reorganize a table is to remove and restore the data using the EXP and IMP commands.

REVOKE: A SQL command for removing security privileges.

role: A set of privileges that can be assigned to or removed from a user.

ROLLBACK: A command that removes all changes since the last commit.

row: A component of a database table. It contains the actual data, compart-mentalized in columns.

row ID: A pseudocolumn that contains the physical address of a row. Retrieving a table row using its row ID is the fastest method available.

schema: Everything created by a single user ID in Oracle9i (tables, grants, roles, indexes, relationships, and objects).

script: A file that contains more than just a single SQL or SQL*Plus command.

SGA: System Global Area. The memory area used by Oracle9i.

SQL: Structured Query Language. An English-like set of commands for defining database objects and querying and modifying data in those objects.

synonym: An alternate name for a table or view. Synonyms can be private (for use only by their creator) or public (for use by any user).

table: A set of related columns and rows in a relational database.

tablespace: A portion of the database that Oracle9i reserves for your tables. One database can have many tablespaces, and each tablespace may contain many tables, indexes, procedures, or other objects. Each tablespace is mapped to one or more physical files.

third normal form: A set of rules specifying how tables and columns in a relational database relate to one another.

tree diagram: *See* Entity Relationship Diagram.

unique index: Enforces unique values across all rows in a table. Unique indexes are automatically generated for primary-key constraints.

user: A unique login name in Oracle9i. A user's capabilities inside the database are determined by the user's role assignments.

user ID: *See* user.

view: A query that is named in the database so that it can be used as if it were a table. Views can be used anywhere tables can be used, except for some restrictions on adding, removing, or changing rows from views that join tables.

virtual private database: A structure that allows you to create the illusion of individually owned databases within a single database. Oracle Internet Directory is one example of a virtual private database structure.

Web page: A screen of data, graphics, music, and so on that appears on the World Wide Web (Internet) or on an intranet. This is a general term referring to any document on the Web. It may be an order entry form, a database report, a video, a text document, or any number of other possibilities. The length of one page is totally flexible, and the document contains HTML tags.

World Wide Web: A portion of the Internet dedicated to documents in HTML format. The Web, as it is often known, is a versatile, colorful, and highly interactive area.

XML: eXtensible Markup Language. Similar to HTML, but more versatile because it allows you to design your own language tags and customize the Web document's display based on data and style sheets.

XML parser: The engine that interprets an XML document. If a DTD document is provided, the parser determines the validity of the XML document's markups.

XSL: eXtensible Stylesheet Language. A file containing information about types of data and how to display the data on a Web page. For example, the stylesheet may specify that a street address be displayed in Arial font, boldface, and on a separate line.

Index

● *D* ●

● *J* ●

Notes

FOR DUMMIES®

The easy way to get more done and have more fun

PERSONAL FINANCE

0-7645-5231-7

0-7645-2431-3

0-7645-5331-3

Also available:

Estate Planning For Dummies
(0-7645-5501-4)

401(k)s For Dummies
(0-7645-5468-9)

Frugal Living For Dummies
(0-7645-5403-4)

Microsoft Money "X" For
Dummies
(0-7645-1689-2)

Mutual Funds For Dummies
(0-7645-5329-1)

Personal Bankruptcy For
Dummies
(0-7645-5498-0)

Quicken "X" For Dummies
(0-7645-1666-3)

Stock Investing For Dummies
(0-7645-5411-5)

Taxes For Dummies 2003
(0-7645-5475-1)

BUSINESS & CAREERS

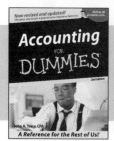

0-7645-5314-3

0-7645-5307-0

0-7645-5471-9

Also available:

Business Plans Kit For
Dummies
(0-7645-5365-8)

Consulting For Dummies
(0-7645-5034-9)

Cool Careers For Dummies
(0-7645-5345-3)

Human Resources Kit For
Dummies
(0-7645-5131-0)

Managing For Dummies
(1-5688-4858-7)

QuickBooks All-in-One Desk
Reference For Dummies
(0-7645-1963-8)

Selling For Dummies
(0-7645-5363-1)

Small Business Kit For
Dummies
(0-7645-5093-4)

Starting an eBay Business For
Dummies
(0-7645-1547-0)

HEALTH, SPORTS & FITNESS

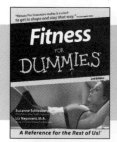

0-7645-5167-1

0-7645-5146-9

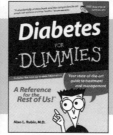

0-7645-5154-X

Also available:

Controlling Cholesterol For
Dummies
(0-7645-5440-9)

Dieting For Dummies
(0-7645-5126-4)

High Blood Pressure For
Dummies
(0-7645-5424-7)

Martial Arts For Dummies
(0-7645-5358-5)

Menopause For Dummies
(0-7645-5458-1)

Nutrition For Dummies
(0-7645-5180-9)

Power Yoga For Dummies
(0-7645-5342-9)

Thyroid For Dummies
(0-7645-5385-2)

Weight Training For Dummies
(0-7645-5168-X)

Yoga For Dummies
(0-7645-5117-5)

Available wherever books are sold.
Go to www.dummies.com or call 1-877-762-2974 to order direct.

FOR DUMMIES®

A world of resources to help you grow

HOME, GARDEN & HOBBIES

0-7645-5295-3

0-7645-5130-2

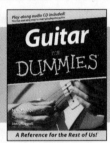
0-7645-5106-X

Also available:

Auto Repair For Dummies
(0-7645-5089-6)

Chess For Dummies
(0-7645-5003-9)

Home Maintenance For Dummies
(0-7645-5215-5)

Organizing For Dummies
(0-7645-5300-3)

Piano For Dummies
(0-7645-5105-1)

Poker For Dummies
(0-7645-5232-5)

Quilting For Dummies
(0-7645-5118-3)

Rock Guitar For Dummies
(0-7645-5356-9)

Roses For Dummies
(0-7645-5202-3)

Sewing For Dummies
(0-7645-5137-X)

FOOD & WINE

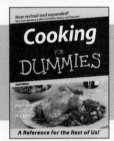
0-7645-5250-3

0-7645-5390-9

0-7645-5114-0

Also available:

Bartending For Dummies
(0-7645-5051-9)

Chinese Cooking For Dummies
(0-7645-5247-3)

Christmas Cooking For Dummies
(0-7645-5407-7)

Diabetes Cookbook For Dummies
(0-7645-5230-9)

Grilling For Dummies
(0-7645-5076-4)

Low-Fat Cooking For Dummies
(0-7645-5035-7)

Slow Cookers For Dummies
(0-7645-5240-6)

TRAVEL

0-7645-5453-0

0-7645-5438-7

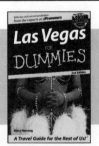
0-7645-5448-4

Also available:

America's National Parks For Dummies
(0-7645-6204-5)

Caribbean For Dummies
(0-7645-5445-X)

Cruise Vacations For Dummies 2003
(0-7645-5459-X)

Europe For Dummies
(0-7645-5456-5)

Ireland For Dummies
(0-7645-6199-5)

France For Dummies
(0-7645-6292-4)

London For Dummies
(0-7645-5416-6)

Mexico's Beach Resorts For Dummies
(0-7645-6262-2)

Paris For Dummies
(0-7645-5494-8)

RV Vacations For Dummies
(0-7645-5443-3)

Walt Disney World & Orlando For Dummies
(0-7645-5444-1)

Available wherever books are sold. Go to www.dummies.com or call 1-877-762-2974 to order direct.

FOR DUMMIES®

Helping you expand your horizons and realize your potential

INTERNET

The Internet FOR DUMMIES
0-7645-0894-6

The Internet ALL-IN-ONE DESK REFERENCE FOR DUMMIES
0-7645-1659-0

eBay FOR DUMMIES
0-7645-1642-6

Also available:

America Online 7.0 For Dummies
(0-7645-1624-8)

Genealogy Online For Dummies
(0-7645-0807-5)

The Internet All-in-One Desk Reference For Dummies
(0-7645-1659-0)

Internet Explorer 6 For Dummies
(0-7645-1344-3)

The Internet For Dummies Quick Reference
(0-7645-1645-0)

Internet Privacy For Dummies
(0-7645-0846-6)

Researching Online For Dummies
(0-7645-0546-7)

Starting an Online Business For Dummies
(0-7645-1655-8)

DIGITAL MEDIA

Digital Photography FOR DUMMIES
0-7645-1664-7

Photoshop Elements 2 FOR DUMMIES
0-7645-1675-2

Digital Video FOR DUMMIES
0-7645-0806-7

Also available:

CD and DVD Recording For Dummies
(0-7645-1627-2)

Digital Photography All-in-One Desk Reference For Dummies
(0-7645-1800-3)

Digital Photography For Dummies Quick Reference
(0-7645-0750-8)

Home Recording for Musicians For Dummies
(0-7645-1634-5)

MP3 For Dummies
(0-7645-0858-X)

Paint Shop Pro "X" For Dummies
(0-7645-2440-2)

Photo Retouching & Restoration For Dummies
(0-7645-1662-0)

Scanners For Dummies
(0-7645-0783-4)

GRAPHICS

PowerPoint 2002 FOR DUMMIES
0-7645-0817-2

Photoshop 7 FOR DUMMIES
0-7645-1651-5

Macromedia Flash MX FOR DUMMIES
0-7645-0895-4

Also available:

Adobe Acrobat 5 PDF For Dummies
(0-7645-1652-3)

Fireworks 4 For Dummies
(0-7645-0804-0)

Illustrator 10 For Dummies
(0-7645-3636-2)

QuarkXPress 5 For Dummies
(0-7645-0643-9)

Visio 2000 For Dummies
(0-7645-0635-8)

FOR DUMMIES®

The advice and explanations you need to succeed

SELF-HELP, SPIRITUALITY & RELIGION

0-7645-5302-X

0-7645-5418-2

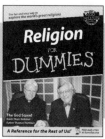
0-7645-5264-3

Also available:

The Bible For Dummies
(0-7645-5296-1)

Buddhism For Dummies
(0-7645-5359-3)

Christian Prayer For Dummies
(0-7645-5500-6)

Dating For Dummies
(0-7645-5072-1)

Judaism For Dummies
(0-7645-5299-6)

Potty Training For Dummies
(0-7645-5417-4)

Pregnancy For Dummies
(0-7645-5074-8)

Rekindling Romance For Dummies
(0-7645-5303-8)

Spirituality For Dummies
(0-7645-5298-8)

Weddings For Dummies
(0-7645-5055-1)

PETS

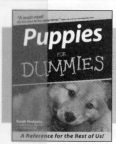
0-7645-5255-4

0-7645-5286-4

0-7645-5275-9

Also available:

Labrador Retrievers For Dummies
(0-7645-5281-3)

Aquariums For Dummies
(0-7645-5156-6)

Birds For Dummies
(0-7645-5139-6)

Dogs For Dummies
(0-7645-5274-0)

Ferrets For Dummies
(0-7645-5259-7)

German Shepherds For Dummies
(0-7645-5280-5)

Golden Retrievers For Dummies
(0-7645-5267-8)

Horses For Dummies
(0-7645-5138-8)

Jack Russell Terriers For Dummies
(0-7645-5268-6)

Puppies Raising & Training Diary For Dummies
(0-7645-0876-8)

EDUCATION & TEST PREPARATION

0-7645-5194-9

0-7645-5325-9

0-7645-5210-4

Also available:

Chemistry For Dummies
(0-7645-5430-1)

English Grammar For Dummies
(0-7645-5322-4)

French For Dummies
(0-7645-5193-0)

The GMAT For Dummies
(0-7645-5251-1)

Inglés Para Dummies
(0-7645-5427-1)

Italian For Dummies
(0-7645-5196-5)

Research Papers For Dummies
(0-7645-5426-3)

The SAT I For Dummies
(0-7645-5472-7)

U.S. History For Dummies
(0-7645-5249-X)

World History For Dummies
(0-7645-5242-2)

Available wherever books are sold. Go to www.dummies.com or call 1-877-762-2974 to order direct.

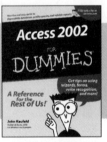